Studies in Christianity and Judaism / Etudes sur le christianisme et le judaïsme : 2

Studies in Christianity and Judaism /
Etudes sur le christianisme et le judaïsme

Studies in Christianity and Judaism / Etudes sur le christianisme et le judaïsme presents publications that study Judaism and Christianity together in an effort to reach an understanding of how the two religions have related and relate to each other as well as studies that offer original insight into some central aspect of the two religions or of one of them. Three groups of studies are envisaged: studies of doctrine, historical studies, and textual studies. Whereas there exist similar publications produced in Canada in a theological context, this Series reflects the specific nature and orientation of the departments of religious studies in Canadian centres of learning. In these departments Christianity and Judaism are studied from the perspective of the history of religions. Such a perspective is not necessarily aligned with one of the two traditions. It tries to transcend traditional antagonisms as well as confessional limitations. After several decades of work from such a perspective, Canadian scholars are now in a position to offer studies that put forward less conventional views of the two religions.

STUDIES IN CHRISTIANITY
AND JUDAISM

Number 2

ANTI-JUDAISM IN EARLY CHRISTIANITY

Volume 1
PAUL AND THE GOSPELS

edited by
Peter Richardson
with David Granskou

Published for the Canadian Corporation for Studies in Religion/Corporation Canadienne des Sciences Religieuses by Wilfrid Laurier University Press

1986

Canadian Cataloguing in Publication Data

Main entry under title:
Anti-Judaism in early Christianity
(Studies in Christianity and Judaism = Etudes
sur le christianisme et le judaïsme, ISSN 0711-5903 ; 2)
Bibliography: v.
Includes index.
Partial contents: v. 1. Paul and the Gospels /
edited by Peter Richardson with David Granskou.
ISBN 0-88920-167-6 (v. 1)

1. Christianity and other religions – Judaism.
2. Judaism – Relations – Christianity. 3. Paul,
the Apostle, Saint – Attitude towards Judaism.
4. Christianity – Early church, ca. 30-600.
I. Richardson, Peter, 1935- II. Granskou,
David M. III. Series: Studies in Christianity
and Judaism ; 2.

BM 535.A57 1986 261.2′6 C86-093124-2

86 87 88 89 4 3 2 1

Order from:

Wilfrid Laurier University Press
Wilfrid Laurier University
Waterloo, Ontario, Canada N2L 3C5

Printed in Canada

Contents

Notes on Contributors

CHARLES P. ANDERSON is Associate Professor of Religious Studies, University of British Columbia, Vancouver, B.C. He is the author/editor of the *Guide to Religious Studies in Canada* and Past-President of the Canadian Society of Biblical Studies.

ERWIN BUCK is Professor of New Testament Studies in the Lutheran Theological Seminary, Saskatoon, Saskatchewan. He is the co-author of *A Complete Concordance to Flavius Josephus*, vol. 1 (Leiden: Brill, 1973).

DANIEL FRAIKIN is Professor of New Testament at Queen's Theological College, Queen's University, Kingston, Ontario. His main publications have been in French theological and pastoral journals.

LLOYD GASTON is Professor of New Testament at the Vancouver School of Theology, Vancouver, B.C. His books include *No Stone Upon Another* (Leiden: Brill, 1970) and *Horae Synopticae Electronicae* (Missoula: SBL, 1973).

DAVID GRANSKOU is Professor of Religious Studies at Wilfrid Laurier University, Waterloo, Ontario. He is presently working on a major study of Johannine irony.

JOHN C. HURD, JR. is Professor of New Testament in Trinity College, University of Toronto, and the author of *The Origin of 1 Corinthians* (London: SPCK, 1965; and Macon, Georgia: Mercer University Press, 1983), together with a number of computer-produced tools in Aramaic and Greek. With Peter Richardson he has recently edited a *Festschrift* for Frank C. Beare, *From Jesus to Paul* (Waterloo: Wilfrid Laurier University Press, 1984).

WILLIAM KLASSEN is Academic Dean of the Inter-Faith Peace Academy in Jerusalem. His main interest is the relation between the Cynics and

Stoics and the New Testament. He edited *The New Way of Jesus* (Newton, Kansas: Faith and Life Press, 1980) and has recently published *Love of Enemies: The Way to Peace* (Philadelphia: Fortress Press, 1984).

BENNO PRZYBYLSKI is Professor of New Testament, North American Baptist Divinity School, Edmonton, Alberta, and the author of *Righteousness in Matthew and his World of Thought* (Cambridge: Cambridge University Press, 1980).

PETER RICHARDSON is Professor of Religious Studies and Principal of University College, University of Toronto, Toronto, Ontario. He is the author of *Israel in the Apostolic Church* (Cambridge: Cambridge University Press, 1969) and *Paul's Ethic of Freedom* (Philadelphia: Westminster Press, 1979). He has recently edited, with John C. Hurd, *From Jesus to Paul*.

E.P. SANDERS is Professor of Religious Studies, McMaster University, Hamilton, Ontario, and has recently been appointed the Dean Ireland's Professor, Queen's College, Oxford. His works include *The Tendencies of the Synoptic Tradition* (Cambridge: Cambridge University Press, 1969); *Paul and Palestinian Judaism* (Philadelphia: Fortress Press, 1977); and *Paul, the Law, and the Jewish People* (Philadelphia: Fortress Press, 1983).

S. G. WILSON is Professor of Religious Studies, Carleton University, Ottawa, Ontario, and the author of *The Gentiles and Gentile Mission in Luke-Acts* (Cambridge: Cambridge University Press, 1973); *Luke and the Pastoral Epistles* (London: SPCK, 1979); and *Luke and the Law* (Cambridge: Cambridge University Press, 1983).

Introduction

Since the Holocaust the question of Christianity's contribution to anti-Semitism has given rise to a vast amount of literature, and since the middle 1960s, with Vatican II's declaration, the issue has become one of the central questions of ecumenical debate. No doubt the inwardness of the 1960s and 1970s has given its own special stamp to the contours of that debate. This period will go down in history as one of the most agonizingly introspective, and not least because of the pain of the re-assessment of Christianity's attitude to Judaism.

The early Christian materials have often been examined to assess their role in the longstanding negative attitude of Christians to Jews. Many of these studies are valuable, but even the good ones are often flawed by being too apologetic, too polemical, or not sufficiently critical. Generally they have focussed on the theological reasons for, or implications of, the statements in the New Testament or in other early Christian literature which might be considered anti-Judaic. The studies which follow emphasize the context and history of early Christianity. While not without presuppositions, they all try to be rigorously critical as they present a reconsideration of many of the classic passages which have contributed to the development of anti-Judaism in Christianity.

The motivation for the early church's sometimes harsh attitude was partly theological—it needed to define itself over against its parent—and partly sociological—it needed to make clear the line which divided the fledgling group of Christian believers from the group with which it was most likely to be confused. That polemic was sometimes fed by historical circumstances, on the one hand mistrust originating in Judaism, on the other hand societal dislike of a religious body that remained separate from the rest of society. The growing separation was also related, both as cause and as effect, to the rapid gentilizing of the church as it developed in the first century. For these and other reasons, a polemic quickly developed from the side of Christianity towards its parent—Israel.

It is of course true that the polemic was reciprocated; indeed in the earliest period the Jewish side of the story was probably the more important, though we have less direct and accessible evidence of it. As time went on, however, it was the Christian side of the polemic which had the most devastating consequences, especially after the Roman Empire officially adopted Christianity. From then on, in greater or lesser degree, there came to be an "official" stance towards Judaism that kept it in a position of subordination, and often of outright persecution.

The essays in this volume, and another to follow soon after, explore a limited range of texts and issues, these being the most important because they have been the most influential. What they reveal is a sense of the dynamic and changing character of the Christian-Jewish debate in the first couple of centuries. They are not completely comprehensive. But the two volumes together offer extensive glimpses into the way in which a group of Messianic Jews in the mid-first century became a triumphalist church which had turned its back on its source by the late third century.

The origin of this volume lies in a conversation in an airport restaurant following the Learned Societies at Québec City in 1976. It had become clear in earlier meetings that a substantial number of scholars in the Canadian Society of Biblical Studies had a clearly defined interest in this question. So it was decided to begin a five year seminar to study "Anti-Judaism in Early Christianity." Fortuitously, as it happened, the same year marked the beginnings of a very large and important international research project situated in McMaster University on the related theme "Normative Self-Definition of Judaism and Christianity." A good part of the strength of the seminar was a result of the enthusiasm generated at McMaster. But the CSBS seminar drew upon scholars across Canada, meeting once a year during "the Learneds" and keeping in touch by correspondence in between.

In its first year or two (at Fredericton, New Brunswick, and London, Ontario) the seminar was wide-ranging in its interests, looking at evidence for the way polemic was conducted in the surrounding world of the first century B.C.E. and first century C.E. Regrettably those papers have not been included. The majority of the papers in this volume come from the session of 1979 on the gospels (Saskatoon, Saskatchewan), and the meeting on Paul in 1980 (Montréal, Québec). The second volume of papers will include those which look at other developments in the late first century and on into the second and third centuries (prepared for the 1981 meeting in Halifax, Nova Scotia, and the 1982 meeting in Ottawa, Ontario). The second volume will also include an interpretive essay by Lloyd Gaston which will draw together some of the strands. The whole collection is prefaced by an examination of recent literature on the topic of anti-Judaism by William Klassen.

The order of papers in this volume is roughly chronological. In dealing with Paul before the gospels we seek to draw a clear picture of the earliest evidence for anti-Judaism, where the critical questions are not quite so vexing. A good bit of that evidence, if not all, shows how it is an *intra muros* debate rooted in the difficult new questions posed by Paul's mission to Gentiles. With the gospels and Acts it is clear that the picture, though bolder in many respects, is less clear with respect to setting, motivation, and historical circumstance. The redactional intentions of the authors become a primary concern, along with the sense of a greater degree of separation. The contributions of the gospels of Luke, Matthew, and John towards the shaping of later Christian anti-Semitism is acknowledged and explored by several of the authors.

The editor is grateful to the contributors (and apologizes to them for unexpected delays in the volume's appearance), to Wilfrid Laurier University Press for its help and advice, to the Canadian Corporation for Studies in Religion, and to Professor Jean Ouellette, the editor of the Monograph Series, "Studies in Christianity and Judaism." This book has been published with the help of a grant from the Canadian Federation for the Humanities using funds provided by the Social Sciences and Humanities Research Council of Canada. We are all grateful for this help; in addition the Editor is personally grateful to the SSHRCC for a Research Grant during his sabbatical leave in 1980-81, which allowed time to begin to work on this volume. The University of Toronto Research Board provided a small grant to assist with the typing, which Mrs. Colleen McColeman, Ms Doreen Morton, and Mrs. Carol Robb have done so nobly, despite the unfamiliar new technology of the computer.

Professor David Granskou was the other coffee drinker in Québec; he played an important role in the seminars and in the early planning stages of the volume. Regrettably, a serious accident that occurred just as the editorial work was beginning interrupted his direct involvement. Fortunately, as the editorial work was concluding, he was once more back to full vigour. Professor Stephen Wilson, who will edit volume 2, and Professor Lloyd Gaston, who will write the summary essay, both contributed substantially to the direction of the seminar and have been involved in the major editorial decisions.

The abbreviations used are basically those of the *Journal of Biblical Literature*. The indices have been prepared by a graduate student at the Centre for Religious Studies in the University of Toronto, Mr. Barry Henaut.

Peter Richardson

1

Anti-Judaism in Early Christianity: The State of the Question

William Klassen

Few topics in the area of New Testament studies have received the amount of attention that the topic of anti-Semitism or anti-Judaism has received in recent times. The importance of the theme, however, is not universally recognized. When we look at standard encyclopaedias we find that an entry under the topic of "anti-Semitism" is missing both in the four volume work *The Interpreter's Dictionary of the Bible* (1962), and also in the supplementary fifth volume (1976) which sought to correct serious omissions. The third edition of the six volume encyclopaedia, *Die Religion in Geschichte und Gegenwart* (1957) treats the topic masterfully in a page and a half while the Schaff-Herzog Encyclopaedia devoted half a column to it. By contrast, the recently published *Theologische Realenzyklopädie* (1978) published by a group of Roman Catholic scholars devotes fifty-five pages to it using six different writers to deal with the history of the problem.

This essay surveys some of the literature, sketches the contours of the debate and seeks to isolate the more important contributions. Recent literature demonstrates that we are dealing with a central question in the relation between Christianity and Judaism. This survey seeks to highlight the major areas in which research has been done as well as to make some preliminary observations about the current state of the question.

Sources

Central to the question of anti-Semitism among the early Christians has been the question of its presence among the Greek and Roman writers prior to the emergence of Christianity. Any analysis of anti-Semitism in the ancient world is constrained by the availability of the sources, literary and otherwise. Ever since the beginning of the twentieth century scholars have depended heavily on the work of Th. Reinach, recently reprinted.[1]

With the publication of the three volume work by Menahem Stern, *Greek and Latin Authors on Jews and Judaism,* now drawing to a close, a reliable and indispensable collection of sources is available.[2] Stern treats the sources from Herodotus to Plutarch in volume 1 and from Tacitus to Simplicius in volume 2. Volume 3 plans to treat difficult problems, geographical texts, and to provide an index to the whole.

The method employed by Stern is to present an introduction to the text, placing the writer into his historical context and looking at the writing in terms of the problems which have been associated with its transmission. Stern then presents the text in the original language using the best text available to him, and offers translations from the Loeb Classical Library series or from other recognized translations. He adds exegetical comments where points need clarification or where textual difficulties have arisen. Although the work will not make redundant the reading of the texts themselves, that reading will be greatly facilitated, and the commentary provided by Stern is always well informed and balanced. Stern's work is an extremely important contribution to the discussion of the place of Jews in the ancient world and one which can be of great benefit to the scholar and untrained student as well.

Alongside this collection which concentrates on what non-Jews were writing should stand an approach based upon the material arising from within the Jewish community itself. The collection of papyri from Egypt assembled by Tcherikover and Fuks is indispensable. The continuing publication of papyri still remains one of the greatest frontiers beckoning scholars.[3] It is evident that sources are available to the current participants in the discussion which were not available to scholars a few decades ago.

Some Classical Treatments

One of the most persistent and articulate analysts of the phenomenon of Jewish Christian relations has been James Parkes. A clergyman who lived and travelled in the Mideast, Parkes was the first in the English-speaking world to raise his voice in favour of recognition of the strong tie which binds Judaism and Christianity. In book after book his careful research observed the interaction between Judaism and Christianity

1 Th. Reinach, *Textes d'auteurs grecs et romains relatifs au judaisme* (1895, reprinted Hildesheim: Olms, 1963).

2 Menahem Stern, *Greek and Latin Authors on Jews and Judaism* (Jerusalem: The Israel Academy of Sciences and Humanities), vol. 1, from Herodotus to Plutarch (1974); vol. 2, from Tacitus to Later Antiquity (1980); vol. 3 is in process.

3 V.A. Tcherikover and A. Fuks, *Corpus Papyrorum Judaicarum* (Cambridge: Harvard University Press; Jerusalem: Massada Press; vol. 1, 1957; vol. 2, 1960; vol. 3, 1964).

and chronicled with uncompromising care the history of their conflict. Although he never held an academic post he nevertheless was responsible for some of the most painstaking scholarship in this area; he never confused ideological campaigns with the hard and demanding role of the scholar. His concern with anti-Semitism began in 1925, and always his interest in the New Testament was in the background. It came to clearest focus in his book, *Jesus, Paul and the Jews,* published in 1936; regrettably it made little impression.[4]

Another person, of very different life experiences and background, who made an equally important contribution to the discussion is Jules Isaac. "Isaac had academic knowledge, the discipline of a scholar, the courage to speak out, and the nobility to offer the healing hand of a friendship which is intent on building for the future."[5] Isaac was baffled by the silence of Christians in the presence of the persecutions of the Jews during the World War. He wrote some pages on this subject and submitted them to Maurice Blondel and André Trocmé.[6] In 1943, while working on the problem, tragedy struck his own family. His wife was captured by the Nazis, and with the exception of two sons his whole family was wiped out. His wife's clandestine note to her husband after being shipped off read: "Save yourself for your work; the world is waiting for it." Against great odds he worked on his manuscript driven by the "passion of an anguished heart." "I viewed my work as a fight for wounded Israel, for brotherhood against hatred. I had a task to fulfill. It was a sacred mission." In 1946 his publisher received the six hundred page manuscript of *Jésus et Israël.* In it he compared the gospel text with what the commentators said about it, and he demonstrated the distortions in the latter. He tried to show that these distortions were largely responsible for the Christians' anti-Semitic conditioning. Most importantly, as a Jew he led the attempts to get the liturgy of the church changed so that it would no longer perpetuate contempt for the Jew. Through several direct meetings with the Pope he was able to achieve some very significant reforms in the liturgy. At age 85 he wrote *The Teaching of Contempt,* the first of his books to be translated into English. He taught Christians to look more carefully at the New Testament and in doing so they became aware—perhaps were taught again by a Jew—that if they want to be children of God they cannot afford to hold their neighbour in contempt.[7]

4 See Alan T. Davies, ed., *Antisemitism and the Foundations of Christianity* (Toronto: Paulist Press 1979), v-xi.

5 Claire Huchet Bishop in her biographical introduction to Jules Isaac, *The Teaching of Contempt: Christian Roots of Antisemitism* (New York: Holt, Rinehart and Winston, 1964), 5.

6 See the moving story of how André Trocmé assisted Jews including Daniel, son of Jules Isaac, in escaping from the Nazi death machine by turning his village into a virtual sanctuary for hundreds of them in Philip Hallie, *Lest Innocent Blood be Shed* (New York: Harper, 1979), esp. 158-60.

7 Isaac, *The Teaching of Contempt,* 8-15.

In giving pride of place to these two outstanding scholars, the one a Christian clergyman and the other a Jewish history teacher, we dare not overlook the scholarly contribution made by men like Herman Strack who worked hard to help his colleagues understand Judaism.[8] In this category also belongs F.J. Foakes-Jackson, who in all his books tried to lead his readers to a fuller understanding and a deeper appreciation of Judaism.[9] In the twentieth century few scholars did that as ably as Adolf Schlatter, whose greatness as a New Testament scholar may appear from the fact that both the massive Kittel's *Theological Dictionary of the New Testament* and also Rudolf Bultmann's *Theology of the New Testament* are dedicated to him. Schlatter's exegetical work is permeated with quotations from Jewish sources, including Josephus, Philo, and the Talmud. We would not phrase our comments today as he did, but his desire to find the key to understanding the New Testament in the Judaism of the first century has been found adequate and essential.

The work of Jakob Jocz, who has lived and worked in Canada for many years, is quite different,[10] for his writings have been directed as missionary tracts towards the Jews. In effect he is saying to Christians that they cannot be saved without Jews, therefore work hard to encourage the Jews to accept the Messiah. The truth in what he is saying is that Christianity has no mission without a forthright confrontation with its own Jewishness.

Interdisciplinary Studies on Anti-Semitism

Space does not permit any detailed treatment of anti-Semitism from the standpoint of other disciplines. Nevertheless several deserve comment. Fundamental to any discussion is Hannah Arendt's work on totalitarianism. For New Testament scholars especially, tempted as we are at times to grasp at simple correlations, it is well to be reminded by Professor Arendt that "Modern antisemitism must be seen in the more general framework of the development of the nation state, and at the same time its source must be found in certain aspects of Jewish history and specifically Jewish functions during the last centuries."[11] The link between the development of totalitarianism and the phenomenon of anti-Semitism can be seen clearly. If it is true that the most virulent form of anti-Semitism has always been seen where Christianity became

8 H.L. Strack, *Jesus, die Häretiker und die Christen nach den ältesten jüdischen Angaben* (Leipzig: Hinrichs, 1910), and many other works.

9 E.g., F.J. Foakes-Jackson, *The Rise of Gentile Christianity* (New York: Doran, 1927).

10 J. Jocz, *Christians and Jews: Encounter and Mission* (London: SPCK, 1966). *The Jewish People and Jesus Christ* (London: SPCK, 1954) is his best known and most satisfactory book.

11 H. Arendt, *Antisemitism: The Origins of Totalitarianism* (New York: Harcourt Brace, 1951), 9.

the governing power or became institutionalized in the state, then a normal conclusion can be drawn: Christianity is not anti-Semitic by definition but only in its distorted form which is defined by Constantine. In that form all kinds of totalitarianism can flourish.

What is sobering is the extent to which the academic community became Hitler's servant in this matter. Scholarship in general played an important role in Germany's crimes against the Jewish people, and unfortunately it cannot be said that Biblical scholarship was free from blame.[12]

Two issues in particular emerge as important in the discussion: Was anti-Semitism a universal phenomenon or did it begin with Christianity? This question emerges repeatedly and therefore receives major attention in this essay. The second question revolves around a different issue: To what extent can Christianity and Judaism be separated? Since both speak about and to the same God it is difficult to separate them neatly from each other. Siamese twins they may not be. But they have developed a kind of symbiosis which is hard to describe in other terms. The definition of each and their self-understandings are always intimately related.

The History of Anti-Semitism in the Ancient World

There has been continuing debate whether anti-Semitism began in the ancient world or whether it began with Christianity. Johannes Leipoldt argued that it emerged after the dispersion; he saw the first witness to it in the Elephantine papyri evidence (410 B.C.E.) that an altar or temple of Jahweh was destroyed. Further evidence is seen in the book of Esther (300 B.C.E.), and the writings of the Egyptian, Manetho (260 B.C.E.), who knew legends defamatory to the Jews.

As a counter-balance Leipoldt noted a strong attraction to Judaism; he refers to the wife of Nero, Poppaea Sabina, whom Josephus called a Jewish *sebomenē* (Josephus uses *theosebēs* in *Ant.* 20.8.11; *Life* 3). The reason anti-Semitism developed so quickly is to be found in "the Jewish revolts against Nero, Trajan, and Hadrian."[13] Jews came to be seen as a threat to the common life, so that Titus did not dare to marry the Jewess, Berenice (Suetonius, *Titus,* 7), and the subsequent developments were such that Christianity could not keep itself aloof from anti-Semitism.

---

12 See Max Weinreich, *Hitler's Professors: The Part of Scholarship in Germany's Crimes against the Jewish People* (New York: Yiddish Scientific Institute, 1946), especially 40-45 and 65-67. See also Alan D. Beyerchen, *Scientists Under Hitler* (New Haven: Yale University Press, 1977). The former was kindly called to my attention by Peter Richardson.

13 Johannes Leipoldt, *Antisemitismus in der alten Welt* (Leipzig: Dörffling & Franken, 1933), summarized in his article, "Antisemitismus," *RAC* 1, 469-76. This quotation in col. 470.

Leipoldt saw this not as a racial matter—for racial discrimination in the modern sense was not known in the ancient world[14]—but rather as a result of Judaism's religious commitments, and particularly because many non-Jews were attracted to Judaism. Although Judaism evoked more antipathy than the cult of Dionysus, or the philosophies of Epicurus or the Cynics, it shared with those movements the disdain and even hatred directed against them by the dominant culture, which led to depreciatory statements directed against it. In the case of Judaism the separatism which kept it alive was seen by its contemporaries as a threat to the ideal of the emerging humanity in which all would share with each other and participate fully in the common life.[15]

A further reason for ancient anti-Judaism was political. Leipoldt observed that the cause of the destruction of the sanctuary to Jahweh in Elephantine in 410 B.C.E. was Jewish friendliness towards the Persians, whom the Egyptians saw as a threat to their independence. Such anti-Judaic sentiments are evident in Alexandria at least up to the time of Trajan and Hadrian.

Finally there is the economic impact of the Jews as they moved beyond their agrarian means of survival to enter business and finance, a move noticed but not fully endorsed by all segments of Judaism. Leipoldt referred to Josephus's description of a Jewish business which earned at about the rate of 900 per cent (*Life* 13:74-76). All of this he sees as food for anti-Semitism even when it does not justify the virulent response it evoked.

The most thorough treatment this topic has received in recent times was published by J.N. Sevenster in 1975.[16] Sevenster seeks to lay bare the roots of anti-Semitism in the ancient world and he pursues the task in four areas: race, social status, strangeness, and politics. The work deserves a detailed analysis and critique for it deals with a fundamental problem and has not received critical recognition.

By contrast, the extensive history of the Jewish people edited by H.H. Ben-Sasson and published in 1976 has only one passing reference to anti-Semitism in ancient times. Esther is cited along with Judith and Tobit as providing "the first evidence of those virulent anti-Jewish attacks that were to become so frequently directed at major Jewish communities there."[17]

---

14 For confirmation from a different standpoint see Frank Snowden Jr., *Blacks in Antiquity* (Cambridge: Harvard University Press, 1970).

15 See especially H.G. Baldry, *The Unity of Mankind in Greek Thought* (Cambridge: Cambridge University Press, 1965); E. Bickermann, *Der Gott der Makkabäer* (Berlin: 1937), 129-31. Arthur Hertzberg, *Anti-Semitism and Jewish Uniqueness Ancient and Contemporary* (1973 B.G. Rudolph Lectures in Judaic Studies, Syracuse University, 1975), says: "The age-old principle from which antisemitism has sprung is that no radically dissenting group can be allowed to maintain itself. This notion has dominated in the Western world" (19).

16 J.N. Sevenster, *The Roots of Pagan Antisemitism in the Ancient World*, NovTSup 41 (Leiden: E.J. Brill, 1975).

17 H.H. Ben-Sasson, ed., *History of the Jewish People* (Cambridge: Harvard University Press, 1976), 160.

Sevenster, however, believes the phenomenon is much more pervasive. He begins by trying to define the term and to bring some precision into the discussion. He discusses extensively the argument that we should distinguish between anti-Judaism and anti-Semitism. The terms "Judaism and Judaize can be used in theological discourse without referring personally to Jews" (3). In this regard he claims that a Christian in order to be a Christian "must be anti-judaistic and a Jew in order to be a Jew must be anti-Christian" (3). Ultimately, however, he argues that even though the word "anti-Semitism" is susceptible to misunderstanding, suggesting to the modern mind a racial distinction, still it is the best term we can use.

Herein lies the major definitional problem of the book. From the present writer's perspective it would have been helpful to explore this dimension more fully. In order to be able to look at the question more dispassionately we might look for other examples in ancient literature of the kind of prejudice that is inherent in the word "anti-Semitism."

One such case is to be found in the New Testament itself where the author of the letter to Titus quotes with approval a common proverb: "Cretans are always liars, vicious brutes, lazy gluttons," and the author adds: "He told the truth" (Titus 1:12). Thus the author lumps together all Cretans and condemns them all! This kind of a general statement allows for no exceptions leading to the stereotyping of a class of people and portrays them all in the same evil mold. How did Christians who had lived in Crete for many centuries deal with such slander? The best way to deal with it is to call it simply what it is: malicious nonsense for which Epimenides should have been censured, not enshrined in the New Testament!

Ordinarily the prefix "anti-" simply means to be opposed to something. In the present intellectual climate, given our awareness of the waves of anti-Semitism which have engulfed Western thought, virtually drowning it in Nazi Germany, we must recognize that anti-Semitism has connotations which other words with that prefix do not have. In our context it is best to reserve the term for hatred of Jews or Judaism. Moderns are familiar with such concepts as "contempt," "prejudice," and "discrimination," and they apply here. This means that any negative assessment of the contribution of Judaism to a given historical debate should not automatically be termed "anti-Semitism." Not every prophet of the Old Testament or writer of the New who criticizes the Israelite people or the Jewish people is to be called anti-Semitic. Those who do criticize by broadside condemnation and those who treat groups of people indiscriminately and whose statements become irrational and project more hatred than understanding can rightfully be called "anti-Semitic," or with slightly less harshness, "anti-Judaic."

Overall Sevenster fails to make clear distinctions consistently. From that standpoint his is an unfortunate book, for it fails far too often to distinguish between the various gradations: uneasiness that outsiders felt towards Jews because they were different or successful, puzzlement that outsiders felt towards Jewish religion, hatred that came out of special circumstances, fear of the Jews among outsiders in part as a result of compulsory circumcisions, or fear among outsiders as a result of Jewish attempts to destroy totally such people as did not allow the Jews exclusive possession of a land which they felt was theirs by Divine right.

One example of confusion of categories must suffice. Sevenster deals with Philo's report that Sejanus wanted, as Sevenster puts it, "to destroy that race completely" (*to ethnos anarpasai thelontos*) (*Leg*. 159-61).[18] On these few words Sevenster bases accusations of "anti-Judaism" and "anti-Semitism" (*Roots,* 11-13). No serious effort is made to ascertain whether Philo is here to be trusted. But Sevenster does go on to say that "if it is correct, it then appears that even in ancient days certain occupants of very high posts could be extremely dangerous to the Jews because of their antisemitism." Furthermore he says: "It has sometimes been suspected, for example, that Pilate's provocation of the Jews in Palestine was partly inspired by Sejanus's antisemitic policy" (13). The "for example" is to help the reader believe that there were other potentates of the ancient world who were also anti-Semitic but who did not have an opportunity to harass the Jews. Surely a careful historian will build his case on evidence which has been analyzed, not on suppositions. Sevenster prefers to use the words "anti-Judaism" and "anti-Semitic" interchangeably, and by looking at isolated pieces of information he creates an impression that anti-Jewish feelings were widespread and already motivated along the lines of Hitler's program.

All of this is meant to bring us beyond the crude anti-Semitism which appears among modern scholars; and our task now is "to uncover the latent antisemitism, the secret arrogance of the non-Jew who sometimes assumes the garment of sympathetic philo-Semitism" (30-31). While he recognizes that "objective historiography . . . to extract the truth from the facts themselves . . . has become more difficult than ever" (31), he has not made the task any easier by bringing in the category of "latency." We may ask: Can the historian ever place his finger on that which is latent? If the arrogance is "secret" what tools does the historian possess which will bring it to the light of day?

---

18 Others have translated this text differently; Colson reads: "[F]alse slanders invented by him because he wished to make away with the nation" (Loeb edition, 1962, ad loc.). Even that is rendering the verb *anarpazō* falsely, for the word can mean "to plunder, kidnap, ravage," but hardly "to destroy." Based on the use of the word in other writers of the time it is better to translate, "because he wished to harass the people." Sevenster himself warns that the word *ethnos* must not be taken as "race." When seen alongside Hitler's deliberate policy to do away with the "race" of the Jews, it behoves the historian to be cautious in the translation of such ancient lines. Josephus's usage of the word does not support Sevenster's translation. Compare also Diodor of Sicily, 1:5.

Although Sevenster recognizes that the word "race" must be used with care (and he criticizes Bell[19] especially for misusing it) he himself uses it throughout in a very fluid manner. He does recognize, however, that "there is not a single indication to be found in ancient literature that antisemitism in the ancient world used the theory of race as a weapon of attack" (56).

It may be that Cicero, following Posidonius, overstated the case, but there surely is evidence in Jewish sources that in large part he is correct when he says: "The Jews are the only people to reject all social contact with other peoples as being enemies, who considered them godless and hated by the gods, who accused them of misanthropy and said they would never sit at table with another nation nor display any good will towards him" (51-52). Surely it is not the historian's task to imply that Cicero felt even more strongly and it was only his cleverness as a rhetorician which causes his restraint. Is it not possible that Cicero too was making certain deductions on the basis of information available to him? And would there not have been Jews who would have read these words as a high compliment to the fact that they had been able to retain that distinctiveness to which Jahweh had called them?

In his treatment of economic status Sevenster concludes that there is no basis in the economic situation for anti-Semitism (88). He does not deal however with an equally important aspect of the economic picture: restrictions on trade with foreigners. Martin Hengel has pointed out that the Hasidic and apocalyptic circles, including Ben Sira, join in a condemnation of many items which could only be purchased from Gentiles.

> After the conquest of Jerusalem by Antiochus III in 198 B.C.E. the orthodox members of the priesthood, presumably under Simon the Just, succeeded in obtaining from the king a regulation which—allegedly on grounds of purity and to protect the sanctity of the Temple—inevitably put considerable limitations on dealings of aliens in the city .... The dispute between Simon's son Onias III, and the financial administrator of the Temple, Simon, a supporter of the Tobiads, ... broke out over a question which also concerned trading in the city .... Restriction on trade with foreigners through ritual prescriptions occurs to a still greater extent after the Maccabean period.[20]

Hengel provides numerous illustrations of this and concludes: "The tendency to prohibit all trading with non-Jews by ritual commands and prohibitions, which amounted to an economic boycott, comes up again in the time of the first revolt in A.D. 66, when the importation of foreign oil and other foodstuffs was prohibited on grounds of impur-

---

19 Sevenster, *Roots,* 30-32. The reference to H.I. Bell is to the German version of his book, *Juden und Griechen im römischen Alexandreia* (2d edition, 1927) although he also lists the book, *Jews and Christians in Egypt* (London: British Museum, 1924; reprinted, Westport, CN: Greenwood, 1972).

20 Martin Hengel, *Judaism and Hellenism* (Philadelphia: Fortress Press, 1975) 1:52.

ity" (53). The question of economic status is far from resolved. Leipoldt's reference (cited above) to a Jewish business which Josephus depicts as having a margin of profit approaching 900 per cent deserves further comment.[21] If one looks at the text in Josephus cited by Leipoldt (*Life,* 13) one finds there a highly tendentious account in which Josephus accuses John of Gischala of a knavish trick. He requested pure oil for the personal use of the Jews in Caesarea. His real motive, Josephus says, was not piety but profiteering of the most bare-faced description; for he knew that at Caesarea two pints were sold for one drachm, whereas at Gischala eighty pints could be had for four drachms. Josephus indicates that he gave his consent in order to avoid being stoned by the mob. "Thus, having gained my consent, John by his sharp practice made an enormous profit."

To cite this as an example of Jewish business ("ein jüdisches Geschäft") strikes me as very odd. It is surely an isolated incident and betrays Josephus's own knavery rather than allowing us any deductions about Jewish business practices.[22] Eventually Leipoldt does conclude that economics played a very modest role in comparison to religion and politics.

Furthermore, there is evidence in 3 Macc. 3:10 of Jewish businessmen going into partnership with Greeks and it is above all important that wealthy Jews had reserved the most desirable seats in the front rows of the theatre in Miletus. It is not unimportant that the wealth of the Jews or their business practices is missing totally in the satires written by their contemporaries. If anything, it was their poverty that was an object of ridicule.

The statement by W. Bousset that the Jew brought with him "his wealth, his superiority and unscrupulousness in business, . . . his skill in taking advantage of situations" and that this evoked "hatred and uncontrolled mob reactions" is totally without foundation.[23] The conclusion which Sevenster reaches is worth noting: "Not one single writer of antiquity mentions [wealth or commercial practices] when pouring forth his hatred and contempt of the Jews" (59).

The nub of the matter has to do with religion and religious practices. But in most religions there is an economic fall-out, and that is certainly true of Judaism. The first to have complained about the unsocial behaviour of the Jews seems to have been Hecataeus of Ab-

---

21 Leipoldt, *RAC* 1, 472.

22 A possible example of applying the anti-Semitic arguments of one's own milieu to conditions of nineteen centuries ago is provided by Charlotte Klein. She quotes Lagrange: "Undoubtedly, as today, they [the Jews] had the monopoly in certain forms of trade, not to speak of the management of finance," *Anti-Judaism in Christian Theology* (Philadelphia: Fortress, 1978), 36, quoting from *Le Messianisme chez les Juifs* (Paris, 1909), 276. The matter of Josephus's reliability as a historian is one which has received serious study in recent times. See e.g., Shaye Cohen, *Josephus in Galilee and Rome: His Vita and Development as a Historian* (Leiden: Brill, 1979).

23 W. Bousset, *Die Religion des Judentums im neutestamentlichen Zeitalter* (Berlin, 1906), 87 (76 in the 1903 edition).

dera (end of the fourth century B.C.E.) who has considerable respect for the Jews. By the time Diodor of Sicily (first century B.C.E.) quotes him, however, much more emphasis is laid upon a common humanity and therefore what had been at least in part a virtue for Hecataeus is no longer seen as such: "A form of life encouraging seclusion from mankind and hatred of aliens" (*apanthrōpon tina kai misoxenon bion*).

To be properly understood, the accusation of strangeness has to be looked at in the light of those aspects of Old Testament law which forbade contact with paganism or pagans and which commanded the total rooting out of the inhabitants of the land. In a situation where the Jews were no longer the conquering people but the conquered, the remnants of these instructions expressed themselves through refraining from social contacts and separation from what were considered evil persons. Ancient society, like modern, often shows great tolerance for the individual dissenter (unless like Socrates he has power, influence, and followers!) and even to some extent for communities of dissenters. What it could not and cannot tolerate is any strangeness based on depreciation of those being estranged, and any use of violence against those who do not accept the value system.

Hecataeus and those who followed him translated into their own words what they saw as anti-social behaviour on the part of the Jews. It can only be described as anti-Semitic if it proves to have no basis in Israelite law or behaviour. The extent of over-reaction on the part of non-Israelites may be noted; but it can hardly be correct historical procedure to castigate the accusation without seeing the basis for the fears. It is not enough then to see with Sevenster the fundamental cause for anti-Semitism in the sovereign self-sufficiency of Judaism. We must also see the way in which that expressed itself and the way in which it was perceived by those who were not Jews.

The strangeness of the Jews threatened the outsider also at another point. For with the emergence of Rome as the dominant power the Jews negotiated and received special privileges: exemption from military service, some diversion of taxes to the Temple, etc. Sevenster's way of dealing with this matter shows him totally insensitive to social realities. One can stress the aberrations of Roman justice if one likes, for there were many instances in which the Romans did not treat the Jews fairly; but, according to Josephus, during the siege of Jerusalem Titus reminded the Jews that the Romans had never impeded their extraction of tribute for God and the collection of offerings. He noted that the Jews had therefore become richer at the expense of the Romans and that they now used that money to attack the Romans (*Wars,* 6:335).

Any one who belongs to a privileged minority knows the animosity that can come from such a status. Exemption from military service, relaxation of taxes, special laws, Temple tax protected by Rome as it made its way to Jerusalem, interdiction of inter-marriage, all of these are bound to bring strong feelings of antagonism from those who do not belong to the group. A historian knows that in retrospect the reaction is never fully justified. Why should the Reformers of the sixteenth century advocate the death penalty for a small group of people who refused military service and refused to have their infants baptized? Because even when—and perhaps especially when—motivated by religious zeal, authorities cannot tolerate deviance.

Sevenster's approach therefore lacks precision in the use of words and fails to enter into the social dynamics of the situation. It is a catalogue of sources brought together with an extreme bias and serves little good for a thorough study of this problem. He assumes that he has demonstrated the existence of considerable anti-Semitism in the pagan world but leaves at least this reader quite unconvinced that it is as widespread or as virulent as he assumes. The roots may be there, but little evidence is provided of the nourishment. Above all his book does not portray the infinite variety in Judaism itself and the attempts made by many devout Jews to head off this "anti-" feeling without compromising in any way the essential nature of Judaism. Sevenster has taken a collection of texts and arranged them according to certain categories. Helpful as they may be, the book would have been more valuable from a historical point of view if he had set the statements into their historical context and given some heed to social factors.

Finally a word must be said about the sources which Sevenster uses. He is almost totally dependent upon the collection of Reinach.[24] He also uses the papyri of Egypt collected by Tcherikover and Fuks[25] and the so-called Acts of the Alexandrian Martyrs published in the 1890s.[26]

Fortunately, as noted above, we are no longer confined to Reinach. The excellent collection of all sources dealing with Jews in the ancient world published by Professor Stern provides the scholar with an objective commentary, accurate texts and adequate translations which will make it possible for the reader to assess the evidence and to see the interrelations between certain texts. Even then, of course, it is necessary to study each quotation in the light of the events which informed it, the place where it was written, the wider social context in which it appeared, to whom it was addressed, and by whom it was written. It is now possible for scholars to make careful judgments about the existence of anti-Semitism in the ancient world.

Conversion to Judaism

When we recognize Judaism as a minority group which had (and has) a divinely appointed role in history it is even more necessary to assess the

24 See above note 1.

25 See above note 3.

26 Sevenster, *Roots,* 15; Tcherikover and Fuks, *Corpus,* 2:55.

factors which went into its rejection by the dominant society. In some of these we can recognize the inevitable clash between visions of good and evil. In some however we must also raise the question whether Judaism was true to its own calling.

Take as an example the way in which new members were brought into the religion of Judaism. There was a debate which ran for many centuries over the necessity of circumcision. The rite was also associated with inter-marriage, as can be seen by the attempt to strike a matrimonial alliance after the rape of Dinah (Gen. 34) which ended so tragically and pained Jacob so deeply. Does not that strange fragment in Exod. 4:24-26 have its place in this discussion as well? The book of Esther also reports (8:17, LXX) that the people were circumcised out of fear of the Jews. Judaism was deeply divided by the act of John Hyrcanus who forced the Idumeans to be circumcised or be evicted from their land (128 B.C.E.; see Josephus, *Ant.* 13:257). Those who rejected this act of Hyrcanus called the Idumeans *hemiioudaioi* (Josephus, *Wars* 4:270-82; *Ant.* 14:403) and according to a number of writers this act was widely rejected.[27] It brought about the distinction between true proselytes and those who merely appeared to be such.

Some would have been opposed as well to the forcible circumcisions of Mattathias described in 1 Macc. 2:45. That this form of "Judaizing" was known in the pagan world can be assumed since Strabo himself reports that Aristobulus acquired additional territory and did many good things for his country including "bringing over (converting) to them a portion of the Iturean nation, whom he joined to them by the bond of circumcision."[28]

It is likely that the Hasidim sought support for such a course of action from Gen. 41:55, for according to one interpretation[29] Joseph forcibly circumcised the Egyptians. The narrative is inconsistent at a number of points and provides evidence of a Hasidic tendency.

Aptowitzer is certainly right when he sees evidence of a protest against forcible circumcision in the Psalms of Solomon (12 and 13), and he is also correct when he says that no one would want to maintain that such proselytes would be considered genuine by anyone. There is abundant evidence that coercion in the act of circumcision was rejected by Judaism as a whole.[30] It is the same totalitarian error committed later by Constantine who forced people to become Christians.

---

27 V. Aptowitzer, *Parteipolitik der Hasmonäerzeit im rabbinischen und pseudepigraphischen Schrifttum* (Vienna: Kohut Foundation, 1927), 46-47; 222-23.

28 On this text see Stern, *Authors,* 1:271.

29 *Gen. Rab.* 90, near end.

30 V. Tcherikover says about the severe policy that it aroused fierce hostility from the Greeks "to the Jews as a whole . . . and the echoes of this hostility can still be heard in the harsh censures of some scholars." He attributes these censures to the historian's admiration for Greek culture and to the theologian's approach. This makes it easier for such scholars to evaluate "the political achievements of the Hasmoneans by their destructive acts, and ignores their constructive achievements" (*Hellenistic Civilisation*

To be sure, the approach of John Hyrcanus was a distinct modification of the directives given in Deuteronomy and Exodus on how the conquering Israelites are to treat the vanquished. They are commanded to:

(1) Destroy all their holy places (Exod. 23:24; Deut. 7:5; 12:3; Exod. 34:13; Judg. 2:2).

(2) Kill all inhabitants, known as the *herem* (Deut. 7:2; 20:17). "When the Lord your God delivers them into your power and you defeat them, you must put them to death. You must not make a treaty with them or spare them." Not only the altars and high places are to be destroyed but the seven nations are named. In another source it is granted that only the males are to be put to the sword. Permission is granted to "take the women, the dependents, and the cattle . . . and to plunder everything else in the city" (Deut. 20:14). In the cities which lie close to Palestine not one creature shall be left alive. Only "the trees of the field are not men that you should besiege them" (Deut. 20:19).

(3) Reject all inter-marriage; this forms the centre of Ezra's reform movement (Deut. 7:3-4; Exod. 34:15ff.; Josh. 23:12; Judg. 3:5).

The first two of these were not practised after the time of David. And the third was always a difficult matter. Any group which seeks to continue cannot treat it lightly (see the defence in 1 Maccabees of Maccabean deviations).

The themes of exclusivity and tolerance have played a unique role in the relations between Jews and non-Jews. Behind them stand the various strands of Hebrew history which depict God on the one hand as wiping out all who stand in the way of Israel's conquest, and on the other hand commanding Israel to do so. The oldest norm for the way in which Israel is to relate to other nations is: Do not come to terms with them; do not make peace with them.

As G. Schmitt has demonstrated, the basic theme of the Old Testament and one which has remained a ruling principle in Judaism is that exclusiveness does not yield to tolerance.[31] This is one of the reasons why Judaism continues to survive with such rigour and tenacity.

If exclusiveness leads to intolerance it is also true that exclusiveness is the characteristic found offensive most often. Intolerance has been rejected by the majority of devout Jews because it contradicts the

---

and the Jews, [New York: Atheneum, 1975], 247-49). Morton Smith has argued that Hyrcanus was imitating Rome, see "Rome and Maccabean Conversions: Notes on 1 Macc. 8," in E. Bammel, ed., *Donum Gentilicium; N.T. Studies in Honour of David Daube* (Oxford: Clarendon Press, 1978), 1-7.

31 G. Schmitt, *Du sollst keinen Frieden schliessen mit den Bewohnern des Landes; Die Weisungen gegen die Kannaanäer in Israelsgeschichte and Geschichtsschreibung, BWANT* 91, (Stuttgart: Kohlhammer, 1970).

view of Jahweh found in Isaiah and many other parts of the Old Testament. Where exclusiveness is incapable of building tolerance and trust it must be discarded decisively and energetically. It does not deserve to survive even as a wish. Exclusiveness has made it extremely difficult to persuade non-Jews that Jews are strong enough to allow other religions to flourish alongside them, and that whatever the Old Testament says the Jewish faith also invites all persons to live under the rule of Jahweh. Instead outsiders became afraid of certain Jewish expansionists. The same holds true for Christianity whose concern for exclusivity when enforced by a Constantinian model has led to great intolerance towards Jews.

It would be naive to assume that such a fear was not felt by the "great Society." One thinks of the irrational fear so widespread in the first few centuries of the Christian movement, or of the fear in the sixteenth century that the Anabaptists would be non-violent only until they had power to work all kinds of harm on the larger society. One aberration feeds many fears, and the response is often that the majority subsequently ridicules what is sacred to the minority. The historian would do well to study the after-effects of the act of Hyrcanus and observe in particular how seldom circumcision is discussed in a negative way by non-Jewish writers before the Maccabean revolt. It is not the historian's role to condemn or praise. He/she deals with causes and effects and with origins insofar as they can be traced. The historian also can detect how certain values can lead to difficulties in human interaction.

Anti-Semitism in the New Testament

The myth that the scholar can approach religious texts objectively without allowing his or her own biases to interfere was first seriously doubted, even before it was firmly entrenched, by Schleiermacher in the beginning of the nineteenth century. All scholars are conditioned by the society in which they live, and there can be no doubt that the present wave of interest in anti-Semitism in the New Testament is determined to a large extent by the wave of quite justified shame that Christian interpreters have with respect to the Holocaust. No group of interpreters is exempt from this judgment. In this discussion Roman Catholic interpreters have taken a very large place, as have German interpreters.[32]

Many have been deeply moved to what Franz Mussner called a drastic *Umdenken*[33] which borders on a radical conversion. This reas-

32 See Franz Mussner, *Traktat ueber die Juden* (Munich: Kosel Verlag, 1979), who provides abundant references to literature. Still one of the best is the book by the Catholic priest, Edward H. Flannery, *The Anguish of the Jews* (New York: Macmillan, 1965).

33 Mussner, *Traktat,* preface et passim.

sessment, while led by Germans and Catholics, has not been confined to them; Lutherans also have had to come to terms with Luther's totally unchristian statements about the Jews.[34] From the Catholic side the question has been vigorously pursued by those like Gregory Baum or Charlotte Klein who have their roots in Judaism,[35] or Rosemary Ruether[36] whose studies in the ancient church led her back to the New Testament. By contrast, the Jewish scholar Samuel Sandmel comes out much less dogmatically about anti-Semitism in the New Testament. He argues strongly against the idea that there may be a connection between pagan and Christian anti-Semitism,[37] and he concludes that we must rise above that tendency.

Others who studied the New Testament and were led to explore the Jewish roots of its writers could not avoid the question of whether the picture of Judaism derived from the New Testament was accurate. It was also questionable whether the writers of the New Testament had overreacted to the mother faith from which they were increasingly separated by force of history—or simply by the fact that Christianity was beginning to form its own distinct ethos.

Fortunately the process of debate and discussion has fostered group projects of dialogue and discussion in which Jewish scholars have engaged Christian scholars in an unprecedented way.[38] Christians

---

34 Edgar Mills, *Martin Luther and the Jews. A refutation to his book, "The Jews and their Lies,"* (Vienna: Europäischer Verlag, 1968). Reinhold Lewin, *Luthers Stellung zu den Juden* (Berlin, 1911; reprinted Aalen: Scientia Verlag, 1973). Johannes Brosseder, *Luthers Stellung zu den Juden im Spiegel seiner Interpreten* (Munich: Max Heuber Verlag 1972), is a study of the interpretation and reception of Luther's writings and comments in the nineteenth and twentieth centuries especially among German-speaking peoples. Towards the end of his life Luther pressed the state to put an end to three forms of blasphemy: the mass, the proclamation of the Anabaptists, and synagogue worship. See H. Bornkamm, "Luther: Leben und Schriften," *RGG* (3d ed., 1960), 4:403.

35 G. Baum, *Is the New Testament Anti-Semitic?* (Glen Rock, N.J.: Paulist Press, 1960; 2d ed., 1965); Charlotte Klein, *Anti-Judaism in Christian Theology*, trans. E. Quinn (Philadelphia: Fortress Press, 1978).

36 R. Ruether, *Faith and Fratricide: The Theological Roots of Anti-Semitism* (New York: Seabury Press, 1974). Compare the essays which respond to her: A. Davies, ed., *Antisemitism and the Foundations of Christianity* (Toronto: Paulist Press, 1979).

37 S. Sandmel, *Antisemitism in the New Testament?* (Philadelphia: Fortress, 1978), 5, 168.

38 K.H. Rengstorf and S. von Kortzfleisch (eds.), *Kirche und Synagoge, Handbuch zur Geschichte von Christen und Juden* (Stuttgart: Ernst Klette Verlag, 1968); W. Eckert, N.P. Levinson, and M. Stöhr, *Jüdisches Volk-gelobtes Land*, vol. 3: *Abhandlungen zum christlichen-jüdischen Dialog* (Munich: Kaiser Verlag, 1970) and by the same editors: *Antijudaismus im Neuen Testament? exegetische und systematische Beiträge* (Munich, 1967). H. Gollwitzer, M. Palmer, and V. Schliski, "Der Jude Paulus und die deutsche neutestamentliche Wissenschaft," *EvT* 34 (1974), 276-304. M. Barth, J. Blank, J. Bloch, F. Mussner, and R.J. Zwi Werblowsky, *Paulus—Apostat oder Apostel? Jüdische und christliche Antworten* (Regensburg, 1977). P. Lapide, F. Mussner, and U. Wilckens, *Was Juden und Christen von einander denken: Bausteine zum Brückenschlag* (Freiburg/Basel/Vienna: Herder, 1978). Marc H. Tanenbaum, Marvin R. Wilson, A. James Rudin, *Evangelicals and Jews in Conversation, on Scripture, Theology, and History* (Grand Rapids: Baker, 1978). In comparison to the foregoing the volume, *The Church Meets Judaism* by Otto Piper, Jakob Jocz and Harold Floreen (Minneapolis: Augsburg, 1960) reads like a book from another time. Piper alone tries to take the

have not only read Jewish writers but have often felt that unless they read them they could not really understand the New Testament. Gone forever is the stance of Christian scholars who assume that an understanding of the New Testament is somehow the special province of the Christian scholar. The writings of Joseph Klausner,[39] David Flusser,[40] Geza Vermes,[41] and others have provided too much understanding for us to ignore them or to disparage them in any way whatever.

With the creation of the state of Israel, Jewish scholars, fortunately, have been able to work with a degree of freedom not felt before. As long as Jewish scholars were living in a predominantly Christian society, no matter how open it may have been, they were inhibited from stating their position clearly.

A major turning point in the discussion has been the reversal of the Catholic church's position between 1965 and 1975. Those of us not from that religious group sometimes fail to understand the guilt associated with the Good Friday liturgy and the kind of catechetical teaching associated with the accusation that the Jews had killed Jesus. Nevertheless we all have profitted from the ongoing process of reeducation. To look afresh at the New Testament from the perspective of the Holocaust can have a very wholesome effect on the lingering remnants of anti-Jewish feelings. As evidence of this one can cite the forthright response of David Flusser to the writings of Ulrich Wilcken in which the process of dialogue reached a new openness and candour.[42]

---

historical existence of Judaism seriously. For the rest it is a blatant attempt to use Luther to promote evangelism to the Jews! Piper argues that the church's role is "not to make the Jew a Gentile Christian, but to make the Jew a true Jew" (52). "[I]t is primarily our task to make him [the Jew] aware of his dignity, his responsibility, and his obligation as a Jew" (53). H. Goldstein, ed., *Gottesverächter und Menschenfeinde? Juden zwischen Jesus und frühchristliche Kirche* (Dusseldorf: Patmos, 1979). H.H. Henrix, ed., *Jüdische Liturgie. Geschichte-Struktur-Wesen,* Quaestiones disputatae 86 (Freiburg: Herder, 1979). L. Klein, ed., *Judentum und Christentum; Lebendiges Zeugnis* 32/1-2 (Paderborn: Bonifatius-Einigung, 1977). R. Rendtorff, ed., *Arbeitsbuch "Christen und Juden." Zur Studie des Rates der Evangelischen Kirche in Deutschland* (Gutersloh: Mohn, 1979). (These last three I know only as abstracted in *NTA* 24 (1980), 310-13.)

39 J. Klausner, *Jesus of Nazareth* (London: George Allen, 1929); *The Messianic Idea in Israel,* 3 vols. from 1909-23.

40 D. Flusser, *Jesus,* first published in German in 1968, went through many editions and translations. Very poorly translated into English (New York: Herder and Herder, 1969), it is now unfortunately out of print. See also his *Judaism and Christianity, Collection of Essays* (Jerusalem: Academon Press, 1974). His piece, "Das Erlebnis ein Jude zu Sein," in *Richte unsere Füsse auf den Weg des Friedens: Für Helmut Gollwitzer* (Munich: Kaiser, 1979), 15-25, should be read by any Christian who wants to understand the New Testament.

41 G. Vermes, *Jesus the Jew* (London: William Collins, 1973).

42 On the debate between David Flusser and Ulrich Wilckens see: D. Flusser, "Ulrich Wilckens und die Juden," *EvT* 34 (1974), 236-43; U. Wilckens, "Das Neue Testament und die Juden," ibid., 602-11; R. Rendtorff, "Die neutestamentliche Wissenschaft und die Juden. Zur Diskussion zwischen David Flusser und Ulrich Wilckens," *EvT* 36 (1976), 191-200.

While such interfaith discussions are to be warmly welcomed there is much evidence in the polemical work of Rosemary Ruether that much still needs to be done within the circle of Christian scholars on their understanding of the Jewishness of Christianity. The volume edited by Alan Davies in which eleven scholars debate with Professor Ruether and in which she responds to their critique is basic to our discussions. The major issues are there isolated and the fundamental question of methodology directly addressed in an exemplary way. The present writer would agree with John Meagher that there is in principle nothing wrong with writing in a polemical manner, but also that such writing is especially vulnerable to the distortion of history.[43]

The issue therefore deserves the broadest possible discussion. The popular works which seek to inform the public about this critical issue, the revision of the liturgy, the analysis of how our handbooks have been slanted in an anti-Judaistic manner, and above all our understanding of the person of Christ, both the historical Jesus and the Christ of faith—all are of vital importance.

When the work is done correctly we will be finished with all references to a "superior" or inferior religious outlook and we will see ourselves as equal co-workers in a vineyard planted by God.[44] And we will see from our common understanding of God's purpose that whether that vineyard will survive depends on our faithfulness to his covenant. Commitment to that covenant and its demand for the righteousness and *shalom* will transcend whatever may divide, and the term "anti" will be displaced with the prefix "co." Surely it is clear that those who spend their energies fighting against something, building walls of separation rather than building ways of understanding and the common life, have missed the point of God's intervention in history, whether it be in the gift of Torah, the liberation from slavery, or the presence of Jesus Christ.

Like siblings in a common family, Judaism and Christianity have had centuries of bitter rivalry. In the meantime the world has become very small indeed. The tragedy of history is that these two high religions have spent much time thrashing each other instead of rejoicing in the world which God has given them. Their guilt over the past, however, should now be able to yield to a healthy respect for each other, enabling each to deal honestly with the other.[45]

---

43 James Parkes says about Ruether's book: "As a book it is written too hastily, and as a scholarly work, it is too slipshod" (Alan Davies [ed.], *Antisemitism,* xi); see also the contribution by John Meagher, "As the Twig was Bent: Anti-Semitism in Greco-Roman and Earliest Christian Times." Note the forthright challenge to her thesis that to believe in the Messiahship of Jesus is to be anti-Jewish in T.A. Idinopulos and R.B. Ward, "Is Christology inherently Antisemitic?", *JAAR* 45 (1977), 193-214.

44 Note, for example, David Flusser's statement that "Christianity surpasses Judaism, at least theoretically, in its approach of love to all men," in "A New Sensitivity in Judaism and the Christian Message," *HTR* 61 (1968), 127. See also Sandmel, *Antisemitism,* 161, on this question.

45 While recognizing that the relationship between early Christianity and Judaism was

For New Testament scholars this means looking at the text of the New Testament with historical integrity. It is not good historical method to find classical anti-Semitism in the New Testament. In the New Testament writers are trying to delineate differences while taking many similarities for granted. Those common areas bound Judaism and Christianity together inextricably.[46] They still do. A study of the New Testament will have integrity only insofar as it focusses on that central theme and allows all other themes to illuminate the freedom which Jahweh's rule brings.

If there is anything which this age demands, if there is anything which gives reason for hope, it is this: Christian and Jew, each within the common religious dialogue and also independent of it, each faithful to his own belief and his own way of life, bear common witness together before the world that they possess tidings from the divine realm; they go through history as corporeal evidence of the truth of God .... Confronted with a world which for two centuries now has set itself against the word of God, per se, to a degree which increases terrifyingly, the church and Israel—each in its proper way and in its place—have a common witness to bear; at *all* times, even contrary to appearances, God remains king over the whole earth.[47]

"polemic-apologetic," G. Lindeskog has also stressed the deep commonality which they shared. Taken in the usual meaning of the term as a collective hatred towards Jews or as a wholesale enmity against them insofar as they are Jews, it is simply wrong to claim that there is anti-Semitism or anti-Judaism in the New Testament. See G. Lindeskog, "Anfänge des jüdischchristlichen Problems. Ein programmatischer Entwurf," in Bammel, ed., *Donum Gentilicium,* 255-75.

46 See Pinchas Lapide, "Das christlich-jüdische Religionsgespräch," in the *Gollwitzer Festschrift* (note 40), 40-48.

47 H.J. Schoeps, *The Jewish Christian Argument: A History of Theologies in Conflict* (New York: Holt Rinehart and Winston, 1963), 8.

2

Paul Ahead of His Time: 1 Thess. 2:13-16

John C. Hurd

Introduction

Any study of anti-Judaism in the New Testament must at some point come to terms with 1 Thess. 2:13-16. In the *RSV* the passage reads:

And we also thank God constantly for this, that when you received the word of God which you heard from us, you accepted it not as the word of men but as what it really is, the word of God, which is at work in you believers. For you, brethren, became imitators of the churches of God in Christ Jesus which are in Judea; for you suffered the same things from your own countrymen as they did from the Jews, who killed both the Lord Jesus and the prophets, and drove us out, and displease God and oppose all men by hindering us from speaking to the Gentiles that they may be saved—so as always to fill up the measure of their sins. But God's wrath has come upon them at last!

Unfortunately we cannot move directly to consider what Paul meant by these words, for this passage presents a notable problem which has made it the subject of considerable scholarly debate.

The Problem

The basic problem is the attribution of the passage. Two types of evidence incline many scholars to believe that Paul could never have written the words quoted above.

Paul's Attitude Towards Judaism

The accusation that the Jews "killed . . . the Lord Jesus," that they "displease God," that they "oppose all men," that they "fill up the measure of their sins," and that "God's wrath has come upon them" has no precise parallel in the other writings attributed to Paul. On the contrary, in his fullest discussion of the position of Judaism within the purposes of God (Rom. 9-11) he wrote, "Has God rejected his people? By no means! I myself am an Israelite, a descendant of Abraham, a member of the tribe of Benjamin. God has not rejected his people whom he foreknew" (11:1-2). And, more poignantly, "I could wish that I myself were accursed and cut off from Christ for the sake of my brethren, my kinsmen by race" (9:3). He continued, "They are Israelites, and to them belong the sonship, the glory, the covenant, the giving of the law, the worship, and the promises; to them belong the patriarchs, and of their race, according to the flesh, is the Christ" (9:4-5). These passages seem directly to contradict the passage we are presently considering.

Furthermore, although the point is often missed in traditional Protestant readings of Paul's letters, Paul himself did not have an attitude of revulsion towards his preconversion days. Quite the reverse. When Paul made the magnificent comparison between his former life within Judaism and his new life as a Christian in Phil. 3:4-7 he did not contrast bad and good, but rather a very considerable good and an infinitely better good. Indeed, he considered that his Jewish credentials were impeccable and his zeal far above average, so that he could say of himself, "As to righteousness under the law blameless" (Phil. 3:5). It is the obvious value of his initial statement which is the point of the paradoxical contrast between his former state and the present suffering which was his lot as a consequence of "knowing Christ Jesus my Lord" (Phil. 3:8).

That the attitude towards Judaism expressed in Philippians was not simply the product of the rhetorical structure of his argument is shown by his autobiographical reflections in Gal. 1:13-17. Here Paul mentioned his persecution of the earliest church as he had in Philippians, but in neither place does he take these acts to be part of the sin of Israel. Rather he cites them as evidence of his zeal, albeit misguided. He wrote, "For you have heard of my former life in Judaism, how I persecuted the church of God violently and tried to destroy it; and I advanced in Judaism beyond many of my own age among my people, so extremely zealous was I for the traditions of my fathers" (Gal. 1:13-14). There is no hint of condemnation here, either of himself or of Judaism.

Thus we conclude that in the other Pauline letters Paul's attitude toward Judaism both theologically and autobiographically stands in sharp contrast to the sentiments expressed in the Thessalonian passage.

Anti-Judaism After 70 C.E.

On the other hand, the earliest passages—not considering for the moment 1 Thess. 2:13-16—in which we find systematic and pervasive anti-Judaism are found in documents which date after the Jewish revolt and the resulting destruction of the Temple. Matthew provides numerous clear examples.

> Woe to you, scribes and Pharisees, hypocrites! for you build the tombs of the prophets and adorn the monuments of the righteous .... Thus you witness against yourselves that you are the sons of those who murdered the prophets. Fill up, then, the measure of your fathers. You serpents, you brood of vipers, how can you escape being sentenced to hell? Therefore I send you prophets and wise men and scribes, some of whom you will kill and crucify, and some you will scourge in your synagogues and persecute from town to town, that upon you may come all the righteous blood shed on earth, from the blood of innocent Abel to the blood of Zechariah the son of Barachiah, whom you murdered between the sanctuary and the altar. Truly, I say to you, all of this will come upon this generation. O Jerusalem, killing the prophets and stoning those who are sent to you! (Matt. 23:29-37)

Moreover, Matthew is the source of those words which modern Christians wish had never been written, "His blood be on us and on our children!" (Matt. 27:25). The parallels with the Thessalonian passage are obvious and numerous.

It is not necessary to rehearse the long and sorry process by which Christians came to view Judaism first as a rival and then as a scapegoat. The development can be traced through numerous passages in the New Testament, the Apostolic Fathers, and other early Christian writers. After the destruction of the Temple and the horrors resulting from the first Jewish revolt it became a commonplace to believe that all this was the direct judgment of God directed at Israel for its part in the death of Jesus.

Thus the Thessalonian passage is anomalous and seems out of place if taken as an utterance of Paul, but it fits well with the post-70 C.E. attitude of the church. If we picture Jewish-Christian relations as developing smoothly from the earliest days in which Christians thought of themselves as a sect within Judaism to the point at which Christianity, having survived considerable persecution, took its place as the official religion of the Roman Empire and in turn participated in the persecution of Jews, then our passage is an anomaly when dated from the time of Paul.

Previous Solutions to the Problem

Non-authenticity of 1 Thessalonians

In the nineteenth century Ferdinand Christian Baur attempted to sort out the New Testament documents on the basis of internal evidence, rather than on the basis of tradition. He noted our passage in 1 Thessalonians, and he commented on it with considerable perception.[1] To him it seemed clear that the "wrath" which had come upon the Jews must be the destruction of the Temple. He used, that is, the same technique by which modern scholars date the gospels of Matthew and Luke as post-70 C.E., and he concluded that 1 Thessalonians cannot have been written by Paul. His was an "all-or-nothing" approach; he did not dissect and rearrange the Pauline material in the manner of later nineteenth-century scholars. His decision with respect to 1 Thessalonians was parallel to his decision with respect to 2 Thessalonians, Ephesians, Philippians, and Colossians, not to mention 1 and 2 Timothy and Titus. He was of the opinion that a considerable number of New Testament documents had been wrongly attributed to Paul.

Baur's identification of the *Hauptbriefe* (Romans, 1 and 2 Corinthians, and Galatians) became traditional in the Tübingen School, and indeed, except for the Dutch school which believed that Paul left no literary remains at all, subsequent critical scholarship has always assigned at least these four letters to Paul. Moreover, a number of modern scholars have followed Baur's lead in rejecting 1 Thessalonians, mainly on the evidence of 2:16.[2] This negative decision has two virtues. First, it treats the letter as a unified whole and thus avoids the inherent improbability of partition theories. Secondly, it solves at one stroke the difficulties outlined above. Unfortunately for our peace of mind, however, most later scholars have come to believe that the rejection of 1 Thessalonians raises more problems than it solves. In very many respects 1 Thessalonians is similar to 1 Corinthians, a letter of undoubted authenticity. Further, it gives every appearance of being a real letter addressed to a real-life situation. In addition, much of the letter is occupied with the affectionate relationship between Paul and his congregation. It seems hard to imagine a later author concerning himself with these matters. Thus in spite of 2:13-16 most scholars today accept the authenticity of 1 Thessalonians.

Theories of Interpolation

In the last twenty years two independent proposals have been put forward which attempt to solve the problem of 1 Thess. 2:13-16 by rejecting the authenticity of just this passage while accepting the remainder of 1 Thessalonians as genuine. In 1961 Karl Gottfried Eckart suggested that 1 Thess. 2:13-16 was, like 2 Thessalonians, the product of a later age, and that 1 Thess. 4:1-8, 10b-12, and 5:12-22 were liturgi-

1 F.C. Baur, *Paul, The Apostle of Jesus Christ* (2 vols.; 2d ed.; London: Williams and Norgate, 1875-76), 2:87-88.

2 These include Noack, Volkmar, and Holsten from the Tübingen School, and in the twentieth century apparently only Andrew Q. Morton, but not on theological or historical grounds.

cal in origin and thus also inauthentic.[3] His disposal of 2:13-16, however, was a by-product of his main concern which was to divide 1 Thessalonians into two original letters: the first, a letter of recommendation which Paul had sent with Timothy; the second, a letter rejoicing at Timothy's return. The major reason that he rejected the authenticity of 2:13-16 is its similarity to 1:2-10, not the theological and autobiographical considerations outlined in the previous section, above.

In 1971, however, Birger A. Pearson published his influential article "1 Thessalonians 2:13-16: A Deutero-Pauline Interpolation."[4] He carefully considered the verb "has come" (*ephthasen*) in 2:16 and concluded that it must refer to some event in the past with respect to its author. And he asked, "What event in the first century was of such magnitude as to lend itself to such apocalyptic theologizing? The interpretation suggested by Baur and others is still valid: 1 Thess. 2:16c refers to the destruction of Jerusalem in 70 A.D."[5] He then showed how verses 13 to 16 hang together, and he discussed the elements in verses 14 to 16 which he took to be uncharacteristic of Paul. Verse 13 itself, which is characteristically Pauline, is, he argued, a reworking of 1:2-5. He concluded, "The method of our hypothetical interpolater is strikingly similar to that of the author of 2 Thessalonians, *viz.*, to use Pauline words and phrases from a genuine letter in order to provide a putative 'Pauline' framework for a new message."[6] Thus he excised the passage from its context and assigned it to the period after 70 C.E., the period which gave birth to sentiments such as those reflected in Matthew's gospel, as noted above.

The theory of interpolation seems to offer the best of both worlds: we are allowed to keep 1 Thessalonians as an authentic letter of Paul, but the historical and theological difficulties posed by our passage are resolved by assigning it to a later period. Eckart's article seems arbitrary and by itself does not arouse much enthusiasm. Pearson's work, however, represents a very considerable advance. He shows himself sensitive to the historical problems which were outlined in the previous section. Further, he recognizes the inherent improbability of interpolation theories and accepts the proposition that the burden of proof rests upon the scholar who would challenge the integrity of the text. For this reason he has marshalled a very considerable series of arguments in order to tip the probability in favor of his thesis. Not only does he deal with the traditional historical problems but he also has made use of recent form-critical work on Paul's letters. Thus he has used structural considerations to argue that the suspected passage breaks the flow of

3 K.G. Eckart, "Der zweite echte Brief des Apostels Paulus an die Thessalonicher," *ZTK* 58 (1961), 30-44.

4 B.A. Pearson, "1 Thessalonians 2:13-16: A Deutero-Pauline Interpolation," *HTR* 64 (1971), 79-94.

5 Ibid., 83.

6 Ibid., 91.

Paul's letter composition. Moreover, he recognizes that any theory of interpolation must show two things: (1) not only that the passage in question does not connect to its context, but also (2) that the context reads more smoothly with the passage removed. Thus he discusses the way in which 1 Thess. 2:12 prepares for 2:17-20.

He may be right. Nevertheless, the solution is not a comfortable one. Normally the transmissional evidence of a Pauline text (i.e., the external evidence) supports the evidence which we derive from analyzing the contents of the text (i.e., the internal evidence). In this case, the two vectors point in opposite directions, and the argument has to be that the internal evidence overbalances the external. This result is, of course, possible, but it cannot be accepted as anything more than a tentative solution to a bad situation.

Furthermore, although Pearson's case is probably the best that can be built in favor of the theory of interpolation, his argument has a number of weaknesses in method, although they are by no means of his own devising. Many scholars base arguments for the non-authenticity of material attributed to Paul on the dissimilarity between that material and the undoubtedly genuine letters. This argument is widely used, for example, with respect to the Pastoral Epistles. By contrast, however, some material traditionally ascribed to Paul is alleged to be post-Pauline because it is too similar to genuine Pauline material. Thus 2 Thessalonians is considered a slavish imitation of 1 Thessalonians, and Ephesians of Colossians.[7] These are two very different arguments. The first is the normal and expected line of reasoning for dealing with questions of authenticity. The second is far more difficult to sustain. Moreover, Pearson alternates between the two arguments. Whatever strikes him as unlike the *Hauptbriefe* he lists as evidence for the first. Whatever appears to be Pauline he takes as evidence for the second. These two arguments do not support one another; they pull in opposite directions. We are therefore left with the question, "Who is it who says unexpected things and sounds so much like Paul?" Other difficulties in his solution will be considered below.

Harmonizing Theories

In spite of the thoroughness of Pearson's argument, most scholars who have written since the appearance of his article, as well, I suspect, as most of those who have not, still hold to the integrity of 1 Thessalonians. There are a number of approaches which can be taken. In the first place, Paul's remarks about Judaism in his other letters can be used

7 On 2 Thessalonians as a copy of 1 Thessalonians see, e.g., C. Masson, R.H. Fuller, W. Marxsen, H. Braun, R. Bultmann, H.J. Schoeps, E. Fuchs, and G. Bornkamm. On Ephesians as a copy of Colossians see the work of E.J. Goodspeed and his followers, e.g., L. Mitton, D. Riddle, and F.W. Beare.

to blunt the sharpness of the statements in our passage. Alternatively, the positive attitude of Paul toward Judaism which was maintained earlier is not universally admitted. Some scholars take Paul's outburst in Rom. 7:24, "Wretched man that I am! Who will deliver me from this body of death?" to refer to his life within Judaism. Further, it must be allowed that our quotations from Romans 11 (above) were somewhat selective. In the same chapter Paul also wrote, "Israel has failed to obtain what it sought" (v. 7); "Through their trespass salvation has come to the Gentiles" (v. 11); "Their rejection means the reconciliation of the world" (v. 15); "They were broken off because of their unbelief" (v. 20); and "God did not spare the natural branches" (v. 21). A third approach is to argue that the anti-Judaic material quoted from Matthew above is not new with that writer but goes back to the earliest church or even to the ministry of Jesus itself.[8]

Thus by the first two lines of argument our passage is interpreted to sound more like his other writings and by the last argument, more like the attitude of his contemporaries. It is not necessary to deal with these theories individually. Their shortcomings will be discussed in the next section.

A New Proposal

Structural Considerations

An important departure in Pauline studies was accomplished by the Paul Seminar of the SBL which met from 1970 to 1975 under the leadership of Nils A. Dahl. At the suggestion of Robert W. Funk the seminar was formed to address itself to the question, "What does it mean that Paul's writings are in the form of letters?" They were able to assemble a large amount of work which had been done in a disconnected way by scholars working individually on the subject of letter structure. They considerably advanced the problem and in turn gave rise to the Epistolography Working Group. As a result of this work the letter structure of 1 Thessalonians may be summarized more or less as follows:

(1) Salutation	1:1
Senders—Recipients—Greeting	
(2) Thanksgiving	
A. Thanksgiving	1:2-10
B. Letter Body	2:1-12

8 So J. Bernard Orchard, "Thessalonians and the Synoptic Gospels," *Bib* 19 (1938), 19-42. He gives a table of parallels between the Thessalonian letters and, for the most part, Matthew. He believes that the Matthean source material was used by Paul and that Matthew is the earliest of the gospels.

C. Eschatological climax (with renewed Thanksgiving)	2:13-16
D. Travelogue	2:17-3:8
E. Thanksgiving renewed	3:9-13
(3) Paraenesis	4:1-5:22
(4) Close	
A. Peace Wish	5:23-24
B. Greetings	5:25-27
C. Benediction	5:28

It was the analysis of the central section by Robert Funk with which Pearson took issue. He noted that (2) C seems anomalous and that in his other letters Paul passed directly from letter body to the travelogue. By itself such an argument is not impressive, both because we have so few letters from Paul and because each of them exhibits anomalous features. Moreover, letter structure is least clear in the body section of a letter, since by its very nature the body reflects the special needs for which the letter was written.

Structure, however, can be considered on a number of levels. Another approach to structure is more helpful in the present instance. There are a number of basic rhetorical forms which Paul used as the mold for his thought. I have discussed several of these patterns elsewhere.[9] The pattern which has relevance for the passage under discussion is in the A B A pattern, or as I call it, "the sonata form." There are a number of instances in Paul's letters where he discusses one point, digresses to a second point, and then closes the discussion with a recapitulation of the first point. The history of the various partition theories for 1 Corinthians is in the main the history of the failure to recognize this habit. For example, Paul discussed the eating of meat offered to idols in 1 Corinthians 8, he then discussed the rights of an apostle in 1 Corinthians 9, and then in 1 Cor. 10:1-11:1 he recapitulated his attitude toward idol meat. Those who partition 1 Corinthians into two or more letters invariably separate 1 Corinthians 8 from 1 Cor. 10:1-22 on the grounds of the dissimilarity of the two discussions of the same subject. Again, 1 Corinthians 12, 13, and 14 are an example of the same phenomenon. Chapter 13 is a digression on the theme introduced in chapter 12, although this fact is frequently missed. Chapter 14 is clearly a return to the subject matter of chapter 12, but from a different point of view.

Now let us turn to 1 Thess. 2:13-16. The similarity between this passage and 1 Thess. 1:2-10 was noted by both Eckart and Pearson, and was taken as evidence for considering the latter passage an interpolation. We may outline this similarity as follows:

9 J.C. Hurd, "Concerning the Structure of 1 Thessalonians," an unpublished paper for the Paul Seminar of the SBL, Los Angeles, 1-5 September 1972.

1 Thess. 1:2-10	***1 Thess. 2:13-16***
A. *We give thanks to God*	A. *We* also *give thanks to God*
B. always for you all, *constantly*.	B. *constantly*
C. knowing . . . your election;	C. that when you received
D. for *our gospel came* to *you*	D. the *word of God* which *you heard from us*,
E. *not* only in *word*,	E. you accepted it *not* as the *word* of men
F. *but* also in power	F. *but* as what it really is, the word of God,
G. and in the Holy Spirit and with full conviction	G. which is at work in you believers.
H. And *you became imitators* of us and of the Lord,	H. for *you*, brethren, *became imitators* of the churches; . . .
I. for you received the word in much *affliction*. . . .	I. for you *suffered*
J. (The success of the missionaries)	J. (The suffering of the missionaries)
K. You turned to God from idols,	K. hindering us from speaking to the Gentiles
L. to serve a living and true God and to wait for his Son, . . .	L. that they may be saved . . . .
M. who delivers us from the *wrath* to come.	M. But God's *wrath* has come upon them at last.

When we approach Paul's letters from the point of view of their rhetorical form, we should not begin with the assumption that Paul would not repeat himself. On the contrary, we find that in many places he did in fact repeat himself, although always with significant differences. Once this point has been observed, we can say that the sequence of parallels listed above shows that in 2:13-16 Paul ran through the same sequence of thought that he had used in 1:2-10, varying the phraseology and attributing a different effect to the reception of the gospel. (In 1:7-8 the gospel brings joy and success to the new missionaries; in 2:14b-15 it brings suffering.) Thus the second passage is by no means a slavish imitation of the first. There is between the two passages the difference which we might expect to find between a Pauline theme and its recapitulation. The parallelism outlined above seems sufficiently close therefore to allow the conclusion that 1 Thess. 1:2-2:16 has as its gross structure the pattern A B A, with 2:1-12 as the middle member. Each of the three panels in this triptych is marked at the opening by a formal structural signal and each closes with an eschatological climax: "wrath" (1:10), "kingdom and glory" (2:12), and "wrath" (2:16).

In passing we may also note that the same sort of parallelism exists between 1 Thess. 2:17-20 and 3:9-13 with 3:1-8 as the middle member. Again the three panels end with eschatological climaxes: "Our Lord Jesus at his coming" (2:19), "stand fast in the Lord" (3:8), "at the coming of our Lord Jesus" (3:13).

Thus from the point of view of literary structure the material which follows the opening salutation (1:1) and precedes the paraenetic material (4:1-5:22) consists of a double triptych. The first triptych concerns Paul's joy and thanksgiving at the news brought by Timothy of the survival of the Thessalonian congregation. The second triptych concerns his desire to see them again, including both his attempts to visit them in the past and his hopes for the future. From a structural point of view therefore 1 Thess. 2:13-16 is by no means anomalous. While Paul's structures are not so regular that they can be predicted, the type of repetition represented by our passage has numerous parallels at other points in Paul's letters. Recapitulation was one technique used by Paul to develop important arguments.

The Hermeneutical Unit

In my opinion much of Pauline study could be improved if scholars were more precise in their recognition of the hermeneutical unit. Texts are extremely complex entities, built up of words, sentences, paragraphs, and other larger structures. James Barr in his book, *The Semantics of Biblical Language,* complained that biblical scholars often take words out of their specific context and invest them with universal theological meaning.[10] A similar observation could be made at a higher level. Frequently sentences or paragraphs are compared from one Pauline letter to another with little regard to the historical circumstances which gave rise to each letter or to the particular structure of argument in which the passages are embedded. Quite simply, the hermeneutical unit is the letter. Most Pauline scholars will agree to this statement in principle, but its significance in practice does not seem to be widely understood.

We begin the study of Paul by attempting to delineate by the use of letter-form analysis those units of Pauline text which constitute individual letter occasions. Of course, for the most part, these divisions correspond to those recognized by tradition. In the case of 1 Thessalonians most scholars have no hesitation in considering the text a single letter. This conclusion is fully supported by the study of letter struc-

10 James Barr, *The Semantics of Biblical Language* (London: Oxford University Press, 1961), 206-62 and *passim.*

ture. The next step is to interpret the parts of each letter in terms of the other parts. Each letter is an organic whole made up of interdependent parts, to use Paul's familar analogy of the body. As applied to a given letter this principle has two aspects.

(1) *The external world.* For my book, *The Origin of 1 Corinthians,* I summarized scholarly opinion concerning the so-called "parties" at Corinth mentioned by Paul in 1 Cor. 1:12 and elsewhere.[11] This exercise turned out to be most enlightening; it became clear that on this subject there is a complete spectrum of scholarly opinion. By some scholars Paul is pitted against the Apollos Party; by others, against the Cephas Party; and still others, against the Christ Party. The parties themselves are assigned points of view which vary all the way from Jewish legalism to gnostic libertinism. Concerning 1 Corinthians 1 to 6, I concluded, "What does the oral information describing the situation in Corinth mean? Perhaps it is not too harsh a judgment to say that more often than not the answer which scholars have given to this question has been determined more by what each scholar has brought to 1 Corinthians than by what he has learned from the letter."[12]

Of course, knowledge of the ancient world is important to the interpretation of a Pauline letter. But the religions, philosophies, parties, sects, and racial heritages were so many and so varied that there is no single obvious background against which to place Paul's letters. Discoveries which have enlarged our knowledge of certain movements or areas of thought have produced, understandably but illogically, corresponding fads within Pauline scholarship. But the link between particular schools of thought or religious practices and Paul must be established by beginning with the text of his letters, not with the study of the Hellenistic world. The background material is logically secondary to our primary source information, Paul's own letters. Secondary sources are valuable, but they cannot take precedence over primary. The order of examination is first the primary material and then, after that has been studied in its own right, the secondary. Thus, to take a parallel example, we cannot use the Acts account of Paul's troubles with Jews in Thessalonica (Acts 17:1-14) as the basis for interpreting 1 Thess. 2:13-16. Nor can we use the parallels with Matthew as grounds for abridging the primary text material. Instead we must begin by trying to determine the extent to which the text of 1 Thessalonians makes sense as it now stands.

(2) *Harmonizing.* It is a fact which can be verified by even the most cursory sampling of Pauline scholarship that most scholars interpret a passage in a Pauline letter by comparing it to Paul's utterances on the *same* subject in *other* letters, rather than by comparing it to his utter-

11 J.C. Hurd, *The Origin of 1 Corinthians* (London: SPCK, 1965), 96-107.
12 Ibid., 107.

ances on *different* subjects in the *same* letter. The texts of Paul's genuine letters are taken to be a single corpus on the basis of which Paul's theology is reconstructed. D.E.H. Whiteley, in his book *The Theology of St. Paul,* even goes so far as to present Paul's thought in the sequence of the medieval theological curriculum.[13] He begins with the doctrine of creation and ends with the doctrine of last things. And on each topic he, like scholars before and after, takes the passage in which Paul deals in most detail with the doctrine in question and harmonizes with it the briefer passages on the same topic in other letters. This widespread procedure is based on two convictions: (1) that Paul's thought was essentially unchanged during the period of the letters, and (2) that the sequence and the dating of his letters is irrelevant or at least indeterminate. It is not necessary to trace the history of the process by which these assumptions became established in Pauline scholarship, but only to observe that they profoundly affect the interpretation of the letters and that, if they have any validity, they must be established by the examination of the individual letters without an initial assumption of their mutual homogeneity. Such an assumption may be supported by this examination or it may not. In any case, homogeneity must be recognized to be a hypothesis and not an axiom. Again, the primary hermeneutical unit is the individual letter.

In analyzing the contents of 1 Corinthians I discovered numerous points at which the interpretation of the letter was limited or determined by passages in other letters. Some scholars argued, for example, that Paul could not have had a high view of asceticism and a correspondingly low view of marriage in the light of his positive remarks about family relationships in Colossians and Ephesians (especially Eph. 5:21-33).[14] Again, the interpretation of 1 Cor. 15:29 as proxy baptism is rejected by many scholars because they believe that such an automatic view of the effect of baptism is contradicted by such passages as Romans 6. Yet if 1 Corinthians is analyzed as an independent system, it appears that there are two other passages in which just such an automatic view of the effect of sacraments appears. In spite of his sin the incestuous man will be "saved in the day of the Lord Jesus" (1 Cor. 5:5). The only thing that can be said in this man's favour is that he had been baptized. Similarly, many Corinthians "are weak and ill and some have died" (1 Cor. 11:30) as a result of their failure to "discern the body" (1 Cor. 11:29-30). Of itself the eucharistic sacrament has the power to give life or to cause death in the thought world of 1 Corinthians.[15]

Having reached this point, it hardly needs to be pointed out that the objections to 1 Thess. 2:13-16 catalogued by Pearson and others are drawn entirely from passages outside of 1 Thessalonians, in particular

13 D.E.H. Whiteley, *The Theology of St. Paul* (Oxford: Basil Blackwell, 1964).
14 Hurd, *Origin,* 160.
15 Ibid., 135-37.

from Romans 9 to 11. The argument they propose is not that the passage conflicts with material found elsewhere in 1 Thessalonians but that it conflicts with what is known about Paul on the basis of his other letters. Naturally, if we are convinced that both Romans and 1 Thessalonians are genuine letters of Paul, we will attempt to trace a relationship between them. But we cannot begin by assuming that the relationship is an identity. And, in any case, we must first analyze 1 Thessalonians in its own right.

Apocalyptic Anti-Judaism

The most obvious observation that can be made about 1 Thessalonians is that it is a highly apocalyptic document. Paul summarized the religious pilgrimage of the Thessalonians by saying, "You turned to God from idols, to serve a living and true God, and to wait for his Son from heaven, whom he raised from the dead, Jesus who delivers us from the wrath to come" (1 Thess. 1:9-10). Paul mentioned their conversion and the parousia but nothing between. When Paul heard of their anxiety over the death of one of their number, he wrote:

> For the Lord himself will descend from heaven with a cry of command, with the archangel's call, and with the sound of the trumpet of God. And the dead in Christ will rise first; then we who are alive, who are left, shall be caught up together with them in the clouds to meet the Lord in the air; and so we shall always be with the Lord. (1 Thess. 4:16-17)

The language is highly apocalyptic and evokes a host of other images and conventional patterns. It is clear that Paul believed at this time that most Christians would survive to the parousia. The parousia itself will be a time of wrath and vengeance. Concerning non-Christians Paul wrote, "Sudden destruction will come upon them as travail comes upon a woman with child, and there will be no escape" (5:3). But to the Thessalonian Christians he wrote, "You are not in darkness, brethren, for that day to surprise you like a thief. For you are all sons of light and sons of the day; we are not of the night or of darkness" (5:4-5). Here we have the normal apocalyptic view of the present age in which only the righteous remnant will receive salvation; the wicked world which surrounds the saved community will receive its just condemnation in the Day of Judgment. In that Day there will be an eschatological reversal: the first will be last and the last first.

Paradoxically, one of the ways by which the saved community reassures itself of its chosen status is by the afflictions which it suffers at the hand of the established world order. As Paul wrote, "You yourselves know that this is to be our lot. For when we were with you, we told you beforehand that we were to suffer affliction; just as it has come to pass, and as you know" (3:3-4). Those who suffer now will rejoice in the new age; those who bring suffering on the church will suffer in the Day. Not only is suffering a mark of God's approval, it is also one of the items which contribute to the just condemnation of the non-Christian world. Note that this view of suffering is different from that expressed in the letter to the Philippians. In that letter suffering produces likeness to Christ (Phil. 3:10); it is part of an imitation-of-Christ theme. In 1 Thessalonians, however, suffering is an evil inflicted on the church by wicked and sinful men. These men are responsible for their own actions and thus are justly condemned in the eschatological hour. And they are also under the control of Satan, who, among other things, has been preventing Paul from revisiting the Thessalonians (1 Thess. 2:18).

I do not see any shades of gray in Paul's thought as expressed in this letter. Everything is darkness or light (5:4-8). The alternatives are wrath or salvation (5:9). The paraenetic material in chapters 4 to 5 concerns almost solely the relationship of Christians to one another. Only at one point did Paul mention the attitude of Christians to outsiders: "See that none of you repays evil for evil, but always seek to do good to one another and to all" (5:15). The Christian is to hold himself aloof from the world. He is not to become involved in its ways or attitudes. He is not to allow the goodness which he is obligated to cultivate to be in any way modified by the evil of the world outside.

To identify the narrowness of vision of 1 Thessalonians is not to attribute to Paul a meanness of spirit. On the contrary, within the limits established by his apocalyptic world view Paul exhibits immense affection and concern for his congregation. In one of the most moving expressions to be found anywhere in his letters he wrote, "Being affectionately desirous of you, we were ready to share with you not only the gospel of God but also our own selves, because you had become very dear to us" (2:8). The whole letter overflows with the loving concern of a father for his own children (especially 2:11). There is evidence, as we shall remark later, that at a later point in his career Paul learned to extend this same love to all men and to hope for their salvation.

Within this apocalyptic framework 1 Thess. 2:13-16 makes eminently good sense. The churches in Judea are suffering; the Thessalonians are suffering by imitation. Paul had told them to expect suffering. The Thessalonians' countrymen are the cause of their suffering, and this fact will be held against them in the Day. The Jews in a parallel fashion are the cause of the suffering inflicted on the churches in Judea and, to some extent at least, on Paul. Paul had no need to catalogue the sins of the Gentiles; they were well known. Paul had been brought up in a tradition which was highly critical of the Gentile world. For Paul the sins of the Jews belonged to a different category, however. They related entirely to God's plan of salvation. According to our text the Jews displease God because they killed the prophets and the Lord Jesus. They "oppose all men"—a common anti-Semitic slogan. Paul used this epithet, however, in a theological way: they oppose the Gentiles by hindering Paul in his apostolic mission to bring to them God's message of salvation. The "measure" of sins to be attributed to the Gentiles did not need rehearsal; for the Jews it was their attempt to frustrate God's plan of salvation which would serve to justify their condemnation in the apocalyptic Day.

That all non-Christians would perish in the Day was an apocalyptic axiom for Paul and the Thessalonians at the point at which our letter was written. Paul attempted in a limited way to work back from this fact to an explanation of the circumstances which would justify it. If his explanation does not persuade us, it is because we do not share the same apocalyptic world view. His diatribe against the Jews quite properly offends us. But we are not thereby justified in improving his letter by removing the offending passage. The passage is part of the apocalyptic logic which is woven into the fabric of the whole letter.

It remains to say a word about the verb "has come" (*ephthasen*). The verb form is an aorist, and most probably refers to an event in the past. In the classical period the verb *phthanō* did not mean "to come" but "to come ahead of" some other event specified or implied in the context. It is true that in the hellenistic period this precise use of the word faded and instances can be found in which it means no more than "to come." However, it is significant that in the seven occurrences of this verb in the New Testament the comparison of two events is either specified, implied, or allowed by the context.[16] There is, in fact, a second occurrence of this verb in our letter (4:15) where it is denied that the living will *arrive ahead of* the Christian dead at the parousia. In 2:16 it seems probable that Paul was referring to some event which had just occurred which for him was a foretaste of the greater wrath which belongs to the apocalyptic Day. What event Paul had in mind is not clear to us. Several suggestions have been made.[17] We must, however, guard ourselves against the fallacy of supposing that the text ought to be referring to the event which seems to us the most obvious candidate: the sack of Jerusalem and the destruction of the Temple. At any point in time the future is almost completely hidden. If we connect the text with the events of 70 C.E., we must first make it probable on other grounds that it was written after 70 C.E., not vice versa. The history that Paul knew stretched only backwards from the point at which he stood. The future was to him only an apocalyptic certainty. Those who are familiar with the mentality of apocalyptic sects know that it takes no very special occasion to convince the believer that the end of the age is at hand and that the apocalyptic woes have begun.

I have in my possession a newspaper published by a modern apocalyptic sect which consists of reports of various disasters—car wrecks, earthquakes, tornadoes—as evidence of the nearness of the Day. Significantly, the paper is undated.

---

16 Matt. 12:28//Luke 11:20; Rom. 9:31; 2 Cor. 10:14; Phil. 3:16; 1 Thess. 2:16; 4:15.

17 See Pearson, "1 Thessalonians 2:13-16," 82-83, nn. 20-22.

Conclusion

We end, therefore, with a picture of Paul and his converts as an apocalyptic community eagerly awaiting the Lord and his angels, who would deliver them from the wicked world around them. Their apocalyptic faith had its virtues and its shortcomings. The love which its members exhibited to one another was admirable. As I have argued elsewhere, Paul's conviction that the relationships which would characterize the kingdom should be effective in the present led him to eliminate sexual differences in his communities, a view with which the church has not yet caught up.[18] On the other hand, this early Christian sect was conditioned to hold a negative view of non-members. Thus Paul's view of the Gentile world on the one hand and of Judaism on the other does not measure up to our standards of Christian humanity. This fact should not surprise or disturb us, but should serve to remind us how great is the interval in time between his day and our own. He was an ancient man, albeit an amazing man. We would be grateful to him if he had left us just this one letter. But, as I have hinted above, it is my conviction that there is evidence that Paul grew in his appreciation of the wideness of God's love and came to hope for the inclusion of all men in God's salvation.[19] But this observation takes us to other letter events in other times.

In sum, 1 Thess. 2:13-16 shows us that there was a time in Paul's career when, under the influence of an apocalyptic hope, Paul was ahead of his time in expressing a historical-theological anti-Judaism. Some decades later similar views became more widespread and have been characteristic of the Christian church throughout most of its history.

---

18 Hurd, *Origin*, 276-77, 282.

19 See C.H. Dodd, "The Mind of Paul: II," in his *New Testament Studies* (Manchester: The University Press, 1953), 118-26.

3

Paul and the Law in Galatians 2-3

Lloyd Gaston

What is at issue in this volume on anti-Judaism is not the positive gospel of the apostle to the Gentiles but the negative shadow side of a Pauline "theology of Judaism." Samuel Sandmel described Paul's situation as follows: "The practical issue was Should new converts be compelled to observe the Jewish practices? The theoretical, theological issue was What was the 'true nature' of Judaism, and in the light of that true nature, what place, if any, was there for Jewish observances *in Judaism*?"[1]

Merely to raise the question of whether or not such a "theology of Judaism" is Pauline or Marcionite, and to do so in a discussion of Paul's most polemical letter, is to embark on an impossible undertaking for a single paper. Let it then be considered only an experiment attempting to identify the issues which would have to be raised if many of the traditional assumptions concerning Paul's "theology of Judaism" in Galatians 2 and 3 were to be challenged.

"Has God rejected his people?" (Rom. 11:1). "Do we then render obsolete the law through this *pistis*?" (Rom. 3:31). Does Paul "teach all the Jews who are among the Gentiles to forsake Moses, telling them not to circumcise their children or observe the customs" (Acts 21:21)? An affirmative answer to these or similar questions would represent theological anti-Judaism. And yet W. Barclay only sums up a commonplace of our exegetical tradition in titling his exposition of Gal. 2:14-17 "The End of the Law."[2] The first question is answered decisively in the affirmative in an influential essay by G. Klein.[3] Klein's

1 S. Sandmel, *Anti-Semitism in the New Testament?* (Philadelphia: Fortress, 1978), 7, his italics.

2 W. Barclay, *Galatians* (Edinburgh: St. Andrew Press, 1958), 20. A similar influential popular work, W. Bousset on Galatians in *Die Schriften des Neuen Testaments* (Vol. 2, Göttingen: Vandenhoeck und Ruprecht, 1907), 47, gives as a heading for 2:19-21 "Bewusster Bruch mit dem Gesetz."

3 G. Klein, "Individualgeschichte und Weltgeschichte bei Paulus," *Rekonstruktion und*

thesis is also a provocative illustration of how this line of interpretation radically calls into question not only Judaism but also the scriptural status of what Christians call the Old Testament and the faithfulness of God to his promises and God's righteousness *ante Christum natum.* If the theological implications of the traditional view are immense, the major exegetical problem is that we must assume Paul was guilty of a "fundamental misapprehension"[4] in his teaching about the law. But what would happen to our interpretation if we were to start from the premise that Paul knew at least as much about "covenantal nomism" and Jewish "soteriology" as E.P. Sanders?[5] It would then be impossible to say, as does the latest commentary on Galatians,[6] that Gal. 2:16 is a "denial of the orthodox Jewish (Pharisaic) doctrine of salvation." In any case, this premise will be assumed in the present exegetical experimentation.

Gal. 2:15-21 Translated and Interpreted

The passage I have been assigned on which to put the premise to the test is one of the most difficult in the Pauline corpus, Galatians 3. Like many other interpreters,[7] I find it impossible to consider Galatians 3 except in the context of 2:15-21 (just as it is impossible to understand Romans 4 except in the context of 3:21-31). Since translations are to a large extent the distillation of long-standing exegetical trends, and since it is precisely these traditions which are being called into question,

---

Interpretation (Munich: Kaiser, 1969), 180-224. This essay has been widely discussed but in my opinion not yet successfully refuted. Cf. K. Berger, "Abraham in den paulinischen Hauptbriefen," *MTZ* 17 (1966), 47-89; H. Boers, *Theology out of the Ghetto* (Leiden: Brill, 1971), 74-82; M. Barth, "Die Stellung des Paulus zum Gesetz," *EvT* 33 (1973), 496-526; W.G. Kümmel, "'Individualgeschichte' und 'Weltgeschichte' in Gal. 2:15-21," in B. Lindars and S.S. Smalley (eds.), *Christ and Spirit in the New Testament* (Cambridge: Cambridge University Press, 1973), 157-73; H. Gollwitzer et al., "Der Jude Paulus und die deutsche neutestamentliche Wissenschaft," *EvT* 34 (1974), 276-304; P. von der Osten-Sacken, "Das paulinische Verständnis des Gesetzes im Spannungsfeld von Eschatologie und Geschichte," *EvT* 37 (1977), 549-87; M. Barth, "St. Paul-A Good Jew," *Horizons in Biblical Theology* 1 (1979), 7-45.

4 H.J. Schoeps, *Paul* (Philadelphia: Westminster, 1961), 213-18.

5 E.P. Sanders, "Patterns of Religion in Paul and Rabbinic Judaism," *HTR* 66 (1973), 455-78; ibid., *Paul and Palestinian Judaism* (Philadelphia: Fortress, 1977).

6 H.D. Betz, *Galatians* (Philadelphia: Fortress, 1979), 116. In addition we have used the commentaries of E.D. Burton, F. Mussner, H. Schlier, R. Bring, A. Oepke, P. Bonnard, and the following articles: R. Bultmann, "Zur Auslegung von Galater 2:15-18," *Exegetica* (Tübingen: J.C.B. Mohr, 1967), 394-99; M. Barth, "Jews and Gentiles: The Social Character of Justification in Paul," *JES* 5 (1968), 241-67; U. Wilkens, "Was heisst bei Paulus: 'Aus Werken des Gesetzes wird kein Mensch gerecht'?" *Evangelisch-katholischer Kommentar zum NT. Vorarbeiten. Heft 1* (Zürich: Benziger, 1969), 51-77; J. Lambrecht, "The Line of Thought in Gal. 2:14b-21," *NTS* 24 (1978), 484-95.

7 Cf. especially K. Berger, "Abraham," 47-49.

we shall begin with an alternative translation of Gal. 2:15-21. This means that some vital issues are discussed only in the notes to the translation. An alternative translation also immediately presupposes an exegesis of all other passages where the word or concept appears. But a beginning has to be made somewhere, and this translation has been made with the knowledge of other passages and the belief that the translation can be consistently justified. Finally, in the light of the initial compact "statement of theses" in Galatians 2, we shall look briefly at some aspects of Paul's discussion of the law in Galatians 3.[8]

(15) We who are Jews by birth and not sinners from the Gentiles, (16) knowing (therefore)[A] that a (Gentile)[B] human being is not justified from works of law, but (rather)[C] through the faithfulness of Christ Jesus,[D] we too became believers[E] in Christ Jesus, in order that we might be justified from the faithfulness of Christ[D] and not from works of law, because (as it is written:)[F] by works of law "all" flesh "is not justified" (Ps. 143:2). (17) But, since[G] seeking to be justified in Christ we ourselves too have been found to be (Gentile) sinners,[H] is consequently[I] Christ in the service of sin? Of course not! (18) For[J] since[G] I again build up that which I tore down, I commend myself openly as an "apostate."[K] (19) For[J] through the law I have died to the law, in order that I might live to God. (20) I have been co-crucified with Christ. I live yet (really) no longer I, but (rather) Christ lives in me. What I now live in the flesh, I live in the faithfulness of the Son of God,[D] who loved me and delivered himself for me. (21) I do not set at nought the grace of God; for since[G] through law is (the) righteousness (of God),[L] consequently[I] Christ has died as a free gift.[M]

Notes on the Translation

A: Omit *de* with p[46] and Nestle-Aland[26], or in any case do not translate "but," as the implied contrast between "being Jews" and "knowing" exists only in the mind of the modern interpreter. *Eidotes hoti* "is frequently used to introduce a well known fact that is generally accepted," BAG[2], 556, l.e.

8 With respect to the situation in Galatians, I assume that it was written during Paul's Ephesian period to the churches of North Galatia, which were completely Gentile. Many of these Galatian Christians were beginning to Judaize (not to convert to Judaism), probably along lines that are clearer in Colossians. Recognition of this situation is much more important than any attempt to identify "opponents." (In particular, the situation in Corinth, where the rival apostles are Jewish Christians but where Judaizing and the law are not issues at all, is quite different and may not be used to cast light on Galatians.) While the troublemakers who try to get the Galatians to Judaize are probably themselves Gentile Judaizers, this is not crucial for understanding the situation. It is not certain whether they are members of the Galatian churches or come from outside. In any case they are in no sense to be understood as coming from James. Paul's argument is not with Jewish Christians, in Antioch or Jerusalem, or with Jews, but with the Galatian Judaizers. He does not argue with his opponents, even at second hand, but only calls them names (Gal. 5:10-12; 1:6-9) and urges that they be cast out (1:6-9; 4:30). All of Paul's arguments in Galatians must be understood as being directed to the Galatian Judaizers and not to those who "court zealously" (4:17), "trouble" (1:7; 5:10, 12), or "compel" (6:12-13) them.

B: In general Paul uses Adam or *anthrōpos* to discuss the situation of specifically non-Jewish humanity. In any case, this meaning is suggested here by the contrast found in the *kai hēmeis* and *kai autoi* of 2:16,17.

C: *Ean mē* is an ellipsis, for the conjunction should properly introduce a subjunctive verb (BAG², 211, 3.b.): "if (he is) not (justified) through ...." It is not here exceptive, cf. Burton, 121.

D: The correctness of this translation, reintroduced in modern times by J. Haussleiter (*Der Glaube Jesu Christi und der christliche Glaube* [Leipzig, 1891]), and advocated most forcefully by K. Barth in his *Römerbrief*, cannot be substantiated here. Cf. E.R. Goodenough, "Paul and the Hellenization of Christianity," in J. Neusner (ed.), *Religions in Antiquity* (Leiden: Brill, 1967), 35-80; G.M. Taylor, "The Function of *Pistis Christou* in Galatians," *JBL* 85 (1966), 58-76; M. Barth, "The Kerygma of Galatians," *Int* 21 (1967), 131-46; G. Howard, "On the Faith of Christ," *HTR* 60 (1967), 459-84; "The 'Faith of Christ,'" *ExpT* 85 (1974), 212-15; J.J. O'Rourke, "Pistis in Romans," *CBQ* 34 (1973), 188-94; H. Ljungman, *Pistis* (Lund: Gleerup, 1964), 38-40.

E: The aorist denotes a specific action in past time as distinguished from the constant "knowing."

F: For *hoti* as an indication of a quotation, cf. 3:11; Rom. 3:20 (*dioti*), etc. and J. Bonsirven, *Exégèse rabbinique et exégèse paulinienne* (Paris: Beauchesne, 1938), 343. That Paul does not use the LXX's *pas zōn* is probably because he uses *zaō* in a theological sense in 2:19-20.

G: There are three (four counting 2:14) conditional sentences in this section, all with *ei* + indicative, *realis* (BDF, 372). Paul can write unreal periods (BDF, 360, but there they are called "remarkably scarce") as in Gal. 1:10; 3:21; 4:15, but then the protasis should be an augmented indicative, and the apodosis should contain *an*. Paul uses the *realis* in Gal. 3:29; 4:7; 5:15; 6:3, although the protases of the *realis* in 3:18; 5:11 clearly represent an unreal case. We will assume here the truth of the protasis unless there should appear to be strong reasons to the contrary, and since the sense "is often closely bordering on causal 'since'" (BDF, 372:1), we shall for the moment somewhat provocatively translate *ei* as "since."

H: That the word *hamartōloi* is used here in the sense of Gentile—those not under the covenant—is shown by the clear usage in 2:15. The word is rare in Paul and can in every sense be understood to refer to the situation of Gentiles (Rom. 3:7; 5:8, 19; 7:13). Cf. in the New Testament also Mark 14:41 par.; Luke 6:32-33 (par. in Matthew, *ethnikoi*); 24:7; and for earlier usage *Pss. Sol.* 2:1; 17 *passim*; *Jub.* 23:23f.; 4 Ezra 4:23; 1 Macc. 1:34; Tob. 13:6; etc. For the sense, cf. Rom. 1:18-32; Eph. 2:1-3; 4:17-19.

I: Reading in both cases ἄρα not ἆρα. That a question can follow this particle in 2:17 is stated by BDF, 440:2.

J: The *gar* here and in 2:19 is to be given its normal force, in spite of *RSV* and Lambrecht, "Line of Thought," 491-93.

K: It is very misleading to translate *parabainō, parabasis, parabatēs* as "transgress, transgression, transgressor," insofar as these imply the inadvertent or regretted breaking of a commandment. Both Judaism and Christianity (though very seldom in Paul) can speak of the forgiveness of sins, or atonement following repentance, but *parabasis* is much more serious. Contrary to what is said by many commentators, neither in Galatians 2 nor elsewhere is *parabatēs* simply equivalent to *hamartōlos.* The LXX speaks frequently of *parabainein tēn diathēkēn* (Josh. 7:11, 15; 23:16; 4 Kg. 18:12; Ezek. 16:59, etc.; cf. *As. Mos.* 2:7), and the concept means not so much law-breaker as covenant-breaker. In rabbinic terminology it is equivalent to "casting off the yoke" or "denying the covenant," a conscious and deliberate denial of the right of God to give commandments and thus a self-exclusion from the covenant. Even if true, it is very misleading to say, as does J. Schneider, *TDNT* 5, 741, 739, "In the NT the *parabatēs* is one who transgresses a specific divine commandment" and "Transgression is sin only where there is disregard for the *entolē* of God." It is not only the presence or absence of law (Rom. 4:15) but the intention and effect which are important (Rom. 5!). The church fathers who used this word when a technical concept of apostasy developed were therefore correct, and even if it involves a certain anachronism this translation will be used here.

L: An adequate discussion of this important concept cannot be provided here. Fundamental to the understanding here presupposed is the starting point in the usage especially of 2 Isaiah and the Psalms, as advocated by H. Cremer, *Die paulinische Rechtfertigungslehre im Zusammenhang ihres geschichtlichen Voraussetzungen* (2d ed., Gütersloh: Bertelsmann, 1900). This understanding has been carried forward by A. Schlatter's commentary on Romans, *Gottes Gerechtigkeit* (Stuttgart: Calwer, 1935) and (with modifications) by E. Käsemann, "Gottesgerechtigkeit bei Paulus," *ZTK* 58 (1961), 367-78, and by others. I would understand the phrase "righteousness of God," then, to mean something like "the power of God for salvation" (Rom. 1:16), through which God's "grace might reign" (Rom. 5:21). Some passages in which the word *dikaiosynē* appears without qualification by genitive or adjective also must be understood as speaking of God's righteousness; only a detailed exegesis of the context can decide.

M: *Dōrean* cannot be translated "in vain" for the following reasons:

(1) The Greek word in itself always means "gratis, for nothing, without recompense, as a gift," and is so used by Paul (Rom. 3:24; 2 Cor. 11:7), and elsewhere in the NT (Matt. 10:8; 2 Thess. 3:8; Rev. 21:6; 22:17).

(2) Paul uses other words to express the concept "in vain, to no purpose": *eis kenon* (2 Cor. 6:1; Gal. 2:2; Phil. 2:16 bis; 1 Thess. 3:5), the adjective *kenos* (1 Cor. 15:10, 14 bis, 58; 1 Thess. 2:1), or *eikē* (Rom. 13:4; 1 Cor. 15:2; Gal. 3:4; 4:11).

(3) Because the Hebrew *ḥnm* can have the related meaning "gratuitously, undeservedly, without cause," *dōrean* too can be used in the LXX in this sense (1 Sam. 19:5; 25:31; 1 Kgs. 2:31; Job 1:9; Pss. 35:7, 19 [=John 15:24]; 69:4; 109:3; 119:161; Isa. 52:5; Lam. 3:52; Sir. 20:23; 29:6, 7) alongside the meaning "gratis, without payment" (Gen. 29:15; Exod. 21:2, 11; Num. 11:5; 2 Sam. 24:24; 1 Chron. 21:24; Mal. 1:10 [probably, cf. 2 Sam. 24:24]; Isa. 52:3; Jer. 22:13; 1 Macc. 10:33). Prov. 1:17 and Ezek. 6:10 (cf. W. Zimmerli, *Ezechiel* [Neukirchen: Neukirchener Verlag, 1969], 141) do not have *dōrean* in the LXX. We can sum up the discussion to this point by citing Burton (*Galatians,* 140-41): "*dōrean* means not 'without result,' a meaning which it apparently never has . . . but 'without cause,' 'needlessly' as in John 15:25."

(4) Ignatius, *Trall.* 10, cited by BAG² in the sense of "in vain," can be used as a test case. R.M. Grant, *The Apostolic Fathers; Vol. 4 Ignatius of Antioch* (Camden: Nelson, 1966), translates: (If Jesus' death was not real,) "then I die in vain. Then I lie about the Lord." But Ignatius is not speaking of a purpose he hopes to achieve by his death. On the contrary, he is saying, "I die gratuitously, as a gift, having received nothing, if in fact Christ has not really died for me" or less likely, "I die needlessly, without a cause, if that to which I witness in my death is not true."

(5) While the second LXX meaning is a possibility for Gal. 2:21, the most natural sense of "Jesus died without cause" would be that no one had any grounds for killing him. If we understood "without cause" theologically to mean that humanity had no cause to deserve such a death, then the meaning is very close to the first, Greek meaning. Accordingly we translate, as in Rom. 3:24, "as a free gift."

The question of the relationship of Gal. 2:15-21 to Paul's reply to Cephas in Antioch (2:14) has long been discussed. H.D. Betz,[9] who analyzes Galatians according to Graeco-Roman rhetorical principles, gives a fairly decisive literary answer by calling the section the *propositio,* a statement of theses which prepares for the following *probatio,* arguments from Scripture. The function of the *propositio,* according to Betz, is also to sum up the preceding *narratio* of facts concerning Paul himself—and (I would add) "the gospel preached by me" (1:11), "the gospel I preach among the Gentiles" (1:16; 2:2), "the gospel to the uncircumcised" (2:7). It is unfortunate that Betz connects the summary

9 Betz, *Galatians*, 113-14.

primarily with the Antioch affair after all, as if Paul's argument were essentially with Cephas rather than with the Galatian Judaizers, and as if Paul were more interested in correcting Cephas's "gospel to the circumcised" than in defining his own "gospel to the uncircumcised" (2:7). I agree that the *propositio* sums up the preceding *narratio,* but it sums up the whole narration, not just the last event recounted, and if anything it has special reference to 1:15-16.

The problems caused by understanding this section as primarily addressed to Cephas are insuperable, though seldom recognized. Paul is then seemingly denying that *Jewish* Christians should keep the commandments, in breach of the agreement just described. The "works of law" are made to refer to a Jewish "doctrine of salvation," against all the evidence. Galatians 2:18 is made to refer to *Cephas,* in spite of the grammar. Further, it is assumed that Cephas was guilty of a serious violation of one or more commandments. In order to make a connection between Paul's "tearing down" of the whole Torah and Cephas's actions in Antioch, assumptions are made which simply are not justified by the sources.[10] Even if the Zealots might have opposed all contact with Gentiles, and even if the *ḥaberim* refused to sit at the same table with the ᶜam-ha-arets, there is no commandment binding on all Jews anywhere in Bible or Mishnah which prohibits eating with Gentiles.[11] Whatever happened in Antioch, then, it did not provide Paul with an occasion to make a sweeping statement about the abolition of commandments for Jewish Christians or for Jews.[12]

This section begins with sentences in the first person plural (2:15-17) and ends with sentences in the first person singular (2:18-21), including two with an emphatic *egō* (19, 20a). It begins explicitly with "we Jews" and ends impressively with "I, Paul." Is there a transition where "we" means "we Jewish Christians"? Or, in the light of the distinctive apostolates reported in 2:7-9, should we think of some of the "we's" as referring specifically to "we who are engaged in the Gentile

10 "Table fellowship with Gentiles had become a serious transgression of the law" (Bring, *Galater,* 84); "die Übertretung einzelner Gebote, wie es sich Petrus in Antiochien hatte zuschulden kommen lassen" (Bultmann, "Auslegung," 398); "the statutes of the law which Paul had declared to be invalid" (Burton, *Galatians,* 130); "the Halakha which forbids Jews and Gentiles to eat together" (A.T. Hanson, *Studies in Paul's Technique and Theology* [London: SPCK, 1974], 28). The unconscious attempt to interpret Gal. 2:11-14 in the light of Mark 7 is of course completely illegitimate. Nothing is said at all about the food eaten but only about the company. Acts 10:28; 11:3 reflect a similar misunderstanding. Cf. G.F. Moore, *Judaism* (Cambridge: Harvard University Press, 1927-1930), II, 75.

11 And some statements which presuppose it, e.g. Ber. 7:1.

12 I would understand it in general accordance with B. Reicke, "Der geschichtliche Hintergrund des Apostelkonzils und der Antiochia-Episode," *Studia Paulina in honorem J. de Zwaan* (Haarlem: Bohn, 1953), 172-87; D. Bronson, "Paul, Galatians, and Jerusalem," *JAAR* 35 (1967), 119-28; R. Jewett, "The Agitators and the Galatian Congregation," *NTS* 17 (1970), 198-212; W. Schmithals, *Paul and James* (London: SCM, 1965); and G. Howard, *Paul: Crisis in Galatia* (Cambridge: Cambridge University Press, 1979).

mission"? Paul speaks about himself (and his co-workers?) and to the Galatians, and about himself as a model to be imitated by the Galatians (4:12); unless there are compelling reasons to the contrary we would not expect a "we" in the sense of "the Jerusalem church and I." Paul is then not ascribing his own views to Cephas and he certainly is not writing a "theology of Judaism" in this section. That this is the case can only be shown by a closer examination of the flow of his *propositio.*

Commentary

Verses 15-16. The distinction between Jew and Gentile is a fundamental one for Paul and is not to be dissolved in favour of a "third race."[13] The closest correlate to the phrase "Jews by nature/birth" is found in the writing which is even more Pauline than Paul, Eph. 2:3: "children of wrath by nature/birth." It is to this bleak situation that Paul speaks and in comparison with which the Jews have an advantage. As in Rom. 3:1-2, that advantage is here expressed in terms of knowledge based on Scripture. It should not be necessary to cite passages from the Hebrew Bible, Qumran texts, or sayings of the Tannaim to show that the knowledge of verse 16a is specifically Jewish knowledge. Of course the positive counterpart would state: "but rather through the faithfulness (*'mwnh* = *alētheia* LXX)" and "righteousness of God," as in Ps. 143:1. While a stronger case can be made for verse 1 being in Paul's mind when he cites Ps. 143:2 in Rom. 3:20,[14] it is also a possibility in Gal. 2:16.[15] Even without this support, however, we must translate "the faithfulness of Christ," moving now to specifically Christian knowledge.

I find it very doubtful that "when Paul thinks of works of law, he thinks of existence as a Jew."[16] Markus Barth[17] insists that the phrase, which appears in no Jewish writing,[18] must be interpreted from the only context where it does appear, Romans and Galatians, as meaning the adoption by Gentile Judaizers of selected commandments understood as prerequisites for salvation. Even more important is the considera-

13 Cf. e.g. D. Zeller, *Juden und Heiden in der Mission des Paulus* (Stuttgart: Katholisches Bibelwerk, 1973). This is of course the exact opposite of the thesis argued by Klein. Cf. also P. Richardson, *Israel in the Apostolic Church* (Cambridge: Cambridge University Press, 1969), 22-25.

14 Cf. R.B. Hays, "Psalm 143 and the Logic of Romans 3," *JBL* 99 (1980), 107-115.

15 Note the conjunction of the two concepts in such passages as 1QH 4:30-31, "I know that a human being has no righteousness . . . to the Most High God belong all deeds of righteousness," or the last petition of the Avinu Malkenu prayer: "be gracious unto us and answer us, for we have no (good) deeds; deal with us in righteousness and faithfulness (*ṣdqh wḥsd*), and save us."

16 J.B. Tyson, "'Works of Law' in Galatians," *JBL* 92 (1973), 423-31; the quote is from 430.

17 M. Barth, *Ephesians* (Garden City: Doubleday, 1974), I, 244-48.

18 1QS 5:21; 6:18; syr. Bar. 57:2 contain close verbal parallels but are quite different in substance.

tion that the common understanding of the phrase only perpetuates "the view of Rabbinic religion as one of legalistic works-righteousness."[19] The classic study of the phrase is by Ernst Lohmeyer,[20] who begins by stating that the only natural grammatical possibility is a *genitivus auctoris* ("die vom Gesetz gewirkte Werke"). He then, however, creates a problem since it is presupposed that the phrase *must* mean "Werke, die das Gesetz fordert." In the context of an experiment which questions traditional assumptions, perhaps we should look carefully at the first of Lohmeyer's alternatives. The phrase *erga nomou* occurs three times in this verse and in Rom. 3:20, 28 as the opposite of *pistis christou* as a means of justification. In Gal. 3:2, 5 it is the opposite of *akoē pisteōs* as a means of supplying the Spirit, and in 3:10 those "from works of law" are under a curse, contrasted with those "from *pistis*" who are blessed. An important clue[21] is found in the one passage where the singular is used, Rom. 2:15. Gentiles have "the work of the law written on their hearts," and from the context (1:18-2:16) it is clear what that work is: "the law works wrath" (4:15). As God's or Christ's faithfulness is expressed in a work done for our blessing, so the law apart from covenant also does works for our cursing. It is then at least possible to understand "the works of the law" in a way that does not refer to Jews keeping commandments but to God punishing Gentiles. We leave the question open for now, pending a more thorough study.

The sentence which began with a distinction between Jews and Gentiles continues in the same way, as is shown by the contrast contained in the *kai hēmeis* and the *kai autoi* of verse 17. This means that the "human being" of which the sentence speaks is specifically a Gentile human being. This and the purpose clause (*hina*) have led Barth[22] to speak of Jews who, having come to know that Gentiles are justified by the faithfulness of Christ, therefore also became believers out of a kind of envy (cf. Rom. 11:11)! But it is not at all clear that Paul means to include Jewish Christians like Cephas in the "we's" of verse 16 and even more doubtful if Cephas or the Jerusalem church would have agreed with the formulation. The language is that of the Gentile mission and not that of "the gospel/mission to the circumcised" (2:7, 8). The true parallel to the purpose clause I believe to be 1:16, which speaks of the Son of God being revealed in Paul "in order that I might preach him among the Gentiles." Paul uses the first person in 2:16-17 not to speak about Jews or Jewish Christians but in order to state fundamental theological theses that apply to himself in relation to the Gentile Galatians. It is Paul and not Jewish Christians as such for whom faith in

19 Sanders, *Paul and Palestinian Judaism,* 35-39.

20 E. Lohmeyer, "Gesetzeswerke," *ZNW* 28 (1929), 177-207.

21 Cf. R. Walker, "Die Heiden und das Gericht; Zur Auslegung von Römer 2, 12-16," *EvT* 20 (1960), 302-14.

22 M. Barth, "Jews and Gentiles," 247.

Christ and commissioning to the Gentiles coincide. The content of Paul's revelation is that "God would justify the Gentiles from the faithfulness [of Christ]" (3:8), and therefore he too became a believer. Paul too is justified, not on the basis of the faithfulness of God on Sinai but through the faithfulness of Christ on Golgotha. Paul describes in the purpose clause of verse 16 what happens to Gentile believers as a result of Paul's own commissioning and believing, something which is more than the knowledge of verse 16a, but he continues to use the first person "we." Does that mean that Paul so identifies with the Gentiles to whom he is sent that he himself in a sense has become a Gentile? Rather than being only the statement of a condensed theological thesis, verse 16 even more recounts Paul's own history (Paul's, not Cephas's), and therefore the pronoun referring to him (we) shifts in meaning as the story progresses.

Verse 17. This suggestion of a shift in the significance of "we" at least has the advantage of making some sense of the following verses. Verse 17, in which the word "sinner" must have the same meaning as in verse 15, makes clearer what was implied in verse 16 by drawing out a false implication. When "we too" became believers, it meant that "we ourselves too" have been found to be sinners, i.e. Gentiles. It does not, however, follow from this acknowledged fact that Christ is in the service of sin. As often in Paul, such a false conclusion is simply vehemently denied and not argued. We can also note that the justification "in Christ" of verse 17 justifies our translation "the faithfulness of Christ" in verse 16.[23]

Verse 18. This famous *crux* is such only for the interpreter who insists that the law must be the object of the verbs and who wants to connect it with Cephas's action in Antioch. In spite of the deliberate shift to the first person singular, most interpreters[24] manage to read the sentence as if it began: "you, Cephas." Many commentators have difficulty with *gar*, but in our view verse 18 follows from verse 17 and leads to verse 19. Paul is referring here, of course, to building or tearing down not the law but the *church.* He uses the concept of building (*oikodomeō, oikodomē*) otherwise always[25] of the church, which he (Rom. 15:20; 2 Cor. 10:8; 12:19; 13:10) or others (1 Thess. 5:11; 1 Cor. 8:1, 10; 10:23; 14:2, 3, 4, 5,

---

23 In general, I would like to argue that the phrase "justification *by faith*" is not the correct translation of any Pauline phrase. The verb *dikaiō* is found with an indication of means in Rom. 3:24, "by (dative) his grace"; 5:9, "by (*en*) his blood"; 1 Cor. 6:11, "in (*en*) the name of the Lord Jesus Christ"; Gal. 5:4, "by (*en*) the law" (negated). It can be argued that *ek pisteōs christou* (Rom. 3:26) means "by Christ's faithfulness," as does the simple *ek pisteōs* (Rom. 3:30 bis; 5:1; Gal. 3:8, 24) or *pistei* (Rom. 3:28). We note also "in Christ" rather than "by faith" in such central passages as Rom. 6:6-7; 2 Cor. 5:21; Phil. 3:8-9; etc.

24 E.g. Burton, *Galatians,* 130-31.

25 Probably also in 2 Cor. 5:1; cf. J.A.T. Robinson, *The Body* (London: SCM, 1952), 76-77.

12, 17, 26) build up. This is occasionally contrasted with tearing down the church: Rom. 14:20 (*katalyō*); 2 Cor. 10:4, 8; 13:10 (*kathairesis*). In Galatians Paul has twice referred to his earlier persecution of the church, seeking to destroy it (1:13, 23, *portheō*). Verse 18 makes explicit the change in Paul's status from being under the covenant to a Gentile, of which verse 17 spoke. That does not make Christ an agent of sin, because concomitant with the shift Paul began to build up the church he had previously persecuted. In what sense is Paul an apostate? The following verse explains.

Verse 19a. "For *through the law* I have died *to the law.*"[26] This paradoxical formulation raises the question of the different senses in which Paul uses the word *nomos,* comparable to the wide range of meanings of Torah in early Judaism. The parallel passage in Rom. 3:21-31 contrasts the "law of works" and the "law of faithfulness,"[27] and says that the law testifies to the righteousness of God which has now been made manifest (also) apart from the law. A thorough discussion would show that Paul uses the word in at least the following senses: (1) the covenant of grace on Mt. Sinai and the election of Israel but only Israel; (2) the administration of order and retribution over the whole creation, through the principalities and powers; (3) as equivalent to Scripture, the revelation of God, whose righteousness and saving power now extends also to the Gentiles in Jesus Christ; and (4) that not only from which Gentiles are redeemed (sense 2) or by which they are redeemed (sense 3) but also that for the fulfillment of which they are redeemed (Gal. 5:14; 6:2, 13; Rom. 8:4; 13:8-10). In the present sentence Paul states that he is an apostate in that by means of the faithfulness of Christ (sense 3) he has deliberately cast off the yoke of the covenant (sense 1). Amazed at this positive use of *nomos,* Bultmann pointed to Rom. 7:4 as the closest parallel:[28] "Therefore, brothers and sisters, also you have died to the law *through the body of Christ,* in order that you might become another's, his who has been raised from among the dead, in order that we might bear fruit for God." Paul is an apostate and commends himself openly as such without apology, for his life is subordinate to his calling to proclaim the righteousness of God among the Gentiles.

Verses 19b-20. This is probably the most important single verse for understanding Paul's theology, and it therefore cannot be discussed in detail here. In its present context it not only sums up Paul's own self-understanding in the *narratio* but is a statement of the life to which

26 It is only by an illegitimate application of Rom. 7:9-10 and 2 Cor. 3:6 to Paul himself that interpreters can say of this verse that "the true purpose of the law is indeed to kill man" (Bring, *Galater,* 95; cf. R. Bultmann, *Theology of the New Testament* [New York: Scribner's, 1954], I, 267).

27 So J.A. Bengel, *Gnomon,* on Gal. 2:19, "*per legem* fidei, *legi* operum. Rom. 3,27. Non sum injurius in legem: lege nitor, non minus divina."

28 Bultmann, "Auslegung," 396. Note however that in Romans 7 Paul is speaking of Gentiles moving from sense 2 to sense 3.

he calls the Galatians in the following: "I beseech you, become as I am, for I also have become as you are" (4:12).

Verse 21. I am of course embarrassed by the boldness of this radically different translation. I am especially troubled by the sharp contradiction to 3:21,[29] but I am even more troubled by the contradictions to lexicography in the usual translation of *dōrean.* If the translator's work is properly done, then the exegete will simply have to make the best of it. It is not only the word *dōrean* in Rom. 3:24 that suggests a parallel between this statement of theses (prior to discussing Abraham) and the later and clearer Rom. 3:21-31. That section ends: "Do we then render obsolete the law through this faithfulness? Of course not, but we rather confirm the law." Paul's apostasy from the covenant (law in sense 1) could very well be seen as a denial of the grace of God, and these are not the only two passages where he has to defend himself against such a false conclusion. It is surely a better formulation in Romans to say that Christ's death as a free gift is an expression of the righteousness of God to which the law *witnesses* (sense 3), now made manifest *outside* the context of the Sinai covenant (sense 1). Nevertheless, the formulation in Gal. 2:21 is also a possible one, particularly in the light of the usage of verse 19, and it does in fact provide a good transition to what will be said in chapter 3. We can so understand the verse, and if the translation is correct we must so understand it.

It is in the light of these fundamental statements (about himself) that Paul goes on to speak of their scriptural basis (for the Galatians). "Righteousness" has been used in the sense of God's righteousness (2:21), which will be the case also in what follows. The word *pistis* (faithfulness) has been used three times with the genitive "of Christ" or "of the Son of God" (2:16 bis, 20) and can now be so understood even when the genitive is not explicit. *Pistis* appears in the context of an act of God which is called "justifying," the opposite of which is "works of law" which do not justify (2:16 ter). Not only "works of law" but also "law" is something to which it is good to have died. On the other hand, "law" can also be the means of dying (to the law) and living to God (2:19), and the "law" contains the gospel of the righteousness of God, expressed in Christ's death as a free gift. The parallels to many of these concepts in Rom. 3:21-31 are evident. As in Romans, so also in Galatians, the initial statements prepare for the discussion of Abraham.

If we come to Galatians 3 with these presuppositions our understanding of the text will be quite different than if we come with a different set of presuppositions. It might be helpful to list what some of the traditional assumptions have been. It is usually assumed that Paul is attacking a position of his opponents, who used the figure of Abraham to argue that we are saved through merits, through the doing of

29 If Paul were completely consistent in his use of prepositions, we could point to the use of *dia nomou* here as in 2:19, and not *ek nomou* as in 3:21 and 2:16 ter; 3:2, 5, 10, 18.

commandments specified in the law. Paul then counters by using Abraham as a model of faith to be imitated by the Galatians, who would then for their faith receive a similar reward of being called righteous. Paul is understood to be contrasting two fundamental types of human activity, that of believing (in Christ) and that of doing (God's commandments), the one which leads to blessing and life, and the other which leads to a curse and death. The problem with the law is its unfulfillability, which is the point of the citation of Deut. 27:26, pronouncing a curse on everyone who does not do every last commandment. Paul profoundly disagrees with a statement of the Torah (Lev. 18:5), which he proceeds to contradict by citing a passage from the prophets (Hab. 2:4). The principles involved in the contrast between believing and doing are universally valid, not only for those being addressed but also and even especially for Jews. According to the usual understanding, Paul then goes on to a brief digression on the history of Israel in 3:15-29, a passage which concerns the Galatians only in the sense of an example to be avoided. The law came to Israel on Sinai long after the time of Abraham, at best given only indirectly by God (3:19-20), at best only a temporary restrainer (3:22-25), but a fulfilment of no promises (3:17-18, 21). Now that faith has been revealed, i.e. that Christ has come, there should be no more Jews or Greeks and certainly no more law, for the third race has been founded in Christ, in which the principle of faith apart from law reigns supreme.

Let us see how chapter 3 might look if it is to be understood not from the presuppositions just listed but in the light of 2:15-21. Paul begins with an appeal to reality: the Galatians have received the Spirit (and that not "from works of law" but "from preaching of faithfulness"); and then he raises the question of possibility: how can this be? what is the scriptural justification for the gift of the Spirit to Gentiles?

The starting point and the conclusion of Paul's argumentation from Scripture are clear. His gospel, the gospel he preaches among the Gentiles, the gospel to the uncircumcised, is found already in Scripture, in the law.[30] The content of that gospel is that "God would justify the Gentiles from faithfulness," and its form is that of a promise, that "in (Abraham) all the Gentiles will be blessed" (3:8). The fulfilment of that promise and the reality of that gospel do not occur for Paul before or outside of but only in Christ, who died "in order that for the Gentiles the blessing of Abraham might become a reality in Jesus Christ, in order that we might receive the promise, i.e. the Spirit, through the faithfulness" (3:14). The contrast throughout Galatians 3 is not between legalism and faith but between law (as that from which Gentiles are redeemed) and promise (as God's act of righteousness in Christ).

30 For a discussion of how Paul hears the promise of the expression of the righteousness of God for Gentiles in Gen. 15:6, cf. L. Gaston "Abraham and the Righteousness of God," *Horizons in Biblical Theology* 2 (1980), 39-68.

The enclosing verses speak explicitly of Gentiles, and one would expect that the enclosed verses, which speak of the law as curse, would also speak of the situation of Gentiles. Schoeps complains of Paul that he does not see the connection between covenant and commandments;[31] I would say that it is precisely because Paul does see this connection that his description of law outside the context of covenant is so bleak. This is reinforced by the possibility that he was accustomed to viewing the Gentile world through the glasses of Shammai and apocalyptic.[32] In any case, the bracketing verses speak of the blessing of Abraham for the Gentiles, which corresponds to the curse of the quotations from Deut. 27:26 and 21:23.[33] Since the ones "Christ has redeemed from the curse of the law" are called explicitly Gentiles in verse 14, the curse of verse 10 must also be one which lay upon Gentiles. Paul is able to find this in the LXX (not the MT) of Deut. 27:26, which inserts the word *pas* twice: *everyone* is under a curse, including Gentiles, who do not do *all* the commandments, not just those incumbent on God-fearers. One might think that those who do remain in the commandments "to do them" would be under a blessing,[34] for those "who do them" are promised life (Lev. 18:5). Indeed, in another context Paul does use Lev. 18:5 in this positive sense: "For Moses writes that the human being who does the righteousness which is from Torah will live by it" (Rom. 10:5). A further connection is made by the parallel "will live" in Hab. 2:4.[35] The contrast here is not between believing and doing but between those whose life is based on the works of the law (Gentiles) and those whose life is based on the faithfulness of God

31 Schoeps, *Paul*, 213-18.

32 Cf. L. Gaston, "Paul and the Torah," in A.T. Davies (ed.), *Antisemitism and the Foundations of Christianity* (New York: Paulist, 1979), 48-71.

33 Deut. 21:23 provides the scriptural basis for the statement that Christ became a curse for us in order that we might receive a blessing. It is an example of "interchange in Christ" (cf. M. Hooker, "Interchange in Christ," *JTS* 22 (1971), 349-61). It must be emphasized that this is not an historical description of the circumstances of Jesus' death, although such an understanding often unconsciously influences the way the Synoptic trial narratives are read.

34 One interesting answer to the question of why Paul speaks of the curses and not the blessings of the covenant when writing to Gentiles is given by M. Wyschogrod, "The Law: Jews and Gentiles," in P.D. Opsahl and M.H. Tanenbaum (eds.), *Speaking of God Today* (Philadelphia: Fortress, 1974), 3-14. If he were writing in another context, I cannot believe that Paul would not have affirmed the statement of Ps. Sol. 14:1-3, "Faithful is the Lord to them that love him in truth, to them that endure his chastening, to them that walk in the righteousness of his commandments, in the law which he commanded us that we might live. The pious of the Lord shall live by it forever."

35 For the proper translation of this important verse, cf. D.M. Smith, "HO DE DIKAIOS EK PISTEŌS ZĒSETAI," in B.L. Daniels and M.J. Suggs (eds.), *Studies in the History and Text of the New Testament* (Salt Lake City: University of Utah Press, 1967), 13-25; and H.C.C. Cavallin, "The Righteous Shall Live by Faith: A Decisive Argument for the Traditional Interpretation," *ST* 32 (1978), 33-43. Paul omits the genitive after *pistis* in order to allow his understanding in terms of the faithfulness of Christ established in chapter 2.

(Christians; also Jews?). The latter group will "do them" (cf. 5:14; 6:2; Rom. 8:4; 2:13)[36] and as "righteous" ones "will live." As the word *alla* shows, verse 12b cannot be understood as a prooftext for verse 12a. In a paradox comparable to 2:19, the sentence must say: "The law (sense 2) is not 'from faithfulness' but on the contrary those who do the law (sense 4) will not be under the curse but will live." The law apart from covenant is not "from faithfulness" but Lev. 18:5 is, for it is to be understood in the light of Hab. 2:4. All of this is very compressed and will be expressed more adequately in Romans. In the context of Galatians, Paul wants to speak not of the promise of Torah but of the promise in Torah to Abraham, and therefore the word *nomos* is used here consistently to refer to law outside the covenant, the law which works wrath (Rom. 4:15), the curse of the law as it applies to Gentiles.

That Paul is speaking of Gentiles who need to be redeemed from the law is shown most clearly as the argument progresses to speak of "the elements of the world."[37] The Gentile Galatians once "served [as slaves] gods who essentially are not," beings further identified as "the weak and impotent elements, whom you wish to serve [as slaves] anew" (4:9). Paul also says that "we minor children were enslaved under the elements of the world" (4:3). We are helped in identifying these "elements of the world" by Colossians, where they (2:8, 20) are also called "principalities and powers" (2:10, 15) and "angels" (2:18), who enforce specific regulations (2:20, etc.) and who have a "certificate of indebtedness" which condemns all those who do not submit to their regulations (2:14), a curse of their law, so to speak. In Galatians, slavery to pagan gods (4:9) means being "under the elements of the world" (4:3), "under guardians and administrators" (4:2), "under the custodian" (3:24), "imprisoned under sin" (3:22). It is, however, also said that the same people were "held in custody under the law" (3:23-24) until Christ came "in order that he might redeem those under law" (4:4-5). There is also reference to a law administered by the angels of the nations (3:19), apart from the covenant.[38] This identification of pagan gods with elements and angelic administrators and with the law as such shows the sense in which the word must be understood in much of Galatians 3. This is the law under which Christ became a curse for us, for according to Paul he was crucified by "the rulers of this age" (1 Cor. 2:8); this is the

36 E.P. Sanders sees correctly that Paul's point here is not to contrast human believing and doing, but he does not note that the two references to "doing" put them into his category of "doing the law" (E.P. Sanders, "Paul and the Law: Different Questions, Different Answers," in *Paul, the Law, and the Jewish People* [Philadelphia: Fortress, 1983]). He was probably misled by his assumption that in Rom. 10:5 and Gal. 3:12 "Paul is disagreeing with the statement of the law" in Lev. 18:5. See Sanders, "On the Question of Fulfilling the Law in Paul and Rabbinic Judaism," in E. Bammel, C.K. Barrett, and W.D. Davies (eds.), *Donum Gentilicium* (Oxford: Clarendon, 1978), 103-26, especially 104.

37 Cf. especially E. Schweizer, "Die 'Elemente der Welt' Gal. 4,3,9; Kol. 2,8.20," *Beiträge zur Theologie des Neuen Testaments* (Zürich: Zwingli, 1970), 147-63.

38 Cf. L. Gaston, "Angels and Gentiles in Early Judaism and in Paul" (forthcoming).

law from whose curse (3:10) Christ has redeemed the Gentiles (3:13-14). When Paul speaks of the law in this specific sense of how it relates to Gentiles, he says nothing whatsoever against the Torah of Israel or about the significance of the law for Jews or Jewish Christians.

The law in the sense of the covenant made with Israel (sense 1) was not in fact the fulfilment of the promise and gospel which interests Paul. That law is not "against the promises" (3:21) but neither is it *for* this specific promise. For the Galatians it is simply irrelevant, unless they are to become converts to Judaism, a possibility Paul vehemently opposes. I would understand the word *nomos* to be used in this sense in 3:17, 18, 21 ter, and 5:3. Paul says nothing whatsoever about the significance of *nomos* in this sense for Israel or for Jewish Christians, but he speaks only of its irrelevance for the Gentile Galatians.

Finally, Paul can also use the word *nomos* in the positive sense of God's revelation (sense 3), although this never occurs explicitly in Galatians 3. If our translation of 2:21 is correct, then the law contains the gospel of the righteousness of God, which resulted in Christ dying as a free gift, and in 2:19 it is through the law that Paul died to the law. The righteousness of God for Gentiles is for Paul a promise in Scripture before it is a reality in Christ, and Paul's whole argument concerning the promise of God made to Abraham presupposes a concept of "the law of faithfulness" (Rom. 3:27) or "the law of the Spirit of life" (8:2). As Paul can use the word *nomos* in Gal. 4:21 in the sense of Scripture, so the word *graphē* is used in the sense of Torah in 3:8, 22; 4:30. It is only because of the situation addressed that Paul does not say that "the *law,* knowing beforehand that God would justify the Gentiles from faithfulness, proclaimed the gospel beforehand to Abraham" (3:8).[39] We can also note that *nomos* in the sense of what Christians have been liberated to fulfil (sense 4) is found in 5:14 and 6:2.

Conclusion

Trying to sort out the different senses in Paul's use of the word *nomos* is a difficult if not impossible task. H. Räisänen has recently warned that it may not be possible at all and that we shall have to live with a number of anomalies in Pauline thought.[40] E.P. Sanders, however, has made an important advance in urging that we pay close attention to the particular questions to which Paul's various statements about *nomos* provide answers.[41] I would like also to urge that we take seriously the distinction

39 "Statt *graphē* könnte hier (Gal. 3:8) auch *nomos* stehen," G. Friedrich, "Das Gesetz des Glaubens Römer 3,27," *Auf das Wort kommt es an* (Göttingen: Vandenhoeck und Ruprecht, 1978), 107-22, 119. Cf. also *gegraptai* in 3:10, 13; 4:22, 27.

40 H. Räisänen, "Paul's Theological Difficulties with the Law," *StBib* 3 (1978), 321-36; "Legalism and Salvation by the Law," in S. Pedersen (ed.), *The Pauline Literature and Theology* (Arhus: Aros, 1980), 63-83.

41 Sanders, "Paul and the Law."

between Jews and Gentiles and consider that *nomos* might function in relation to one group quite differently than it does in relation to the other.[42] It would of course be simpler for all if Paul had used different words for different aspects, particularly if in fact he speaks about law outside the context of covenant, but of course he could not do so. Because God is one, his law is one, and the more the concept of Torah/Nomos is enriched by wider associations the more different senses the word will acquire. I hope that the discussion above will at least show the necessity of rethinking the issue of how Paul speaks of the law in Galatians 2 and 3.

We began with the question of the assumptions usually made concerning Paul's theology of Judaism in Galatians. If these assumptions are put to one side, what then are the exegetical possibilities for understanding what is being said in the context of a letter addressed polemically to Gentiles? It may be that a more thorough study would in fact support at least some of those assumptions, but in this experiment an attempt was made to suggest radically different options. It may be that questions asked from the perspective of a seminar on Christian anti-Judaism will lead to answers which are quite surprising.

Appendix: Paul as Apostate

It is perhaps necessary to spell out in a bit more detail the reasons for claiming that Paul was consciously an apostate in the technical sense of one who deliberately throws off the yoke of the covenant. Although few would use the word, for most scholars Paul's apostasy is axiomatic.[43] If Paul was "converted" from the Jewish to the Christian religion, if he really did die to the Sinai covenant (the law, Gal. 2:19), then of course he was an apostate. It should be clear that we are speaking of an "Apostat *stricto sensu*,"[44] a technical meaning of the term, a shift from

42 We have become accustomed to understanding the contradiction between "the alleged aim of the law, that it has been given for life, and its alleged effect, that it creates sin and death" (H. Conzelmann, *An Outline of the Theology of the New Testament* [New York: Harper, 1969], 226) in an existential fashion: the one law means death for "man before faith" but life for the believer. If we were to move from an existential to a heilsgeschichtliche distinction, from Bultmann to Schweitzer, we would come much closer to Paul's intention. One could compare the rabbinic phrase about the Torah being for Israel "an elixir of life" (*sm ḥyym*) and for the nations of the world "a deadly poison" (*sm hmwt*); cf. T.W. Manson, "2 Cor. 2:14-17: Suggestions Towards an Exegesis," in *Studia Paulina*, 155-62.

43 To let one example stand for many: "The fact that he gave up his Jewish way of life was also in conformity with his gospel, which did not include the observance of the Torah," in H.D. Betz, "2 Cor. 6:14-7:1: An Anti-Pauline Fragment?" *JBL* 92 (1973), 88-108, especially 101.

44 R.J.Z. Werblowsky, "Paulus in jüdischer Sicht," *Paulus-Apostat oder Apostel* (Regensburg: Pustet, 1977), 135-46, especially 135. For a general definition of apostasy in this sense see E.P. Sanders, "The Covenant as a Soteriological Category and the Nature of Salvation in Palestinian and Hellenistic Judaism," in R. Hamerton-Kelly

election at Sinai to election in Christ, a move which Christians praise and Jews should not hold against him. Did Paul for his own person deliberately turn away from the Torah as covenant and thus from the obligation to keep the commandments, at the same time that he was not turning away from God but on the contrary being obedient to his revelation? It is not easy to answer this question.

That Paul was accused of apostasy by later Jewish Christians is clear.[45] He was accused by Jews (or perhaps Jewish Christians) at the time of Luke (and perhaps during Paul's lifetime) of something much worse: "(Those) zealous for the law have been told about you that you teach apostasy from Moses to all Jews (who live) among the Gentiles, saying that they should not circumcise their children or to walk in the customs" (Acts 21:21). Insofar as Paul was persecuted by Jews and insofar as he himself earlier persecuted the church, it was presumably from zealous motives and on this charge. It would therefore occasion no surprise if also in Galatia he had to meet a similar accusation (2:18). I believe that Paul was completely innocent of this charge, in that he confined his preaching to Gentiles and did not encourage Jews to abandon the covenant. I used to believe that he did not do so himself and agreed with W.L. Knox, "It is clear that Paul throughout his life continued to practise Judaism, and that he expected Jewish converts to do so . . . . On his principles, if he obeyed the law at all, he was bound to obey it as a Pharisee";[46] W.D. Davies, "Paul observed the law and that in the pharisaic manner, throughout his life";[47] F.C. Grant, "Not only in his attitude toward the law, as the source and record of a divine revelation, but in his allegiance to the great religious affirmations of the early Pharisees, Paul remained a Pharisee to his dying day."[48] There is nothing at all inconsistent about an apostle remaining himself a member of the Sinai community keeping commandments while being entrusted with a gospel for Gentiles, calling them into the community of Christ without commandments.

However, perhaps it is not quite so simple. The issue was raised in this paper in an attempt to make some sense of Gal. 2:18. If Paul used to act like a Zealot in seeking to destroy the church (1:13-14), it seems that he could be accused of doing the opposite by now building it up (2:18).

---

and R. Scroggs (eds.), *Jews, Greeks and Christians* (Leiden: Brill, 1976), 11-44, especially 40-41; and for rabbinic references see A. Nissen, *Gott und der Nächste im antiken Judentum* (Tübingen: Mohr, 1974), 44, 62.

45 *Apostatēs tou nomou,* Irenaeus on the Ebionites in Eusebius, *H.E.* 3.27.4. Cf. H.J. Schoeps, *Theologie und Geschichte des Judenchristentums* (Tübingen: Mohr, 1949), 127-35; and G. Lüdemann, "Zum Antipaulinismus im frühen Christentum," *EvT* 40 (1980), 437-55.

46 W.L. Knox, *St. Paul and the Church of Jerusalem* (Cambridge: Cambridge University Press, 1925), 122-23.

47 W.D. Davies, *Paul and Rabbinic Judaism* (London: SPCK, 1955), 70.

48 F.C. Grant, *Roman Hellenism and the New Testament* (Edinburgh: Oliver and Boyd, 1962), 136.

It seems that Paul just this once accepts the accusation, but then goes on to interpret it positively as not denying the grace of God (2:19-21). How far does Paul go in identifying himself with the Gentiles to whom his gospel is addressed?[49] Within Galatians itself, there are passages in which "we" must mean "we Gentiles." The parallel purpose clauses in 3:15 are significant: "in order that *for the Gentiles* the blessing of Abraham might become a reality in Jesus Christ, in order that *we* might receive the promise, i.e. the Spirit, through the faithfulness." When Paul says that Christ came "in order that he might redeem those under law, that is, in order that *we* might receive adoption (as children)," he can hardly be referring to Jews unless he contradicts himself in Rom. 9:4, "They are Israelites, and to them belong the *hyiothesia*. . . ." I find it incredible to think that Paul could say that "we (Jews) were enslaved under the elements of the world" (4:3), in the light of the same phrase in 4:9, but that could perhaps be debated.[50] M. Barth has argued that the verb "to live" in 2:14 should be understood in the fullest sense of life, as in 2:19-20.[51] If that is so, then Paul affirms that there are two ways of having "life" in the fullest sense, *ethnikōs* and *Ioudaïkōs*. (It is very doubtful that Cephas would have agreed with this statement about how he lives, but Paul may really be speaking about himself.)[52] Paul refers to something which can only be called apostasy in Phil. 3:7-9, although of course he is not speaking of works-righteousness. I would argue that Phil. 3:9 must be translated: " . . . that I may be found in him, having my righteousness not from the Torah but through the faithfulness of Christ, the righteousness from God which (leads) to the faith of knowing him . . . ." Here too Paul does not deny the righteousness (=election) given through the Torah to Israel when he affirms another righteousness given through Christ to Gentiles and also chooses the latter possibility for himself. On a more speculative note, when Paul wishes "that I myself were accursed and cut off from Christ for the sake of my brethren, my kinsmen by race" (Rom. 9:3), can we hear the implication that he has been cut off from the covenant for the sake of the Gentiles whose apostle he was called to be?

The reasons for Paul's apostasy presumably have to do with his apostolate. Not to have so identified with those to whom he has been commissioned to preach "his" gospel, that "God would justify the Gentiles from faithfulness," would have caused great difficulties, of which Galatians is a good illustration. The Judaizers thought that there

49 "In the course of his work among Gentiles, Paul came more and more to internalize the Gentile point of view and identify himself with it," H. Räisänen, "Legalism and Salvation," 80.

50 Cf. also the use of "we" and "you" in 3:23-27 and probably in 4:26, 28.

51 M. Barth, "Jews and Gentiles," 246, 250.

52 The whole statement is strange, for while it is almost impossible to understand anything about Cephas's actions "compelling Gentiles to Judaize" (cf. Schmithals, *Paul and James*, 68-72), it fits the Galatian situation perfectly (6:12).

was an advantage to being, like Paul, both a Jew and a Christian, for they did not like being called "Gentile sinners." To make his point, Paul tells how he has for his own person renounced the covenant and become like them a Gentile. What Paul had a right to and freely gave up, the Gentiles should not try to attain, particularly in an amateurish manner. The Galatians might have been in the position of wanting to model themselves on their founder and of accusing him of not preaching what he practises. Paul therefore had to put himself into the same status as that of his converts, if his gospel and person were to be followed. Very significant is Gal. 4:12, "I beseech you, become as I am, for I also have become as you are."

Paul is not as clear as he might be with respect to his apostasy for two reasons. First, he wanted to continue to express his loyalty to Israel. When challenged, he too could boast of his Jewish credentials (2 Cor. 11:22; Phil. 3:4-6; Gal. 1:14). That Paul five times received the punishment of *Makkot* in the synagogues (2 Cor. 11:24) shows that he accepted the jurisdiction of the synagogue and presumably continued to worship there. An apostate who had completely renounced Judaism, like Tiberius Alexander, Philo's nephew, was never beaten in the synagogues. That Paul continued to keep the commandments is probable but not sure. If P. Richardson[53] is right in his understanding of 1 Cor. 9:19-23, perhaps he did not. It may be that Paul wanted to have it both ways, to understand himself as an apostate in relationship to his Gentile converts but as a loyal son of Israel in relationship to Jews.

If Paul was occasionally in his own mind an apostate in the technical sense, much more important for his own self-consciousness was the sense of being one of the few faithful Israelites (Rom. 11:1). If I had to imagine an appropriate setting for Paul's revelation and commissioning (Gal. 1:15-16), it would not be the fireworks of the Lukan accounts but rather Paul all alone late at night pondering the text of the second Servant song (Isa. 49:1-6). It is the consciousness of fulfilling Israel's calling to be the light to the Gentiles which was the driving force in Paul's life, and it was the conviction that now was the time in God's *Heilsgeschichte* for the expression of his righteousness toward Gentiles which was the content of Paul's mystery (well summed up in Eph. 3:3-6). What he holds against his Jewish contemporaries in such passages as Rom. 2:17-24 and 9:30-10:4 is not a lack of zeal (=faith) and certainly not works-righteousness but a lack of understanding of the arrival of the eschatological hour for the Gentiles. This is why the word "apostate" in Gal. 2:18 must be put in quotation marks, as an accusation bitterly accepted once for the sake of a larger loyalty not only to his mission but also to Israel. Paul understood himself, then, to be a faithful Israelite in God's *Heilsgeschichte,* who for the sake of his mission

53 P. Richardson, "Pauline Inconsistency: I Corinthians 9:19-23 and Galatians 2:11-14," *NTS* 26 (1980), 347-62.

relinquished any personal advantages stemming from Sinai to make himself a Gentile sinner.

If Paul was an apostate, did he think that other Jewish Christians should follow his example? In the light of the mutual recognition of two apostolates in Gal. 2:7-9, I would assume not.[54] Most interpreters believe that the Jerusalem church continued to keep the commandments and that Paul respected this. There is however a significant theological issue which may not have been apparent in the first century. To judge from such formulae as 1 Cor. 11:23-25; 15:3-7, and perhaps Rom. 3:24-25, Jewish Christians understood Christ as a confirmation of the covenant and as expiation for the forgiveness of sins. That is, for Jewish Christians Christ probably replaced the Temple as the locus of atonement but not Sinai as the locus of election. For Paul, however, Christ died not so much for our sins as to give life to the dead, and in Paul's "pattern of religion" Christ occupies almost exactly the same place with respect to election as does Sinai within Judaism. The logic of Paul's theology is such as to make Jewish Christianity only a transitional period. In terms of what he does say, however, Paul speaks of apostasy only with respect to himself. He can be understood, at least implicitly, as affirming something like the two-covenant concept of F. Rosenzweig.[55] That is, Paul affirms the new expression of the righteousness of God in Christ for the Gentiles and for himself as Apostle to the Gentiles, without in any sense denying the righteousness of God expressed in Torah for Israel.

---

54 There is nothing, least of all in Galatians, to justify Bring's statement that "Paul had come to the conclusion that when they became Christians Jews must become like Gentiles" (*Galater,* 81).

55 That the suggestion is not completely anachronistic might be shown by Barnabas, who warns against "being like certain people, in that you say (heaping up your sins): 'The covenant belongs both to them and to us (*hē diathēkē ekeinōn kai hēmōn*)'" (4:6). (Unfortunately the manuscript tradition is not at all clear at this point.) Is it too fanciful to think that among the "certain people" Barnabas opposes are heirs of Paul and Ephesians?

4

On the Absence of "Anti-Judaism" in 1 Corinthians

Peter Richardson*

There is little in 1 Corinthians that sounds anti-Judaic.[1] Most other letters of Paul have sections that have been given that label, the more

* I am grateful to the University of Toronto for a leave from administrative and teaching duties in 1980-81, to the Social Sciences and Humanities Research Council of Canada for a travel and research grant, to the École Biblique in Jerusalem and to the American School of Classical Studies in Athens and Corinth for their libraries and facilities. All contributed to the peace of mind that allowed the completion of this paper.

1 Anti-Judaism may operate on several levels: sociological, whether societal or communal, theological, historical, and orthopractic. "Societal" anti-Judaism emerges out of the make-up of the population generally, whether in a broad region or a particular city. The trouble in Alexandria which gave rise to the *Legatio ad Gaium* is a good example, where the hostility arises from the way one sub-group responds to another, or from the way the dominant group treats its minorities (see, e.g. A.N. Sherwin-White, *Racial Prejudice in Imperial Rome* [Cambridge: Cambridge University Press, 1967], chapter 3). By "communal" I mean a conflict which has to do with the Christian community specifically—its racial make-up, its tensions, and its problems, as, e.g. in Galatians: where there are statements that verge on the anti-Judaic, they arise from the tensions between Jewish Christians and non-Jewish Christians, exacerbated by intrusions from outside, and fueled by the specific issues that troubled the church (but see Gaston's essay in this volume). "Theological" anti-Judaism presents itself to us as a theologically grounded expression of opposition to the people or beliefs of Israel (see e.g. the volume of essays edited by W. Eckert, N.P. Levinson, and M. Stohr, *Antijudaismus im Neuen Testament? Exegetische und systematische Beiträge* [Munich: Chr. Kaiser Verlag, 1967]). Within early Christian literature the clearest examples of this are the Gospels of Matthew and John, and the Epistle of Barnabas: this is the most depressing kind of anti-Judaism because it presumes to find a theological rationale for antagonism to Judaism. The "historical" category includes those hostile events that create a response that sounds anti-Judaic. I would imagine the expression in 1 Thess. 2:14-16 to be a case in point (see the essay above by John C. Hurd). Finally, there is "orthopractic" anti-Judaism, an expression of opposition to Judaism or its practices that arises out of disagreement over behaviour. These disagreements occur within the Christian community, though they may be caused by either internal or external problems such as circumcision, menus, invitation lists, sexual practices or the like. For an earlier statement of this

important of which are discussed in other essays in the present volume. But the absence of "anti-Judaism" in 1 Corinthians also deserves some attention. It cannot be argued that there is a chronological reason for this absence, since letters written at about the same time do have anti-Judaic motifs. Nor can it be argued that churches outside Judea and Syria did not have to face the kind of situation that may give rise to anti-Judaic sentiments. It can be maintained, of course, that the reason is simply that there is no Jewish community in Corinth, or that there is no contact between Jews and Christians, or that no Corinthian Jews became Christians. One of the purposes of this paper is to argue against these explanations.

The main purpose, however, is to propose that there is a problem in the relation between Jews and Greeks within the Christian community in Corinth, similar to the problems which have arisen in other churches. Paul does not express himself in the same way in 1 Corinthians as in some other places, it will be argued, because he is being deliberately accommodating, walking a tight-rope between competing parties in the church at Corinth. He is trying very hard to be irenic in this letter—though he does not always succeed—whereas in other letters he becomes argumentative, angry, sarcastic, or "anti-Judaic."

Where we find anti-Judaism in Paul there is generally a strongly relational component to it, involving Jews or Jewish Christians. It is not always possible to distinguish between passages where Paul is dealing with an internal Christian difference of opinion and with relations with non-Christian Jews (see E.P. Sander's essay in this volume). And it is not always possible to determine precisely which problems arise from "anti-Judaism." It is clear, for example, that issues of law and circumcision are likely to presuppose some degree of opposition between Jews or Jewish Christians and Gentile Christians, as in Galatians and Philippians. But as we shall see, the major orthopractic problem in Corinth is food. Is this evidence for opposition of an "anti-Jewish" kind, or is it perhaps evidence that the source of the difficulties in Corinth is entirely Gentile? I shall argue (*contra* Hurd and Sanders) that in Corinth the substantial difficulties do involve differences between "Jew and Greek."

Jews in Corinth

Corinth in the time of Paul was a very diverse city. Of relatively recent Roman re-foundation (44 B.C.E.) after the demolition of the city by

approach see P. Richardson, *Israel in the Apostolic Church* (Cambridge: Cambridge University Press, 1969), 1-8; and for a different set of categories see D.R.A. Hare, "The Rejection of the Jews in the Synoptic Gospels and Acts," in Alan T. Davies, ed., *Antisemitism and the Foundations of Christianity* (New York/Toronto: Paulist, 1979), 27-47, who proposes "prophetic," "Jewish-Christian," and "gentilizing Anti-Judaism."

Mummius (146 B.C.E.), the city had shortly thereafter become the capital of the Roman Province of Achaia (27 B.C.E.).[2] It is likely that it was not as completely destroyed in 146 B.C.E. as most scholars have supposed, and that some of its original inhabitants continued to live in the badly mauled city for the next 100 years. Indeed, it may even be the case that worship at some of its temples did not cease.[3] The population was dominated, at least in the earliest stages, by Romans, mainly freedmen, among whom were some—perhaps many—Greek freedmen. But Greek inhabitants and a multitude of others who were attracted by the economic prospects settled there until, by Paul's time, it was a very large commercial city.[4] Not only were there adherents of the archaic gods and the philosophical schools, there were also initiates into the mystery religions, adherents of eastern cults, and Jews.[5] The inscription from a "synagogue of the Hebrews," though from a later synagogue, is physical evidence of a Jewish community.[6]

There is one good piece of literary evidence for the presence of Jews in Corinth: the *Legatio ad Gaium* (281-82) mentions Corinth as the location of a Jewish "colony." It is odd that there are no other primary non-Christian references to Judaism in Corinth at this period. In the secondary literature there are, apart from obvious and standardized comments, no discussions of Judaism in Corinth in Radin, Morrison, Grant, Juster, Schürer, Hengel, or Smallwood.[7] Regrettably, there is no

2 During Tiberius' reign Achaia and Macedonia were merged into one Imperial province. Claudius separated them again, and restored Achaia to the rank of a Senatorial province.

3 James Wiseman, "Corinth and Rome I: 228 B.C.-A.D. 267," in H. Temporini, ed., *ANRW*, 2.7.1 (Berlin: de Gruyter, 1979), 438-548.

4 See H.S. Robinson, *The Urban Development of Ancient Corinth* (Athens: American School of Classical Studies, 1965); N. Sakellariou and N. Faraklas, *Corinthia-Cleonaea* (Athens: Centre of Ekistics, 1971), 131-59.

5 The literary, epigraphic, and archeological evidence suggests that all the following cults were active in Corinth in the first century C.E.: Aphrodite, Aphrodite Melainis, Bellerophon, Ephesian Artemis, Dionysos, Tyche, Hieron to all the Gods, Herakles, Poseidon, Apollo Klarios, Hermes, Zeus Chthonios, Zeus Hypsistos, Athena, Octavia, Demeter and Kore, Asklepios, Jupiter Capitolinus, Isis Pelagia, Isis Aegyptia, Serapis, Helios, Ananke and Bia, the Mother of the Gods, Hera Bounaia, and Mithras. In addition there was worship of the God of Israel by Jews and Christians. The list could be expanded somewhat if evidence from the nearby Corinthian cities of Isthmia, Kenchreai, Lechaion, Perachora, and Sikyon were included.

6 The inscription is published in B.D. Meritt, ed., *Corinth*, vol. 8.1, Greek Inscriptions 1869-1927 (Cambridge: Harvard, 1931), 78-79 (number 111). It is widely believed that an earlier synagogue may have occupied the same site, but the site cannot be identified.

7 M. Radin, *Jews Among the Greeks and Romans* (Philadelphia: Jewish Publication Society, 1915); W.D. Morrison, *The Jews Under Roman Rule* (London: Unwin, 1890); M. Grant, *The Jews in the Roman World* (London: Weidenfeld, 1973); J. Juster, *Les Juifs dans l'empire romain* (Paris: Libraire Paul Geuthner, 1914), 2 vols.; E. Schürer, *History of the Jewish People in the Age of Jesus Christ (175 B.C.-A.D. 135),* vol. 2, new revised Eng. version by G. Vermes, F. Millar, and M. Black, eds. (Edinburgh: T. & T. Clark, 1979); M. Hengel, *Judaism and Hellenism*, 2 vols. (Philadelphia: Fortress, 1974); E. Mary Smallwood, *The Jews Under Roman Rule* (Leiden: Brill, 1976).

full-scale study of Jews in Greece[8] comparable to the studies that exist of Jews in Rome, Cyrenaica, Egypt, and Babylon.[9]

There is, however, a set of tantalizing allusions: one pair of doors to the Temple in Jerusalem was of Corinthian bronze, described glowingly by Josephus. So remarkable were the doors that they were the only ones not overlaid with gold. They were given to the Temple by Nicanor, whose ossuary has been found.[10] Though there is some doubt about the correct interpretation of the inscription, it appears probable that Nicanor was an Alexandrian. And yet the fact that these doors were of Corinthian bronze prompts a question about the possibility of a connection between those doors—the subject of legend in the Talmud and Tosefta—and the Jews of Corinth. It is hardly likely that Corinthians donated them in view of the inscriptional evidence, but did Corinthian Jews, perhaps, fashion them in bronze before their transport to Jerusalem?[11]

Whatever the answer to that question, we can establish from evidence outside the New Testament the existence of a Jewish

8 For a beginning see the overly cautious article by L. B. Urdahl, "Jews in Attica," *Symbolae Osloenses* 43 (1968), 39-56; and B.D. Mazur, *Studies on Jewry in Greece* 1 (Athens: Hestia, 1935). Despite its promising title E. Maas, *Griechen und Semiten auf dem Isthmus von Korinth* (Berlin: Reimer, 1902) is quite irrelevant for this period. F.S. Darrow, *The History of Corinth from Mummius to Herodes Atticus* (Ph.D. Diss. Harvard, 1906) claims, without specific evidence, that the Jewish community in Corinth dates from the time of Caligula (143-46).

9 On Rome, there is a large literature, among which note: P. Styger, *Juden und Christen im alten Rom: streiflichter aus der ersten Verfolgungheit* (Berlin, 1934); S.L. Guterman, *Religious Toleration and Persecution in Ancient Rome* (London: Aiglon, 1951); H.J. Leon, *The Jews of Ancient Rome* (Philadelphia: Jewish Publication Society, 1960); E. Schürer, *Die Gemeindeverfassung der Juden in Rom in der Kaiserzeit* (Leipzig: Hinrichs, 1879); H. Vogelstein, *Rome,* trans. M. Hadas (Philadelphia: Jewish Publication Society, 1940). On Cyrenaica, S. Applebaum, *Jews and Greeks in Ancient Cyrene,* SJLA 28 (Leiden: Brill, 1979) is now in English; see also J.W. Hirschberg, *A History of the Jews in North Africa.* (2d ed., Leiden: Brill, 1974). On Egypt, see V. Tcherikover, *The Jews in Egypt in the Hellenistic-Roman Age in the Light of the Papyri* (2d ed., Jerusalem, 1963) in Hebrew, and, with A. Fuks, *Corpus Papyrorum Judaicarum,* 2 vols. (Cambridge: Harvard University Press, 1957 and 1960); I.A. Ghali, *L'Egypte et les juifs dans l'antiquité* (Paris: Cujas, 1969). Both Egypt and Syria are covered in E. Ashtor, *History of the Jews in Egypt and Syria,* 3 vols. (Mosad Ha-Rav Kook, 1944-70) in Hebrew. On Babylon, several works of J. Neusner are readily available, including his *A History of the Jews in Babylonia,* 5 vols. (Leiden: Brill, 1965-70). Also useful is J.B. Frey, *Corpus Inscriptionum Judaicarum: Recueil des inscriptions juives qui vont du iii*[e] *siècle avant Jésus-Christ au vii*[e] *siècle de notre ère,* 2 vols. (Paris, 1936).

10 *T.* Yoma 2:4; *b.* Yoma 38a; *y.* Yoma 3:41a. See Clermont-Ganneau, "Archeological and Epigraphic Notes on Palestine," *PEFQS* (1903), 125-31; G. Dixon, "The Tomb of Nicanor of Alexandria," *PEFQS* (1903), 326-32; art. "Nicanor's Gate," *Enc Jud* 12, 1133-35.

11 Evidence of bronze-working has been found in at least two sites in Corinth, both dating from the first century (see Wiseman, "Corinth and Rome," 512). There is a pattern to Jewish settlements, so that in Asia Minor Jewish settlements tend to be found in metalworking towns, commercial centres, towns manufacturing textiles or perfume, and agriculturally-based towns. This pattern may well hold true for Greece as well. See S. Applebaum, "The Social and Economic Status of the Jews in the Diaspora," in S. Safrai and M. Stern, *The Jewish People in the First Century,* CRINT 2.1 (Philadelphia: Fortress, 1976), 701-27.

community—whether large or small we cannot say—in Corinth.[12] Unlike the situation in Alexandria, we can say nothing from external sources about the quality of relations between Jews and Greeks in Corinth.

From the New Testament we can infer only a little more. We cannot say certainly if the Jewish community was rich or poor, whether it was highly segregated or assimilated, whether it was in close contact with Jerusalem, whether it was observant or lax, whether it was syncretistic or not. The evidence of 1 Corinthians is the best we have, and it is either equivocal or silent. The evidence of Acts, which classical and New Testament scholars alike use as the main (sometimes the only) piece of evidence for the presence of Jews in Corinth, suggests a community sufficiently coherent, concerned, and angry to create something like the scene before Gallio. If this inference be fair, then we might be justified in looking at 1 Corinthians in the context of a relatively discrete community of Jews, even though we might wish to allow for a good bit of variation within that community.

Christian Jews in Corinth

Paul established a community of believers in Jesus on the basis of his relatively successful mission in Corinth.[13] He called this group a "church," and with that designation went some degree of self-consciousness as a community (*ekklēsia* appears frequently in 1 Corinthians, beginning with 1 Cor. 1:2: *tē ekklēsia tou theou*).[14] This self-consciousness is one of the dominant characteristics of the Corinthian church.

There is no hard evidence for the make-up of this community; the proportions of Jews and Gentiles is a matter only for speculation. Certainly, it is likely that the church was dominated by Gentiles, of whom some proportion will probably have been God-fearers before Paul's visit.[15] But there were also Jewish Christians, contrary to some claims,[16] evidence for which comes from six kinds of material:

---

12 Not long after Paul's stay the presence of Jews in the area was dramatically increased by the use of Jewish slaves, captured in the Revolt, as labourers on Nero's canal project.

13 A. Schreiber, *Die Gemeinde in Korinth,* NTAbh n.F. 12 (Münster: Aschendorff, 1977), is especially helpful on the community developments in Corinth, though not on the question at issue in this paper.

14 K.L. Schmidt, "*ekklēsia,*" *TDNT* 3, 501-36.

15 In 1 Cor. 12:2 the clause "when you were Gentiles" (*ethnē*) might be taken to imply a uniformly Gentile church. It seems fairer to infer only that the majority is Gentile in origin (cf. 12:13; 1:24). On the textual and grammatical problem, see A. Robertson and A. Plummer, *A Critical and Exegetical Commentary on the First Epistle of St. Paul to the Corinthians*, ICC (Edinburgh: T. & T. Clark, 1914), 259-60; cf. also J.D.M. Derrett, "Cursing Jesus (1 Cor. 12:3): The Jews as Religious 'Persecutors,'" *NTS* 21 (1975), 544-54.

16 See, e.g., E.P. Sanders in the following essay.

(1) Paul, despite the agreement described in Gal. 2:6-10, portrays himself as being concerned for Jews, especially in 1 Cor. 9:19-23.[17]

(2) The reception of the gospel in Corinth is described explicitly in terms which compare and contrast "Jewish" and "Greek" responses (1 Cor. 1:18-25), an argument which should have been put differently if there were no Jewish Christians.

(3) When Paul urges the Christians in Corinth to "give no offence to Jews or to Greeks or to the church of God" (1 Cor. 10:32), he has in mind especially internal relationships in the church ("whether you eat or drink or whatever you do"; 10:31), and the kinds of problems arising therefrom.

(4) It is likely, if not provable, that Cephas had visited Corinth, and so, even if Paul had not made converts among Jews, Cephas would have. There is little or no evidence that Jewish converts would have constituted a second "church." A later paragraph (2 Cor. 10:12-18) seems to apply the agreement dividing the missionary activity (Gal. 2:6-10) to the Corinthian situation and to some person or persons who have been intruding on Paul's field. Such a concern would not need to be expressed unless there were a "Jewish mission in Corinth."[18]

(5) It is certain that Apollos worked in Corinth; he is remembered (Acts 18:24-28) as one who concentrated his attention on Jews. It is also clear that Prisca and Aquila (at least one of whom was a Jew: Acts 18:2) had worked in Corinth. And it is possible that Sosthenes (1 Cor. 1:1) is the same person as the ruler of the synagogue in Acts 18:17.[19] That is, several secondary persons in Corinth were also likely to have carried on a "Jewish mission."

(6) Finally, some of the problems in Corinth are closely associated with Jew/Greek distinctions; the two most obvious are eating problems in 1 Cor. 10:31 (cf. 8:1-12; 9:3-7; 10:1-30; 11:17-22, 33-34), and questions about wisdom and the cross in 1 Cor. 1:18-25 (cf. 1:26-3:4; 3:18-4:5), on both of which more will be said below.

These lines of evidence support the likelihood that the community of Christians in Corinth included some Jews who had been persuaded by one or more of Paul, Cephas, Apollos, Prisca, and Aquila that Jesus is Lord (cf. 1 Cor. 12:3).

---

17 See P. Richardson, "Pauline Inconsistency: 1 Cor. 9:19-23 and Gal. 2:11-14," *NTS* 26 (1980), 147-62.

18 In 2 Cor. 10:13, 15, the word *kanōn* ("rule, standard, sphere of action") almost certainly refers to Paul's understanding of his proper area of work (cf. also "other men's labours," "our field," "another's field"). Paul's view of his proper sphere of action and the view of the "others" and their sphere may not coincide, yet this paragraph makes it likely that there are two kinds of missions in Corinth.

19 According to Acts 18:17 Sosthenes was beaten in the Forum—but by whom? By fellow-Jews? By Christians? By Corinthians generally? E. Haenchen, *The Acts of the Apostles* (Oxford: Blackwell, 1971), 536-37, believes it was the Corinthian crowd.

The Question of Leadership

In discussing anti-Judaism we must, however, go beyond the make-up of the community. Leadership is a fundamental issue in Corinth. It is likely that Apollos and Cephas were themselves considerably greater irritants in the Corinthian situation than is sometimes imagined. The references to Paul, Apollos, and Cephas (all Jews) are highly suggestive. In particular the discussion of "God's field" in 3:6-8 unpacks the reference to Apollos in 3:5, and can hardly be anything but an indication of either scepticism of or suspicion towards Apollos. On top of that, 16:12 ("now concerning Apollos") is the last of the so-called response topics, and indicates serious trouble. Apollos refuses to do what Paul wants him to do, in contrast to Timothy who is ready and willing to follow Paul's instructions (16:10-11; cf. 4:17-21).

We can identify at least part of the reason for the scepticism: Apollos's "wisdom" as Paul says (3:18-23; cf. 1:17) or, as Luke would say, his interpretation of scripture (Acts 18:24, 28). His use of scripture may not be acceptable to Paul; Apollos is the champion of a segment of the Christian community that dwells too much on "wisdom," using an exegesis of scripture too clever by half.

There is less evidence concerning Cephas, but a similar line of argument might suggest, first, that Cephas has been in Corinth (9:5);[20] second, that he has laboured among the Jews of Corinth after Paul's initial activity; third, that a segment of the community views Cephas, not Paul, as the real apostle (cf. 15:5); and fourth, that Cephas has done little to discourage his supporters. In 3:10-14 Paul may be developing a lengthy pun on his own role as the "foundation," despite the claim that Cephas is the rock on which Jesus builds.[21]

Whether this interpretation of Apollos and Cephas be correct (see below) the main point is that the Christian community in Corinth is faced with internal tensions (cf. 12:12-13) between "Jews" and "Greeks."

The quarrelling among Paul's, Apollos's, and Cephas's groups triggers Paul's recollection of two issues. The first is baptism (1:13-17), an issue which appears to have questions of attachment—and therefore leadership—bound up with it. Regrettably Paul does not say who baptized in Corinth. Nor later when he mentions baptism in passing (12:13) does he add materially to our information; indeed, in 15:29 he only adds to the interpretive difficulties.[22] The second issue is wisdom (1:17), and this does receive a sustained treatment in what follows

20 See especially C.K. Barrett, "Cephas and Corinth," in *Abraham unser Vater: Festschrift für Otto Michel* (Leiden: Brill, 1963), 1-12.

21 So, cautiously, C.K. Barrett, *A Commentary on the First Epistle to the Corinthians*, HNTC (New York: Harper & Row, 1968), 87-90.

22 On 15:29 see now J. Murphy-O'Connor, "'Baptized for the Dead' (1 Cor. 15:29) A Corinthian slogan," *RB* 88 (1981), 532-43.

(1:18-4:13; cf. 4:20), with barely a mention later (6:5; 12:8). It would seem that one of the keys to the leadership problem is, then, the question of wisdom.[23]

As soon as the question of wisdom is raised the response of Jew and Greek to the preaching of the word of the cross (1:17, 18) is also raised (1:21-25). When that distinction is drawn, Greeks are associated with wisdom, and Jews with signs. Paul's opening line of attack on the problem of dissensions hints that the source of the difficulty has to do with wisdom-preaching to "Greeks."[24]

When Paul turns to defence in 2:1 he insists that his own preaching was neither eloquent nor "wise," that is, that he did not succumb to the temptation to cast his message in convenient terms. But he rather quickly shifts gears to claim that there is a wisdom element in his message that is legitimate (2:6-3:4), even though not all can perceive it. He claims implicitly that only *his* approach is informed by the Spirit.

In 3:4 he reverts explicitly to the divisions again, this time isolating only two of the three actors, himself and Apollos. And he goes on to describe the problem twice in different ways: Paul plants and Apollos waters; Paul lays a foundation and "another man" (is this Cephas?) builds on it. There can be little doubt that in all of 3:5-17 Paul is saying that Apollos (and perhaps Cephas?) is a secondary worker, building on Paul's basic work, and that, though "he himself will be saved" (3:15), his work may burn up.[25] As he goes on, he re-emphasizes the wisdom element of this pressing problem (3:18-23) and then reiterates the applicability of his analysis of himself and Apollos (4:6-7) to the Corinthian situation. This is true especially in 4:8-13, but it is also present in 4:14-21, where Paul claims to be the sole father who is the source of common teaching and the person to be imitated.

In 9:5-6, Cephas surfaces again in the context of food and drink problems (9:4) and Jew/Greek problems (9:19-23). If the connection between 9:19-23 and 10:31-11:1 is secure, then again we have in this context notions of imitation and church custom, ideas which tie in nicely with 4:16-17 and Paul's claims there.

---

23 U. Wilckens, *Weisheit und Torheit,* BHT 26 (Tübingen: J.C.B. Mohr, 1959).

24 It is relevant to this analysis to note that "signs" is not developed in the same way as "wisdom", and this could be taken as evidence for an absence of Jews in the Corinthian church. It does surface again, however, at 14:22 in a context which is very suggestive of a Jewish "problem." In 14:21, Isa. 28:11-12 is cited—part of a larger passage (Isa. 28-29) used frequently by the early church to explain Jewish/Gentile relations, especially Jewish "hardness." Tongues are a sign to unbelievers, that is to the "people" (*laos*) who have not believed. This is evidence of Paul's concern about Jews, of the general Jewish rejection of the message, and of a continuing concern in Corinth for Jews. It should not be taken as evidence that there are no Jewish Christians in Corinth. See further P. Richardson, *Israel,* 213, and literature noted there.

25 There is a remarkable similarity in eschatological conception between his description of the fate of these "opponents" and the fate of the man caught sleeping with his father's wife in 5:5.

The tensions among the leaders, I suggest, involving Jew and Greek may have led not only to verbal arguments like those reflected in 1 Corinthians (and of course 2 Corinthians also!), but also to the incident that must lie behind Acts 18:12-17.[26] If the incident has a historical basis (as its use in the development of virtually every Pauline chronology suggests) and if it had the basic features attributed to it by Luke (Jews attack Paul, bring him to Gallio and accuse him, whereupon Gallio berates the Jews) an important question arises. Why did the opposition between Jews and Christians not surface in 1 Corinthians as it did, for example, in 1 Thess. 2:14-16 (cf. 2 Cor. 11:21-28)?[27] The closest approach to this in 1 Corinthians is the rather mild 4:11-18, and that passage is basically a personal apologetic without anti-Jewish overtones. (It could be argued that the incident *follows* the writing of 1 Corinthians, but I am not yet persuaded of this view.)

But where does all this lead? This suggests that the divisions in Corinth are not merely the result of incorrect attachments to persons (Paul, Apollos, or Cephas) but of missionary practice and leadership. And these matters involve—almost inevitably—distinctions between Jew and Greek, especially with respect to how the gospel is received and how it is to be implemented in day-to-day living.

Food Problems in Corinth

The most fruitful line of enquiry concerning anti-Judaism in 1 Corinthians has to do with orthopraxy. There is little evidence of conflict over circumcision (only 1 Cor. 7:17-19), over interpretations of law (mentioned, apart from introductory formulae, only in 1 Cor. 9:20; 15:56; cf. 7:19; 14:34), or over the proclamation of the gospel (note, however, Paul's insistence on his own priority). These basic dividing lines which in other letters give rise either to explicit or implicit anti-Judaic statements occupy a small place in 1 Corinthians. The tone is muted. We are faced, however, with a letter-body which is tense with a treatment of divisions in the congregation, apparently in the context of wisdom-questions, and with a paraenetic section, most of which responds to questions raised by Corinth (especially marriage, food, spiritual gifts, the resurrection, the collection, and Apollos), but some of which deals with oral reports (immorality and communal grievances).

The paraenetic section is dominated by the recurring references to food questions and eating practices in chapters 8 to 11. These chapters should all be seen as a single—though fractured—response

26 See O. Broneer, "Corinth, Center of St. Paul's Missionary Work in Greece," *BA* 14 (1951), 78-96; and E. Dinkler, "Das Bema zu Korinth—archäologische, lexicographische, rechtsgeschichtische und ikonographische Bemerkungen zu Apg. 18, 12-17," in *Signum Crucis* (Tübingen: J.C.B. Mohr, 1967), 118-33.

27 E.P. Sanders, in the following essay, rejects this view.

to a single question: "Now concerning food offered to idols . . ." (1 Cor. 8:1). All the issues in these four chapters flow from that starting point, though some of the topics, such as women's veils, are far removed from the original question.[28] Partition theories of 1 Corinthians seem to presuppose too rigid a view of the process of letter writing;[29] in Paul's letters sudden and dramatic shifts of thought often occur.

There are obvious breaks in chapters 8 to 11, just as there are obvious connections. To begin with, it is not hard to see how chapter 8, the last half of 10 and the last half of 11 fit together even though there are important progressions of thought. But the connections of chapter 9 and the first half of chapter 11 are much more difficult.

With regard to 11:2-16, it should be noted to begin with that the short paragraph 10:31-11:1 is an important recapitulation of an earlier formulation found in 9:19-23, though generalized and applied to the Christian community as a whole. The importance of these two sections can hardly be exaggerated. These are the heart of Paul's opinion on the subject matter at hand, indicating his basic approach.[30] The connection between 11:2-16 and 10:31-11:1 is that the former passage functions as an example of the sort of problem which needs to be solved by the approach proposed in his advice to "give no offence." That is, the principle of accommodation can be extended beyond food questions to include male and female participation in worship (11:2-16), as well as the more obviously connected question of food in worship (11:17-34).

Chapter 9 poses a larger problem. Not only does it concentrate on apostolic questions (position, rights, obligations, rewards), but its defensive tone is also out of keeping with the surrounding materials in which practical concern is the dominant motif. Partition theories are at their strongest in chapter 9. There are, however, four observations that can be made in favour of a connection between chapter 9 and chapters 8 and 10.

(1) Chapter 9 is the apostolic form of the food question. For an apostle the question is neither the menu nor the invitation list, but getting one's food from the local congregation. The connection would then be association of ideas: ah yes, food! that reminds me that I have another bone to pick with you . . . .

---

28 John C. Hurd, *The Origin of 1 Corinthians* (London: SPCK, 1965), 115-49, argues cogently for the integrity of 8:1-11:1. Though he suggests that 11:2-16 was occasioned by the Corinthians' letter to Paul (182-86) and that 11:17-34 was a response to oral information (78-80), he still believes that these units are in their correct positions.

29 Robert Jewett, "The Redaction of 1 Corinthians and the Trajectory of the Pauline School," *JAAR* 44 (1978), 389-444. Material which is here considered unitary is in Jewett's hypothesis attributed to four different letters.

30 See Peter Richardson, "Pauline Inconsistency"; and also "Accommodation Ethics," *Tyn Bull* 29 (1978), 90-142 (with Paul W. Gooch); and also Peter Richardson, *Paul's Ethic of Freedom* (Philadelphia: Westminster, 1979), 79-98.

(2) The major question dealt with in chapter 8—food offered to idols—is answered in terms of removing stumbling blocks from a fellow Christian's way. This is seen most clearly in 8:13 where Paul changes to the first person singular: "I will never eat meat, lest I cause my brother to fall." The second person singular which precedes 8:13 gives way to a first person statement concerning the voluntary giving up of a perfectly legitimate course of action. In 9:1 Paul continues the first person singular and extends the concern to specific food questions concerning apostles, which demonstrates that he does the thing that in 8:13 he says he is prepared to do.

(3) The paragraph 9:19-23 is inextricably connected with the rest of the chapter, and states an "apostolic" principle. It is itself intimately connected with 10:31-11:1 which states a similar principle but in a church setting. That is, the ethical principle of chapter 9 coheres with the more broadly conceived ethical principle at the end of chapter 10.

(4) The connection between the end of chapter 9 and the beginning of chapter 10 is less transparent than the other connections, but one element seems to be the worry about "disqualification." Paul has raised this issue in the body of the letter in connection with Apollos (3:15, 18-23; 4:5, 6). Now he raises it in connection with himself (9:27), and finds both warning and solace in the example of Israel (10:6, 11-13).

In other words, chapters 8 to 11 are a complex answer to a single question. The question is about food, an issue which troubled the early Christian churches (Galatians, Romans, Colossians, Acts) because of the practical difficulties of Jewish and non-Jewish Christians associating in the same ritual and social activities. So *prima facie* one would expect chapters 8 to 11 to show signs that the long answer is predicated on Jew/non-Jew differences.

There is evidence that underlying the difficulties over food is just such a factor. While it is possible to claim (I believe correctly) that questions of the "weak" and their "conscience" in chapters 8 and 10 presuppose food matters raised by Jewish Christians in Corinth, the matter is not crystal clear and will not be argued here.[31] But when Paul veers off from the precise question of food offered to idols, he draws closer connections with Jew-Greek questions:

(1) His own apostolic practice is described explicitly in terms of becoming "as a Jew, as under law, as lawless, [as] weak." The connection of this

31 R.A. Horsley, "Gnosis in Corinth: 1 Corinthians 8:1-6," *NTS* 27 (1980), 32-51, argues cogently for a Hellenistic Jewish background to the proto-Gnosticism in Corinth. He believes that the "mission situation in the Corinthian community to which both Paul and Apollos had been apostles would have involved basically two types of people: (1) Hellenistic Jews who had 'joined the movement,' which was in effect a splinter group of the Jewish synagogue; and (2) Gentiles, including *sebomenoi* such as Titius Justus, who had converted to this movement . . ." (41-42).

principle with apostolic food questions, and of those questions (9:3-18) with the earlier food questions in chapter 8 suggests that these food questions in Corinth raised the issues of lawlessness, lawfulness, and Jewishness.[32] To put it differently, matters of Torah were important in Corinth.

(2) The *midrash* of 1 Cor. 10:1-13 may, though it need not, reflect this Jewish focus on the food questions. This passage (like 2 Cor. 3) stands out from the surrounding material as a finely tuned message dealing with Moses, the Exodus, Israel, and the significance of Paul's message for Corinth's Christians. It is hardly accidental that the core of the example is the "supernatural food and supernatural drink," which leads almost directly into the Christian equivalents in the Lord's Supper, the ritual analog to the social questions underlying chapter 8.[33]

(3) It is, then, almost startling when Paul, in 10:31-11:1, repeats and generalizes his apostolic principle of 9:19-23 in Jew/Greek terms. This version of it, intended to apply to all, is cast in terms explicitly adapted to eating problems. The Corinthians are enjoined to imitate his own practice, a practice he has already expressed in terms tied to the Jew/non-Jew, law/non-law, weak/strong distinctions.

(4) Though it cannot be dealt with in detail here, it is likely that 11:2-16 and the vexed problems of veils, authority, angels, and hair is a further explication of Jew/non-Jew problems which are troubling the church. The appeal to tradition in 11:2 and to the churches of God in 11:16 is probably an appeal to Palestinian or Jewish-Christian custom,[34] and hence an attempt to resolve a practical dispute arising from the different weight being given to Torah by Jews and Greeks.

If this is correct, the most contorted paraenetic section in 1 Corinthians revolves around the key Jewish/non-Jewish question of

32 Regrettably, despite the chiastic structure of this section, it is still not possible to be certain to whom "weak" refers, since several structural possibilities are available and lead to different conclusions.

33 Paul makes use of the Exodus events, compares Christian actions with Israel's actions in the wilderness, and reaches the conclusion that a comparable "way of escape" is available for those "upon whom the end of the ages has come." He distances Christians from Jews not by demolishing the received interpretation of a part of Israel's history but rather by claiming that the old things "were written down for our instruction." By comparison 2 Cor. 3 is considerably harsher and more direct, though its midrashic form might profitably be compared with 1 Cor. 10. In this case the comparison is between Paul as a minister of a new covenant and Moses as the minister of the previous covenant. A polemic is being conducted, characterized by the sharp antitheses between the two forms of revelation. While neither passage is strictly speaking anti-Judaic they are both acute theological statements which encourage the reader to adopt negative views of Judaism.

34 The Palestinian origin seems to me required by (1) the logic that "traditions" (1 Cor. 11:2) are not of one's own making but handed on from another source (1 Cor. 11:23; 15:3; 2 Thess. 2:15; 3:6; Gal. 1:14); (2) the use of the expression "churches of God" in 1 Cor. 11:16 (cf. 10:32; 1 Thess. 2:14); (3) the arguments of the passage, especially in 1 Cor. 11:10, which become somewhat clearer if predicated on a Targumic tradition.

food. We might generalize and say that in the Corinthian church Jewish/non-Jewish issues were animating the *orthopractic* questions, though they had not reached (or perhaps better, were not being dealt with on) a theoretical plane, as happened in other places with respect to law or circumcision. Indeed, when these latter two issues are raised in a glancing way in 1 Corinthians (7:17-19 and 9:19-23) they are dealt with as matters of no great consequence.[35]

The point is this: the Jew/Greek distinction (to use Paul's short-hand) is present, but either the raw nerve which triggers Galatians 2 to 3, Philipians 3, or even Romans 4 and 9 to 11, is not, or else the tone is deliberately muted. When Paul deals with the practical questions that arise out of the varied make-up of the congregation he does so irenically.

For the rest, suffice to say that the questions of morality in chapters 5 to 6 and of marriage in chapter 7 support this view. It is possible that chapters 12 to 14, chapter 15, and of course the issue of the collection in 16:1-9, may also give minor support for the view that Jew-Greek distinctions animate the church in Corinth more than Paul admits.

Hypothesis

While one can isolate several kinds of anti-Judaic strands in one or another part of the Pauline literature (see n. 1), at the time of the writing of 1 Corinthians Paul does not express any explicit anti-Judaism. The degree to which there might be some evidence for such a tendency in Paul has already been assessed and may be quickly summarized:

(1) There is no contemporary evidence available of a "societal" anti-Judaism in Corinth. There is surprisingly little information outside the New Testament about the Jewish community in Corinth, but it may have been reasonably large and cohesive.

(2) That there are "communal" tensions in Corinth is clear. There are good reasons for thinking that these have something to do with distinctions between Jew and Greek within the community. The conditions may be ripe for the development of an anti-Judaism located *intra muros.*

(3) There is little explicit "theological" anti-Judaism; where Paul reflects on the theological implications of Judaism he does so in a muted

35 It is barely possible, I suppose, if Cephas has also been in Corinth and carried out there his customary role as apostle of the circumcision, that converts of the Jewish mission and of the Gentile mission behave differently in Corinth, so that the issues which would arise if all Christians were one happy family do not arise. While I do not think this likely, it is possible, and the difficulties of interpretation in Acts 18:14-17 might lend it some support.

way, though the net effect is negative. There is a distancing, but not a real polemic.

(4) What I have called "historical" anti-Judaism is also absent from 1 Corinthians, in spite of the fact that the riot before Gallio might have given rise to an angry outburst in 1 Corinthians, had the conditions been right.

(5) The most fruitful place to look for evidence is on the "orthopractic" side, where behaviour gives rise to problems, and Paul's approach to these troubles involves explicitly an exhortation to give no offence to Jews and Greeks in food matters, along with a consideration of law and non-law matters. It seems also to be allied with questions having to do with leadership, baptism, and wisdom.

The question is this: Why, given the tensions and troubles and evidence of difficulty, is there no outburst analogous to those which intrude upon Galatians, Philippians, 2 Corinthians, 1 Thessalonians, and, in a different fashion, Romans? The suggestion which follows seems to satisfy the data.

In Corinth there are three acknowledged dominant personalities: Paul, Apollos, and Cephas. Each is a Jew, but each has his roots in a different part of the Jewish-Christian community. Paul views himself as falling somewhere in the middle. Cephas, who has been in Corinth, has become the figurehead of a Palestine-oriented, somewhat conservative, probably fearful, and over-cautious group. Apollos has persuaded some by his eloquent wisdom that Christians, even Jewish Christians, can be more experimental and daring. They can go beyond Paul's rudimentary presentation of the cross of Christ and engage both in intellectual speculation and in practical behaviour which demonstrates the better spirituality of those who have moved beyond the rudiments. It may, but need not, be an Alexandrian-oriented group. Cephas, I expect, has limited his concern to Jews; Apollos may, from a Jewish Christian base, be directing his energy to non-Jews. Paul explicitly tells us he tried to appeal to both Jews and Greeks, though the focus of his energy was his mission to non-Jews.

The hypothesis, then, is this. The absence of "anti-Judaism" in 1 Corinthians arises not because there are no Jews but rather because Paul is being deliberately conciliatory, irenic, and accommodating. The stage of development of the Corinthian congregation is such that an intemperate blast might fragment it irreparably. Paul objects to two tendencies, one on either side of him. Because he perceives himself to be in the middle, he is in a position to try to effect compromises, in the interests of the continued health of the congregation. (In addition, because he is the real founder of the congregation, he is the one most "wronged" by the recent developments.)

There is, first, Apollos's tendency towards a loosening of the core beliefs and customs, based on a speculative wisdom which stresses imaginative understandings of the faith. Apollos and his followers are a part of the movement towards too great an assertion of freedom and too small a concern for others. His adherents are concentrated on the non-Jewish side of the church, attracted to his eloquent way of interpreting Torah. The second tendency, on this showing, is Cephas's inclination towards a concern only for the Jewish members of the community, predicated on the conviction that the Palestinian church's needs and perceptions are basic. Those who see Cephas as their mentor are deeply concerned to ally themselves as much as possible with Palestinian customs. In such a situation Paul attempts to conciliate (4:13; 7:17-24; 9:19-23; 10:31-11:1; 12:12-13; 13:4-7).

The evidence of 2 Corinthians might be noted briefly in passing. Matters get worse. The theological polemic in 2 Corinthians 3 is partial evidence for this worsening condition. The presence of "someone" in the congregation who is causing trouble and distress (2:2-11; 3:1; 8:18-24; 10:7-18; 11:4; 12:14-18) may be further evidence. It is likely that in 2 Cor. 10-13 Jerusalem apostles (or at least members of a Palestinian-oriented group) lie behind the deep antagonism of the polemic there. In other words, the later more developed "anti-Judaism" of 2 Corinthians is latent in the situation described in 1 Corinthians. It is given no play at the time of the writing of 1 Corinthians because Paul's dominant concern is to keep the sides together.

Conclusion

If this explanation is correct it sheds some light on accommodation and deliberate compromise as fundamental aspects of the interpretation of 1 Corinthians. The "tone" is apologetic; and tone is important in anti-Judaic statements.[36]

In the Corinthian Christian community reflected in 1 Corinthians there is a problem between Jews and Greeks. It is, however, an *intra muros* difficulty, directed to fellow Jewish-Christians—Apollos and Cephas—who lie to either side of Paul. There is not yet anything in the Corinthian setting which requires vehement polemic.

Finally, a suggestion. The approach of this paper suggests that more research, involving a "sociological" reconstruction of anti-

36 It seems to me possible to adopt yet another set of categories of anti-Judaism: apologetic, defensive, and offensive. Examples of each kind can be found in Paul's letters, in the rest of the New Testament, and in the Apostolic Fathers. Apologetic anti-Judaism would include works (such as *Barnabas* and Justin's *Dialogue*) where the main intent is to explain Jewish institutions or practices in such a way as to deny their validity or undercut their attractiveness. Defensive anti-Judaism would arise when Christians were in danger in some fashion or another (as in Hebrews, Revelation). Offensive anti-Judaism is likely to be found only at a stage when Christianity had a fair degree of self assurance as over against the synagogue (for example Matthew, John, Melito).

Judaism in the early Christian world, needs to be done. It may be possible to reconstruct the emphases of anti-Judaic disputes in such a way that the role of the *intra muros* debates noted above sheds light on the development of *extra muros* anti-Judaism. Or to put it differently, the later more highly motivated "theological" anti-Judaism may be a direct consequence of the relational "orthopractic" anti-Judaism which arose in communities such as Corinth.

5

Paul on the Law, His Opponents, and the Jewish People in Philippians 3 and 2 Corinthians 11

E.P. Sanders

The question of "anti-Judaism" in Paul must take into account at least three topics: his direct comments on his own people, his attitude towards Juda*ism* (considered as a religion or a way of life), and his attacks on his opponents. The principal passages in which these issues arise are well known: Romans 1 to 4 (righteousness by faith, not by law); 9 to 11 (the fate of Paul's kinsmen by race); and 1 Thess. 2:14-16 (opponents, attacks on the law).[1] Full consideration of "anti-Judaism," then, would have to consider the complicated questions of Paul's self-conception (in his role as Christian apostle has he rejected Judaism as a religion and a way of life and also "written off" the Jewish people as being beyond the reach of God's grace?), as well as major and difficult aspects of his theology (the law; the exclusiveness of salvation in Christ).

The principal passages which have led to the discussion of these issues are being dealt with in other contributions to this volume, and I have had ample opportunity to address most of them elsewhere.[2] The symposium from which these essays arise, however, has provided the welcome opportunity to see what light can be thrown on the interrelated questions mentioned above from two passages which have been

1 I omit here the arguments against opponents in the Corinthian correspondence because none of the opponents can be viewed as non-Christian Jews. Galatians and Romans, on the other hand—though this is a view I do not share—are often seen as being against "the Jews and their understanding of salvation" (quoted from G. Bornkamm, *Paul* [London: Hodder and Stoughton, 1971], 95, on Romans). For the view that Romans is against Judaism, see also J.C. Beker, *Paul the Apostle* (Philadelphia: Fortress, 1980), 74-89; on Galatians 2-3 as against Judaism, see, for example, H.D. Betz, *Galatians* (Philadelphia: Fortress, 1979), 116.

2 E.P. Sanders, *Paul and Palestinian Judaism* (London: SCM, 1977), and *Paul, the Law and the Jewish People* (Philadelphia: Fortress, 1983).

less discussed in considering Paul's attitude towards Judaism and Jewish people. In discussing them I shall have to presuppose fuller argumentation which has focused primarily on Galatians and Romans, but I am hopeful that readers will find it useful to consider what we can learn from two passages—Philippians 3 and 2 Corinthians 11—about the complicated issues before us.

Paul and the Law: Phil. 3:4-11

Paul's discussions of the law, particularly those connected with the phrase "justified by faith and not by works of law" (especially Gal. 2:16-3:14; Rom. 3:20-4:25), have often been taken as indicating Paul's view of what is wrong with Judaism.[3] The explanations for Paul's opposing "faith" to "law" as the gateway to "righteousness" have been varied. Perhaps the two most popular have been (1) that the law cannot in fact be fulfilled, so that it brings on those who would follow it a curse, and (2) that fulfilling it is even worse than transgressing it, since that leads to the sin of arrogance and pride. According to those who hold to one of these explanations (or both; they can be combined),[4] the law necessarily leads to frustration and condemnation or to estrangement from the grace of God in favour of a legalistic calculation of merit. Those who see Paul as having held one of these views, or some variant of them, have naturally seen him as criticizing Judaism at the most basic level, for all forms of Judaism expect that Jews will keep the law. How thoroughgoing Paul's critique of Judaism appears to be can be seen, for example, in the treatment of H.J. Schoeps, who concluded that Paul, to bring such serious criticisms against his native faith, must simply have misunderstood it. In Schoeps's view, Paul, as a Diaspora Jew, did not understand the traditional connection of the requirement of the law with the grace shown in the establishment of the covenant.[5]

The problem of "Paul and the law" by no means ends with the question of why he said righteousness is by faith, not by law. There are also serious questions with regard to his own internal consistency. How could he say, on the one hand, that Christians die to the law and, on the other, that its requirement is fulfilled in those who walk by the Spirit (Rom. 7:4-6; 8:4)? How could he say that doers of the law—whether Jew or Gentile, but in neither case Christian—will be justified (Rom. 2:13)? How could he say that "keeping the commandments of God" is what counts, and then exclude circumcision (1 Cor. 7:19)? How could Paul, who at times waxes so vitriolic against those who would require

---

3 E.g., Bornkamm, Beker, and Betz, as in n. 1.

4 H. Hübner, *Das Gesetz bei Paulus* (2d ed.; Göttingen: Vandenhoeck and Ruprecht, 1980), argues that the first of these two supposed objections to the law is advanced in Galatians, the second in Romans.

5 H.J. Schoeps, *Paul* (London: Lutterworth, 1961), 213-18.

the keeping of the law, at other times offer as a summary of the Christian life the rule to "love your neighbour as yourself" (Lev. 19:18), and specify what that means by itemizing four of the ten commandments, even adding "and any other commandment" (Rom. 13:8-10)?[6]

Of the complex of problems surrounding "Paul and the law," the one which needs most to be addressed in connection with the present passage is why he opposed "faith" to "law" as the way to "righteousness," since that very opposition meets us in Phil. 3:9. Further, it is this point which bears most directly on the question of "anti-Judaism" in Paul. It may help if I sketch an answer to this point, as well as to some of the other difficulties with regard to the law, before turning directly to Philippians 3.[7]

(1) When Paul argues that righteousness (usually indicated by the passive verb "be justified") is by faith, not by law, the *topic* is entry to the "in" group, the body of those who will be saved. "To be justified" in these passages means "to transfer from the state of sin to the state of life." Since, for Paul, life is found in Christ Jesus, it follows that it is not found in proselytizing to Judaism. Entry into the "in" group is by "faith in Christ" or by "dying with Christ" (Rom. 6), but not by accepting circumcision and the Mosaic law.

Thus what is wrong with works of law in such passages as Galatians 2 to 3 and Romans 3 to 4 is that accepting and doing the law do not lead to the desired goal—life in Christ. An important consideration for Paul was evidently that he thought that Jew and Gentile alike should have access to salvation on the same footing.[8] God appointed Christ, not the Mosaic law, to provide the possibility of universal salvation. The law is wrong not because it is impossible to fulfil, nor because fulfilling it leads to legalism; it is wrong because doing it does not lead Jew and Gentile alike to salvation in the way appointed by God, sharing the death of Christ.

It must be carefully noted in this context that there is no criticism—in fact no mention—of life under the law. The quality of the religious life as lived by observant Jews is not being evaluated.[9] Paul

6 The most thorough treatment of the theological problems raised by Paul's diverse statements about the law which I have seen is Heikki Räisänen, *Paul and the Law* (Tübingen: Mohr, 1983).

7 The sketch summarizes major aspects of my other treatments of Paul and the law (n. 2 above). The proposal that Paul's diverse statements about the law result from his addressing different questions is appreciably different from the suggestion that he had different meanings of the word *nomos* consciously in mind. For the second view, see, for example, Lloyd Gaston's article, "Paul and the Law in Galatians 2-3" in this volume.

8 See also Peter Richardson, *Israel in the Apostolic Church* (Cambridge: Cambridge University Press, 1969), 134-37.

9 Against the views cited in n. 1 above. Several scholars have objected to understanding Paul's contrast of "righteousness by faith" and "righteousness by law" as being a contrast of two modes of life, one of "doing" and one of "faith." Thus, for example, Gaston, "Paul and the Law in Galatians 2 to 3," in this volume.

is simply maintaining that the traditional entry rite to Judaism—circumcision and acceptance of the rest of the law—does not apply to those who would be new creatures in Christ Jesus. In other contexts he can regard circumcision, the dietary code, and the Sabbath laws as matters of indifference (1 Cor. 7:19; Gal. 6:15; Rom. 14:1-6).

(2) Once Paul ruled out the law as the means of entry to the body of those who would be saved, he had to find another purpose for it in God's plan of salvation. This was obviously troublesome for him. He seems to give more than one answer, and some of his attempted explanations are tortuous. This topic lies outside the scope of the present paper, and I shall only point to the places where Paul wrestles with the problem: Gal. 3:19-24; Rom. 5:20; Rom 7:7-13. While these passages do not appear perfectly harmonious, the underlying thought seems to be that the law is intimately connected with sin, but with a purpose: *so that* all might need the salvation offered through Christ (note the purpose clauses in Rom. 5:20; 7:13; Gal. 3:22, 24). The law, in other words, is assigned a role in God's plan, but a negative one. It seems to be through this line of thought that Paul can sometimes virtually equate the law with sin and death (e.g., Rom. 7:4-6).

(3) When considering proper Christian behaviour, Paul had at his disposal the principle of living by the Spirit (Gal. 5:22) and general hellenistic moral summaries (Phil. 4:8). He often made use of vice and virtue lists which apparently were derived from Greek-speaking Judaism (e.g., 1 Cor. 6:9-11). But, as we saw above, he could also cite the Mosaic law (Gal. 5:14; Rom. 13:8-10; 1 Cor. 9:8-9).

Thus it appears that most, if not all, of the apparent self-contradictions in Paul's statements about the law can be explained by noting the context.

Phil. 3:9 has been considered one of the key passages in support of the view that Paul objected to the law because keeping it leads to legalistic self-righteousness: "not having a righteousness of my own (*mē echōn emēn dikaiosynēn*), based on law, but that which is through faith in Christ. . . ." This has been read particularly in conjunction with Rom. 10:3: "For, being ignorant of the righteousness that comes from God, and seeking to establish their own (*tēn idian* [*dikaiosynēn*]), they did not submit to God's righteousness." The phrases "my own" and "their own" have been individualized and taken to mean that Paul accused the law of leading to self-righteousness, the assertion of personal merit and resistance to grace.[10]

This interpretation of "my own" and "their own" arouses doubt in the first place because it smacks more than a little of anachronism. It may be doubted that the notion of "legalism"—an attitudinal sin which

10 See, for example, Rudolph Bultmann, *Theology of the New Testament* (New York: Charles Scribner's Sons, 1959), I, 26-67

consists in self-assertion—goes back to the first century. Then, too, one should note that Paul in other contexts has no hesitancy in recommending good works and even in assuming that his own would be counted meritorious before God (see 1 Cor. 3:14; 4:5). But, more to the point, reading the phrases "my own" and "their own" in Phil. 3:9 and Rom. 10:3 as referring to the legalistic calculation of merit is simply bad exegesis of the passages. The comparison in Rom. 9:30-10:13 is between two dispensations, each leading to its own characteristic "righteousness." Israel sought a righteousness based on the law. Its fault was not a legalistic attitude, but "ignorance": it did not know of the other righteousness which is based on faith in Christ (10:3-4). "Their own" righteousness is contrasted not to "acceptance of grace in the right spirit," but to "faith *in Christ.*" "Their own" righteousness is *that which is peculiar to Israel,* the righteousness which is not for *every one* who has faith (10:4; for "every one," "all," and "no distinction" see also 10:11-12, five times). What is wrong with Israel's righteousness by law, in other words, is that it is not based on faith in Christ (the true means of entry to the "in" group) and that it prevents Gentiles from being on equal footing with Jews.

The situation is similar in Phil. 3:4-11. Paul's own righteousness (3:9) is the righteousness peculiar to him as a Jew, according to which he was blameless (3:6). But being blameless did not lead to the sinful attitude which we call self- righteousness. On the contrary, it was "gain" (3:7). Righteousness by law, which was formerly gain, became loss to Paul only because it did not lead to the righteousness which comes by faith in Christ and which appears to be the same as being "found in him" (3:9), sharing his sufferings, and becoming like him in his death (3:10). The only thing wrong with the law in these two passages—and, I would add, wherever Paul discusses righteousness by faith and not by law—is that it does not lead to being Christian and, secondarily, that it prevents Gentiles from standing on equal footing with Jews.

If Paul was in any way scandalized by his former religion, it was not for the reason usually adduced—Judaism leads to self-righteousness, legalism, and boasting in one's own merits. He does seem to have objected to its particularism if applied to admission to the people of God. God sent Christ to save the world, to save both Jew and Gentile on an equal basis. The particular requirements of the Jewish law, therefore, could not, in his view, stand at the port of entry to "righteousness"—life in Christ Jesus.

Philippians 3 is important in another respect in considering Paul's attitude towards his native religion. It is one of two passages—the other is 2 Cor. 3:7-18—in which he directly compares the importance and glory of the old dispensation with the new. His attitude towards the law is the same in both passages, and I believe that these two passages best reveal his fundamental attitude towards Juda*ism.* That attitude is simply stated: the law was good; it was given in splendour; fulfilling it was a gain. Now it is a loss and has no splendour at all, since something far greater has come:

> But whatever gain I had I counted as loss for the sake of Christ. Indeed I count everything as loss because of the surpassing worth of knowing Christ Jesus my Lord. (Phil. 3:7-8)

> Now if the dispensation of death, carved in letters on stone, came with such splendour that the Israelites could not look at Moses' face because of its brightness, fading as this was, why should not the dispensation of the Spirit be attended with greater splendour? . . . Indeed, in this case, what once had splendour has come to have no splendour at all, because of the splendour that surpasses it. (2 Cor. 3:7-10)

We see here Paul's black-and-white way of thinking. What was once gain is now loss; what once had splendour now has none at all. Yet we also see the *only* thing he finds wrong with his former religion: it has been surpassed by a new one.

Paul's Opponents

Phil. 3:2-3

These two verses contain some of the severest language in the Pauline corpus, and the question arises whether it is directed against Jews as such or against Christians (whether Jewish Christians or Gentile Christians). The verses read as follows in the *RSV*: "Look out for the dogs, look out for the evil-workers look out for those who mutilate the flesh. For we are the true circumcision, who worship God in spirit, and glory in Christ Jesus, and put no confidence in the flesh."

The words translated "mutilate the flesh" and "true circumcision" are *katatomē* and *peritomē,* often, and more literally, translated "concision" and "circumcision." As has been recognized at least since Lightfoot, the play on *-tomē* is paralleled in Greek rhetoric by similar plays on words or sounds.[11]

Who are the dogs, the evil-workers, those who make incisions and, apparently, call the incision "circumcision"? If we had only Philippians we should almost certainly have to conclude that they are non-Christian Jews, since the "dogs" of verse 2 are contrasted with the "we" of verse 3; and the latter are certainly Christians.[12] There is no clear evidence in Philippians of the object of this invective, since the opponents are not otherwise described. The passage, in fact, presents a difficulty. The transition between 3:1 and 3:2 is sufficiently sharp that

11 J.B. Lightfoot, *St Paul's Epistle to the Philippians* (London and Cambridge: Macmillan, 1868), 142.

12 Some do identify the "dogs" of 3:2 as Jews. Thus F.W. Beare, *The Epistle to the Philippians* (New York: Harper and Brothers, 1959), 101.

many have postulated that the letter as we have it is a composite one.[13] This is an issue which need not be ruled on here. The difficulty for our study, created by the sharp change in subject and tone which begins with 3:2, is this: the opponents in this verse seem to represent a party which is well marked and whose position is well known. The rest of Philippians, however, is singularly without signs of substantial opposition to Paul in Philippi, so that identifying the opponents in mind in 3:2 is difficult. The scant evidence elsewhere makes 3:2 stand out all the more, not only for its tone, but also for its definiteness: *the* dogs, *the* evil-workers, *the* concisers.[14]

Scholars have, to be sure, searched the rest of the letter for clues to the presumed opposition in Philippi and offered reconstructions.[15] The clearest effort is that of Koester, who identifies 3:2-4:1 as the third letter in the Philippian correspondence and reads it as a sustained polemic against opponents in Philippi.[16] On this reading more or less every phrase can be made to yield clues as to their identity and stance. Thus the use of *ginōskein* (3:10) indicates that they are gnostics, while 3:10-12 indicates that they claim eschatological perfection.[17] This sort of reading, which is the same as that customarily applied to Galatians, is possible if 3:2 to 4:1 is in fact the third of three letters. After writing the first two letters (essentially chapters 1 to 2 and 4), Paul heard of a "heresy" in Philippi and wrote a third letter attacking it. Only thus can the absence of the opponents from chapters 1 to 2 and 4 be explained. While this reading is possible, it is not truly convincing and certainly not necessary. It essentially results in attributing to the "opponents" in Philippi the combined characteristics of the opponents in Galatia and Corinth.[18] They favour circumcision and the law and also believe in the kind of eschatological perfectionism which denies the future resurrection. Rather than supposing that such a complicated heresy sprang up (or was introduced and started to take hold) and came to Paul's attention within a very short period of time,[19] it seems better to suppose, as

13 H. Koester opens the article on Philippians in the Supplementary volume to the *IDB* (Nashville: Abingdon, 1976) with the flat statement that Philippians is composed of three letters (665). Scholarly proposals to divide Philippians in some way or other are numerous and varied, but by no means universally accepted.

14 See Lightfoot, *Philippians,* 141: the party was well known, but we cannot determine whether it was in or out of the church.

15 See J.B. Tyson, "Paul's Opponents at Philippi," *Perspectives in Religious Studies* 3 (1976), 82-95, who mediates between the views of W. Schmithals and H. Koester.

16 H. Koester, "The Purpose of the Polemic of a Pauline Fragment," *NTS* 8 (1962), 317-32.

17 Ibid., 323-24.

18 I have Koester's position primarily in view, but the same observation applies to the reconstructions by Schmithals and Tyson. All three, to be sure, try to maintain distinctions among the "heresies," but I think that the criticism holds.

19 Koester places all three letters within "a brief period" during "the Ephesian imprisonment" (*IDB* 5:666). Cf. D. Georgi, *Die Geschichte der Kollekte des Paulus für Jerusalem* (Hamburg: Herbert Reich, 1965), 50: "Shortly after" the composition of the second letter (Phil. 1:1-3:1 and 4:4-7 on Georgi's reconstruction), Paul learned that there was a threatened outbreak of heresy in Philippi.

Richardson has proposed, that Paul has in mind the problems in Galatia and Corinth.[20] On this understanding one would read Phil. 3:2-4:1 as beginning with a sharp attack on known opponents and then becoming increasingly general, although the language is influenced by previous polemic situations.

On any view the attempt to identify those under attack in Philippians raises the problem of date, and we must say something about it, while avoiding the murky waters of Pauline chronology. Richardson puts the composition of Philippians after Paul met opposition in numerous centres, and thus has no difficulty in supposing that it reflects the troubles which are then behind Paul.[21] Scholars who find definite opponents in Philippi place the various parts at slightly different times, but within the general period also represented by Galatians and 1 and 2 Corinthians.[22] The difficulty with this, as Knox pointed out, is that there is no clear reference to the collection with which Paul was then preoccupied,[23] although Georgi finds an oblique reference in 4:10-23.[24] There are so many parallels between numerous elements of Philippians (not just 3:2-4:1) and the Galatian and Corinthian correspondence that it seems difficult to date Philippians before Paul's second visit to Jerusalem, although the absence of a clear reference to the collection makes that formally possible. An early date for Philippians would rule out using Galatians and 1 and 2 Corinthians to help identify the opponents of 3:2 but an early date seems on general grounds unlikely, even though it is difficult to give firm grounds for accepting either the late date (Roman imprisonment) or the intermediate date (Ephesian or other early imprisonment).

For the present exercise, then, I accept Richardson's general proposal for understanding Phil. 3:2: the problem referred to is specific, but not to Philippi.[25] If this be the case, we must look elsewhere to identify those against whom the invective is directed. We shall see that each of the phrases has a close parallel in Galatians or 2 Corinthians.[26]

---

20 Richardson, *Israel,* 113, who actually refers to the troubles in several churches.

21 It appears to me that there is some ambiguity in Richardson's position which arises from not distinguishing the chronology of the letters from the chronology of the missionary activity. Treating the letters in their presumed sequence (*Israel,* 73), he discusses Philippians after Galatians but before Corinthians. Yet to explain Philippians he appeals to Paul's encounters with opposition in, among other places, Corinth. The question, however, should be limited to the sequence of the letters, which presumably reflects when Paul found out about difficulties.

22 N. 19 above. Koester (*IDB,* 5:666) dates Phil. 3:2-4:1 at about the same time as Galatians. On dating Philippians at about the same time as Galatians and the Corinthian correspondence, see also J.C. Hurd, "The Sequence of Paul's Letters," *CJT* 14 (1968), 189-200; Robert Jewett, *A Chronology of Paul's Life* (Philadelphia: Fortress, 1979), 104.

23 John Knox, *Chapters in a Life of Paul* (Nashville: Abingdon, 1950), 86-87.

24 Georgi, *Kollekte,* 46-47.

25 Richardson, *Israel,* 113.

26 The present examination of parallels in some ways repeats that of Koester

Since so much of Philippians 3 is reminiscent of Galatians, I should indicate, without arguing the case, that I accept the general view that the principal opposing missionaries in Galatia were Jewish Christians.[27] Their message was apparently that, for Paul's Gentile converts to be true sons of Abraham, they had to accept circumcision and the law. Paul calls people who hold such a position when he and Titus go to Jerusalem "false brethren" (Gal. 2:4). Whether the "troublers" in Galatia who would compel Paul's converts to be circumcised (Gal. 5:10-12; 6:12) were the same people as the "false brethren" in Jerusalem who would have compelled Titus to be circumcised we cannot tell. They seem to hold, however, the same position materially: Gentile converts should be circumcised.

When we turn to Philippians several phrases merit consideration:

(1) The "dogs" are called "evil-workers," *kakous ergatas.* This precise title to describe Paul's opponents is not to be found elsewhere, but the closest parallel is *ergatai dolioi* ("deceitful workmen," 2 Cor. 11:13). It seems likely, although there are objections to the view, that the deceitful workmen of 2 Cor. 11:13 are the Hebrew "servants of Christ" mentioned in 2 Cor. 11:22-23.[28] In any case the "false apostles, deceitful workmen" in 11:13 are Christian apostles,[29] and not non-Christian Jews.

(2) The play on the word "circumcision" (*katatomē,* concision) in Phil. 3:2 is reminiscent of Gal. 5:12, where Paul refers to circumcision by the term *apokoptō,* "lop off." There is no verbal parallel, but in both cases Paul refers to physical circumcision as "mutilation" (as the *RSV* correctly interprets both terms). We have already seen that those referred to in Gal. 5:12 are probably Jewish Christians.

(3) When Paul says in Phil. 3:3 that "we" boast in Christ Jesus and do not place confidence in the flesh, he implies that his opponents boast in, or put confidence in the flesh (circumcision). This, again, is reminiscent of an argument in Gal. 6:13-14: his opponents, presumably Jewish Christians, "boast in [the] flesh" of the Galatians (referring to circumcision), while Paul boasts "in the cross of our Lord Jesus Christ."

(4) Finally, it appears in Phil. 3:2-3 that his opponents are trying to get Paul's Gentile converts to accept circumcision. If our reading of Galatians (and Romans) is correct, this was a position taken by Jewish Christians, not non-Christian Jews.[30]

("Polemic"), except that, as I have already indicated, he finds significance in many more phrases than do I.

27 The view that they were Gentiles who favoured accepting circumcision and the law (thus, among others, Richardson, *Israel,* 84-97) does not affect the present question.

28 Below, at n. 32.

29 Cf. below, at n. 33.

30 See the section above on the law, especially at n. 9.

There is nothing that will definitely rule out the possibility that, in Philippians 3, Paul uses against non-Christian Jews charges and phrases which are reminiscent of attacks in Galatians and 2 Corinthians against Christians. That position would be probable, however, only if Philippians were written before the controversies in Galatia and Corinth came to Paul's attention—in effect, before the second visit to Jerusalem. After those difficulties came fully to light, the language of 3:2 was almost surely reserved by Paul for his opponents in the Christian movement. The strongest argument for dating Philippians is its close similarity to Galatians, 1 and 2 Corinthians, and Romans. Thus the argument is circular. The language and theology of the letter date it to the intermediate or late period, and after being so dated the language of invective is best understood in the light of Paul's controversies elsewhere. The language and thought place Philippians close to the *Hauptbriefe,* and the problems which are seen in Galatians and 2 Corinthians explain the invective of Phil. 3:2. Thus it is best to read Phil. 3:2 as being directed not against Jews as such, but against some of Paul's opponents in the Christian movement.[31]

2 Corinthians 11

The identity of the opponents in 2 Corinthians is as vexed a problem as one can find in Pauline studies. My last count, which I am sure was by no means complete, provided a list of fourteen different identifications. There is good reason for the difficulty. The principal questions are these: (1) Are the superlative apostles of 2 Corinthians to be connected in any way with the apostles named in 1 Cor. 1:12? (2) Is the content of their message to be explained on the basis of 1 Corinthians (wisdom, emphasis on *charismata*), or has Paul's perception of the difficulty in Corinth changed? (3) Are all the opposing preachers named in 2 Corinthians the same? (2 Cor. 3:1 implies that they bear letters of recommendation and 2 Cor. 11:22-23 speak of Jewish preachers who are servants of Christ. If these two passages are combined, Paul is seen as having difficulty with apostles authorized by Jerusalem. Would he then call such missionaries "false apostles," deceitful workmen disguised as apostles of Christ, and even servants of Satan [2 Cor. 11:13-15]?)[32]

The questions will probably never be resolved to everyone's satisfaction. Luckily, for the present purpose they do not need to be. Whether or not the false apostles who are actually servants of Satan

31 That the opponents in mind in 3:2 were Jewish Christians is also concluded by Koester, Schmithals, and Tyson (nn. 15, 16 above).

32 On this last problem, see especially C.K. Barrett, "PSEUDAPOSTOLOI (2 Cor. 11:13)," in A. Deschamps et al., eds., *Mélanges Bibliques en hommage au R.P. Béda Rigaux* (Gembloux, 1970), 378-96, here 378.

(2 Cor. 11:13-15) are the same as the Hebrew servants of Christ whose work is less worthy than Paul's, but presumably still valuable (11:22-23), it is clear that they are all Christians. It is intrinsically probable that in Paul's day all apostles were Jewish,[33] but here it is not their Jewishness which bothers Paul—it is the trouble they are making in the church at Corinth. As in Galatians and (we have argued) in Philippians, so in Corinthians. Paul's fierce invective is directed against Christians who hold a position which he sees as threatening the gospel. The study of Paul's opponents tells us nothing about his relationship with or attitude towards his kinsmen by race nor towards his native religion as such.

Paul and the Jewish People (2 Cor. 11:24-26)

Despite what may be some rhetorical exaggeration—Paul is in danger from all groups other than Pauline Christians and in every conceivable place (2 Cor. 11:26)—2 Cor. 11:24-26 seems to provide some information about his relationship with his own people and, in fact, about the relationship between Judaism and the young Christian movement. There are actually two bits of information in these verses: he has suffered at the hands of Jews; he maintains physical contact with his own people.

Persecution

There is rather a lot about "persecution" in the Pauline correspondence.[34] In some instances it is hard to know if actual persecution was taking place or if Paul simply has the habit of depicting himself and the Christian churches as subject to persecution by the outside world (thus, for example, 1 Cor. 4:12; 2 Cor. 4:9; 2 Cor. 8:2; cf. Matt. 5:44). Some references, however, are more concrete. Paul himself persecuted the church, apparently in his role as a zealous Pharisee (Gal. 1:33, 23; Phil. 3:6; 1 Cor. 15:9). Further, Paul says that if he still preached circumcision as a Christian apostle he would avoid persecution (Gal. 5:11). The preachers who do preach circumcision, Paul charges, do so to avoid persecution (Gal. 6:12). Finally, there is an allegorical or typological reference to persecution of Christians (or Pauline Christians, those "born according to the Spirit") by others, designated those "born according to the flesh" (Gal. 4:29).

The point which emerges with most certainty from considering these passages is that at least some Jews persecuted at least some

---

33 I assume that those called "false apostles" in 2 Cor. 11:13 were generally called "apostles." For the point that "apostles" were Jewish, note 1 Cor. 15:8-9, where it appears that Paul was not only the "least" of the apostles, but also the last.

34 In this discussion I leave aside all reference to 1 Thess. 2:14-16, which is discussed elsewhere in this volume by John Hurd.

Christians in at least some places.[35] The fixed point is derived from Paul's references to his own activity as a persecutor. It is less certain that all the references to persecution refer to Jewish persecution of some in the Christian movement, but it appears to me likely that they do, and for the purpose of the present paper I shall work on that assumption. It also appears likely that the issue was "circumcision"; i.e., the admission of Gentiles to the "Israel of God" without requiring them to make full proselytization to Judaism.[36]

Following these leads, we can arrive at the following reconstruction: some Jewish Christian evangelists admitted Gentiles to the messianic movement without requiring proselytization; they were persecuted by Jews. Other Jewish Christians escaped Jewish persecution either because they did not admit Gentiles (probably the situation of James) or because they did, but insisted on circumcision (probably the position of Paul's opponents in Galatia). Paul accused these latter of insisting on circumcision in order to avoid persecution, although one may doubt that that was their true motive.

If the situation just sketched is more or less correct, 2 Cor. 11:24 adds a very important piece of information. Paul says that he five times received the thirty-nine stripes. It seems very likely that the administration of the thirty-nine stripes is what is called elsewhere "persecution." It is important to note that, from the Jewish perspective, it was *punishment.*[37]

Assuming that we can connect the "persecution" passages with the specification of the thirty-nine stripes, we still do not know all that we might wish about the relationship between Judaism and the young Christian movement. One would like to understand better just what it was about the Christian movement which some Jews found offensive enough to require punishment. It is fruitless here to search the list of things in Mishnah Makkoth for which the rabbis decreed corporal punishment. For one thing, the rabbis themselves extended the list of those to be punished by the thirty-nine stripes to include those for whom the Bible decreed "cutting off" (*Mak.* 3:15). More to the point, it is intrinsically probable that the Diaspora synagogues had at their disposal only two punishments, ostracism and the thirty-nine stripes.[38]

35 On the general freedom of Palestinian Jewish Christians from official punishment, see S.G.F. Brandon, *The Fall of Jerusalem and the Christian Church* (2d ed.; London: SPCK, 1957), 88-100.

36 That the motive for Jewish persecution of the Christian movement was in some way connected to obedience to the law is, I think, the majority position. The principal alternative—which to me seems unlikely—is that Christianity proclaimed as Messiah one who had been condemned. Thus Arland J. Hultgren, "Paul's Pre-Christian Persecutions of the Church: Their Purpose, Locale, and Nature," *JBL* 95 (1976), 97-104; J.C. Beker, *Paul the Apostle,* 143-44, 182-84, 202.

37 See also Hultgren, "Persecutions," 104.

38 Hultgren (ibid., 104) proposes flogging and imprisonment, the latter on the basis of Luke/Acts.

We know from 1QS 7:1, for example, that in Qumran even blasphemy (according to the Bible a capital offence) was punished by separation from the community. One may reason *qal-va-homer* that the Diaspora synagogues could not and did not execute people guilty of capital offences. The administration of the thirty-nine stripes was probably the only punishment available in the Diaspora to be applied to transgressors who kept showing up in the synagogue. The penalty, in other words, probably covered so many transgressions that the crime cannot be precisely specified just by learning the punishment.

The only clue, as I said before, is Paul's own connection of persecution and the requirement of circumcision.[39] His receiving the thirty-nine stripes fits well with this explanation of the punishment. His career was precisely to bring Gentiles into the people of God without requiring of them observance of the law, and one may hypothesize that he was punished, and punished repeatedly, for doing so. Thus we see that, from the Jewish side, the Christian movement was considered fully Jewish. Converts to it had to be taken seriously, and missionaries who brought in converts without requiring full proselytization were subject to discipline.

Paul's Continuing Contact with his Kinsmen by Race

The depiction in Acts of Paul's missionary activity is well known and has been accepted by most scholars: Paul went first to the synagogue, and then to Gentiles only when he failed to win a hearing among Jews. Nevertheless, it would appear from Acts, many of his converts were Jewish, while many of the rest were "God-fearers," Gentiles who accepted monotheism and Jewish ethics but had not become Jewish.[40] It would be possible, however, to derive quite a different picture from Paul's letters. Paul, in discussing his ministry, speaks exclusively of Gentiles. He is Apostle to the Gentiles (Rom. 11:13), and he was called in order that he might preach Christ among the Gentiles (Gal. 1:16; cf. 2:2: "the gospel which I preach among the Gentiles"). The agreement between himself, Peter, and James was that he, Paul, would go to the uncircumcised (2:7, 9). His task was to win obedience among all the Gentiles (Rom. 1:5), and he could report that Christ had worked through him to win obedience from the Gentiles (Rom. 15:18). He wished to go to Rome in order that he might "reap some harvest among [the Romans] as well as among the rest of the Gentiles" (Rom. 1:13).

---

39 Cf. Richardson, *Israel,* 90.

40 For references see Sanders, "Paul's Attitude toward the Jewish People," *USQR* 33 (1978), 177-78, expanded in Sanders,*Paul, the Law and the Jewish People.* Among recent literature one may cite Beker, *Paul the Apostle*. While Paul was the Apostle to the Gentiles, he was really apostle to Jew and Gentile alike (6). Further, the *ethnē* (Gentiles) in Paul's letters "are on the whole not pure Gentiles but . . . 'God-fearers' " (76).

One might argue that the division between Peter and Paul was geographical, not ethnic, but it appears that Paul took the division in its ethnic sense. His mission was "to be a minister of Christ Jesus to the Gentiles in the priestly service of the gospel of God, so that the offering of the Gentiles may be acceptable" (Rom. 15:16).[41]

With regard to his converts, it is noteworthy that not a single one can be identified from the Pauline letters as being Jewish.[42] Acts, which depicts Paul as apostle first to Jews and then to Gentiles, identifies Crispus, for example, as Jewish, but Paul does not (Acts 18:8; 1 Cor. 1:14). Further, Paul's description of the former lives of his converts does not lend support to the view that they were largely Jews or God-fearers. The Galatians are said formerly to have worshipped "beings which are no Gods" (Gal. 4:8). The Corinthians had been heathen who worshipped dumb idols (1 Cor. 12:2; cf. 6:9-11). The Thessalonians had turned to God from idols (1 Thess. 1:9), and it would appear that the Philippians were not physically circumcised (Phil. 3:2).[43]

It is true that Paul says that "to the Jews I became as a Jew, in order to win Jews" (1 Cor. 9:19), just as he also says that he preached from Jerusalem to Illyricum (Rom. 15:19). Yet his own description of his career (Gal. 1-2) seems to exclude any possibility of his having preached in Jerusalem, just as the Antioch incident (Gal. 2:11-13) shows that in a mixed church he did not live like a Jew. In short, it is hard to know when Paul could have preached in Jerusalem, and it is hard to know when he actually lived like a Jew in order to win Jews, since he clearly

---

41 Some scholars have previously argued that Paul's mission was to the Gentiles (except for possible occasional preahing to Jews), and that the division between Paul and Peter (Gal. 2:9) was ethnographic rather than geographic. See W. Schmithals, *Paul and James* (London: SCM, 1965), 16-62; G. Lüdemann, *Paulus, der Heidenapostel*, Vol. 1 (Göttingen: Vandenhoeck & Ruprecht, 1980), 96; Lloyd Gaston, "Paul and the Torah," in Alan T. Davies, ed., *Anti-Semitism and the Foundations of Christianity* (New York: Paulist, 1979), 48-71, here 55. This leaves to be answered the question of how Paul thought the Jews in the Diaspora would be evangelized. The evidence is too scant to give a certain answer to this question, as the ingenious attempt of Schmithals to provide one shows (*Paul and James*, 50-51). Nevertheless, it appears clear that Paul did not feel the responsibility to be his. Romans 9 to 11 show his great concern for the conversion of his "kinsmen by race," but they also show that, while he was successfully (at least in his own view) preparing "the offering of the Gentiles" (Rom. 15:16; cf. 2 Cor. 2:14), the mission to the Jews, which was not his responsibility, was far less successful, and he had to portray his apostolate to the Gentiles as *indirectly* resulting in the conversion of the Jews (Rom. 11:13-14).

42 The missionary couple, Andronicus and Junia (masculinized to Junias by Greek editors, by accenting, and by many translators: to avoid the possibility that a woman was an apostle?), are called "kin" by Paul, but they were not his converts, as he explicitly says (Rom. 16:7).

43 Having cited this evidence, Gaston curiously says that Paul's converts were former "God-fearers" ("Paul and the Torah," 55). The discrepancy between Paul and Acts is as great on this point as it is on the number of trips to Jerusalem, but the principle of John Knox—in brief, to prefer Paul's evidence to that of Acts—seems not yet to have affected scholarly views of Paul's missionary activity.

did not do so even in Antioch. I do not have at hand a precise literary category for Rom. 15:19 and 1 Cor. 9:19, although a student of rhetoric may. Perhaps the term "hyperbole" will be adequate. Paul depicts himself as preaching to every person on the northern perimeter of the Mediterranean. Possibly 1 Cor. 9:19 really means no more than that Paul observed the laws of *kashrut* in Jerusalem and other entirely Jewish environments. In any case, the statements that he preached in Jerusalem and sought to win Jews do not accord with the rest of his descriptions of his career.

I regard the dominant description of Paul's career and practice which emerges from his letters to be a good deal more credible than the picture derived from Acts. Paul preached to Gentiles, he converted former pagans (idolaters, not God-fearers), and in the mission field he lived like a Gentile. *But* 2 Cor. 11:24 shows that he kept attending synagogue, at least for an appreciable period of his career. The only way to receive the thiry-nine stripes would be to show up voluntarily in a Jewish community and to submit to community discipline. *Punishment implies inclusion.*[44] Thus, for all his "Gentilizing," Paul was willing to be punished as a Jew for offences against the Torah. He, in other words, shared the view of his Jewish contemporaries.[45] The Christian movement, though "a new creation," had not quite quit being a Jewish messianic movement. Paul thought that he was right in bringing Gentiles into that movement without requiring proselytization, but he was willing to be punished as a dissident Jew. God had not yet rejected his own people, as Paul saw it (Rom. 11:1), and neither had Paul.

Conclusion

In the passages we have considered we find no anti-Jewish sentiment. The law is not downgraded because it is bad nor because keeping it leads to legalism and rejection of grace, but because it does not make one a member of the body of Christ. Where there is invective, it is not against Jews as Jews, but against Paul's various opponents within the Christian movement. Paul was engaged in a mission which would help make Christianity a third race, and he was at least partly aware of that (see 1 Cor. 10:32). Yet he maintained his identity as a Jew, considered his converts to be the true sons of Abraham and members of the Israel

44 Agreeing with Vielhauer against Hultgren's criticism (Hultgren, "Persecution," 101 n. 8). Hultgren's statement that "surely Paul did not 'submit' to the Jewish punishments any more than to the Roman" is wrong-headed. Paul did submit to Roman punishment: he did not go to Parthia; he remained in the Empire and must have been submissive to law and punishment. All the more must this have been the case in regard to Judaism in the Diaspora, which—one would have thought this would go without saying—was not the reigning civil power. He had to count himself "in" in order to be punished.

45 Against Hultgren, "Persecution," 102.

of God (Gal. 3:29; 6:16),[46] and looked forward to the time when the natural branches would be grafted back into their own olive tree (Rom. 11:24).

46 It is not necessary here to debate the meaning of "Israel of God," but I read Gal. 6:16 in the light of 3:29. For another view, see Richardson, *Israel,* 74-84, especially 82.

6

The Rhetorical Function of the Jews in Romans

Daniel Fraikin

Anti-Judaism is a negative disposition towards the Jews and the expression of that attitude in action. It is more than ignorance or error; it implies a value judgment. People reject what they dislike or hate, what they perceive as opposed to the values they cherish. This perception is achieved and consolidated, among other things, by teaching and preaching. It is clear that Christian discourse has contributed to the negative evaluation of Judaism and the Jews in the course of history. The concern here is with the Christian discourse preserved in the writings of the New Testament. The question is not, however, how those writings came to be used against the Jews (it would say little about anti-Judaism in the New Testament, for even the Jewish scriptures were turned against the Jews), but whether those writings were themselves originally anti-Jewish, and in what way.

To speak of anti-Judaism as rejection of the Jews and of writings as generating or promoting such attitude is to speak of rhetoric. For rhetoric can be defined as the study of the discursive means by which an orator or a writer can induce or increase the mind's adherence to the theses presented for its assent,[1] and in most cases in view of some action on the part of the audience. When what is proposed is not mere information nor the result of necessary deduction from universally accepted premises but is in the realm of the credible, the plausible, or the probable, the orator or the writer (the author, to be short) mobilizes the value systems of the audience, its emotions, its trust etc., to obtain its adhesion.

There seems to be no New Testament writing whose goal would be to generate a negative attitude towards the Jews. There is no *adversus iudaeos* in the New Testament. But this is not the end of the matter. For

1 Ch. Perelman and L. Olbrechts-Tyteca, *The New Rhetoric. A Treatise on Argumentation* (Notre Dame: Notre Dame University, 1969), 4.

we must ask if some form of anti-Judaism is not part of the argumentative discourse. We could ask, for instance, if anti-Judaism is not part of the agreement between the author and his audience and used to promote Christianity, just as in times of crisis minorities are used as scapegoats in nationalistic speeches. Our concern, then, is the role played by the Jews and Judaism in the transaction between the author and his audience, in the argument by which the author hopes to achieve his goal. That is what we mean by the "rhetorical function" of the Jews.

The focus is here on the Epistle to the Romans. The study of Romans from a rhetorical point of view has just begun. I will rely on the recent work of Wilhelm Wuellner, whose position on the rhetorical genre of this letter I share.[2] Ancient rhetoric, as is well known, recognized three rhetorical genres: the judicial, legal, or forensic genre, in which the audience is asked to adjudicate between right and wrong; the deliberative, political, or symbouleutic genre, in which the audience is asked to decide on what is useful; and the ceremonial or epideictic genre in which the role of the audience is not as well defined. The epideictic speech, to which such things as eulogies, ceremonial discourses, and sermons belong, was considered in the past mainly an occasion for the display of oratorical skills on subjects of little or no importance. Modern rhetoric, however, would understand its function differently.

> The argumentation in epidictic [sic] discourse sets out to increase the intensity of adherence to certain values, which might not be contested when considered on their own but may nevertheless not prevail against other values that might come into conflict with them. The speaker tries to establish a sense of communion centered around particular values recognized by the audience, and to this end he uses the whole range of means available to the rhetorician for purposes of amplification and enhancement.[3]

Wuellner has argued that Romans belongs to the epideictic genre. The role Paul expects the Romans to perform is neither to deliberate nor to adjudicate but "to affirm the communal values which Paul and the Romans share in being agents of the faith throughout the world."[4] Wuellner's arguments need not be repeated here. It can be pointed out, however, that the rhetorical genre is indicated in the words used by Paul to describe his intention: in the *exordium* he speaks of strengthening (1:11) and mutual comforting (1:12), and in the *peroratio*, of having brought back something to memory (15:15). The epideictic genre could not be better described.

This understanding of Romans' rhetorical genre does not prejudge the means by which Paul achieves his goal. It does not preclude

2 Wilhelm Wuellner, "Paul's Rhetoric of Argumentation in Romans," *CBQ* 38 (1976), 330-51; "Toposforschung und Torahinterpretation bei Paulus und Jesus," *NTS* 24 (1978), 463-83.

3 Perelman, *The New Rhetoric*, 51.

4 Wuellner, "Paul's Rhetoric," 337.

the use of sub-genres. It is quite possible that the position which Paul and his audience share was achieved through polemic and suffering which it suits his epideictic purpose to recapitulate. Epideictic discourse is not identical with irenical, contented self-congratulation. The position reached might well have been still the object of a fragile consensus in need of reinforcement. That such is the case in Romans is indicated by Paul's affirmation that he is not ashamed of the gospel (1:16), by the tone of 8:31-39, and generally by the argumentative character of the whole.

What are the communal values which Paul and the audience share and which are being reinforced? Paul speaks of the gospel (1:15). But this can only be the general subject. What counts, as Wuellner again points out, is Paul's choice of *topos,* namely, what he chooses to say about the gospel in relation to his audience and his goal.[5] We shall agree with him, in advance of our main discussion, that the theme of the whole epistle, expressed in 1:16 and at various points in the course of argument, is that the gospel is a power towards salvation for *all* who believe. This choice is obviously related to the situation prevailing between Paul and his Gentile audience and to the ultimate purpose of the letter, which is to enlist their support for his mission to Spain. For what is at stake in this *all* of salvation is the position of the Gentiles in the plan of salvation. *All* means "not only Jews but also Gentiles" (3:29; 4:16; 9:24).

In order to complete the description of the rhetorical situation in Romans, we may anticipate the discussion of the *exordium* and put forward the conclusion that the audience is not the church of Rome in general but specifically Roman Gentile Christians. Then Romans is an epideictic discourse addressed to the Gentile Christians in Rome, intended to strengthen their awareness and assurance of God's election. It is in this discourse that the Jews and Israel play a significant role. How do they appear in this affirmation of the Gentiles?

Before we proceed, however, some precisions are obviously required in the use of the category *the Jews.* The studies assembled in this volume appear in the context of an effort by scholars to reconsider the negative attitude of Christians toward Jews and to replace it by a more considered, well-informed, and perhaps, positive one. It is, in other words, part of a new rhetoric! At this point in our cultural history the audience for this present persuasive discourse is presumed to understand Christians and Jews as two opposed categories. That was not, of course, the original situation. The polarities were between Jews and Gentiles (or Greeks), on the one hand, and between believers in Christ and non-believers, on the other. Thus the assumptions of New Testament discourse do not coincide with those of the present. In our effort to serve the rhetorical needs of the present collection of papers we might be tempted to accept the modern polarity and to discuss the

5 Wuellner, "Toposforschung," 468-69; 476-79.

problem of anti-Judaism in the New Testament in terms of attitudes toward the non-Christian Jews, the nearest equivalent to what Christians understand by Jews today. We can also, however, help break down the present Christian-Jewish polarization by evoking the more complex situation of the origins evidenced in particular in Paul's complex position between Jews and Gentiles. Since what follows is an effort to understand that situation, *Jew* should initially neither imply nor exclude faith in Jesus Christ.

The determination of the role played by the Jews in Paul's argument presupposes an understanding of that argument which cannot be fully substantiated in this article, although some justifications for it will be offered as the reading proceeds. That the following rhetorical analysis requires a stand on the nature of the argument, however, should be clear. In a good discourse the relation of the author to his audience changes as the argument proceeds along its course. This is the case in Romans. It is not accidental that Israel appears only in chapters 9 to ll, and we shall try to explain why it is so. There is a shift of perspective as the argument runs its course. The importance of this for the question of anti-Judaism in the New Testament will be underlined in the conclusion.

The Argument

1:1-15: Paul and his Audience

In the very first verses Paul locates the gospel, and therefore himself as servant of the gospel, in the Jewish tradition by mentioning the prophets and the holy scriptures and the Davidic lineage of Jesus. Only if we imagine Paul as having somehow broken with this tradition can we see in this a special intention to ingratiate himself with a Jewish-oriented audience. Otherwise it is a plain statement of his situation as the author. The scriptures, of course, are not described as Jewish. This is simply assumed. Paul the Christian Jew does not look at the story of God's dealings with his people from a distance. The gospel is inside that space which Paul considers home. It is not the Jewishness of Paul and his people that is singled out but the non-Jewishness of the addressees, the "nations," to whom he was sent to bring them to the obedience of faith (1:5). That *ethnoi* has here the qualitative meaning of non-Jews (Gentiles) rather than the geographical or sociological meaning of other peoples is clear from what Paul writes to the Romans: "among whom you are" (1:6; also 1:13). It would make no good sense to tell the Romans that they are among the nations of the earth! It is implicit, then, that Paul operates with the Jewish distinction between Jews and Gentiles, and that he speaks from the Jewish pole of this distinction to the other pole.

Who is the audience addressed here? Because it is assumed (reasonably) that the church in Rome comprised both Jews and Gentiles, it is also assumed that the audience is singled out as being Gentile because Gentiles were known to be the majority and/or because they were the constituency he had authority to address as the Apostle to the Gentiles. We observe, however, that this is the only epistle in which the Gentiles are specifically mentioned as the addressees, although the mix between Jews and Gentiles in Rome can hardly have been much different from the one in Corinth or elsewhere. It is also the only epistle from which the word *ekklēsia* ("church") is absent, with the sole exception of the still problematic chapter 16, which seems in any case marginal to the argument. There are good reasons, then, to take the text at its plain value and consider Romans as a discourse addressed to the Gentile Christians in Rome, whatever the actual make-up of the Roman community was. We should remember in this respect that the audience, from a rhetorical point of view, is not the actual congregation of people hearing the speech but a construction of the speaker.[6]

We assume, then, from the terms of the *exordium,* that the audience envisaged by Paul is specifically Gentile Christian. The relationship prevailing between the author and his audience is that of a Jewish Christian apostle reaching out to Gentile Christians, using a gospel rooted in the Jewish tradition. The priority of the Jews affirmed in 1:16 is in fact an underlying assumption of the discourse from the beginning, a part of the agreement between the author and the audience, and the background against which much of the argument must be understood.

1:16, 17: The Theme

Verses 16 and 17 are generally recognized as a thematic announcement. We understand it this way: The gospel is a power for salvation for all who believe, i.e. for both Jews and Greeks, because it is through faith. A thematic announcement is best explained by the argumentation which follows, but even the bare theme allows for some important observations. That the distinction between Jews and Gentiles appears at all is significant, although the full meaning of its presence is only disclosed later. The recapitulation of this phrase—"not only the Jews but also the Gentiles" (or the Greeks) (3:29; 4:16; 9:24)—sets our interpretation in the direction in which Paul's argument moves. What is at stake is the salvation of the Gentiles, the extension of God's election to the nations. There is an argument about it precisely because of the Jewish origins of the gospel, and there is still an argument about it at the end of Paul's missionary career because it is still a controversial issue.

6 Perelman, *The New Rhetoric,* 19-23.

When Paul says he is not ashamed of the gospel he can hardly be thinking of the cultural prestige of Rome. The phrase much more likely refers to the obstacles encountered by his missionary activity among the Gentiles, not just the actual persecutions he suffered but the judgment on him which justified the actions of his persecutors. What Paul is exposing in Romans is the position of the Gentiles in God's salvation and the latter takes the form of a justification of that position.

This justification is of course not made on the basis of philosophical premises, with a universal audience in mind. It is done in terms of the Jewish tradition and on the premise of the priority of the Jews. The reason Paul mentions the priority of the Jews to a Gentile audience (according to our hypothesis) is not that the Gentiles could be tempted to boast of their election at the expense of the Jews (a danger recognized in 11:18). This would hardly create the headline in 1:16. Rather, the reason must correspond to what we think is the argument: "not only the Jews but also the Gentiles." Paul's argument presupposes the priority of the Jews, and he means not that all are equal but that the Gentiles have been received within a purpose of God initiated among the Jews. The distinction between Jews and Gentiles is presupposed, and what makes a Jew a Jew is precisely to have been a part of the people of God before the Gentiles came in. What Paul has in mind, in other words, is not a new house in which Jews and Gentiles are both invited, but a house to which the Jews belong *ab initio*.

1:18-3:20: All Have Sinned, Not Only the Gentiles but Also the Jews

From a rhetorical point of view one of the most remarkable features of this section is the second person singular address "to the Jew" in 2:17, which is not paralleled by a similar "to the Gentile." We do not find an evenly distributed reminder to Gentile and Jewish Christians of their sinful condition before Christ (although 6:16-21 shows that Paul could well have addressed the Gentiles in the second person as well). I would like to propose as an explanation that the whole of this section 1:18-3:20 (at least) is really an argument addressed to Jews, for the benefit of the Gentile Roman audience.

The first section, 1:18-32 (except for the first verse, perhaps), is generally recognized as a form of the traditional Jewish indictment of the Gentiles. What function does it play? One could say that Paul borrowed a type of discourse, originally meant to emphasize by way of contrast the holiness of Israel, to describe the sinful condition of the human race. Given the later emphasis on the Jews, Paul is probably here speaking specifically of the Gentiles. What then would be the audience of this indictment? If it is the Gentiles in Rome, why does he use the third person? I find it more likely that this tirade against the Gentiles is addressed to its normal audience, Jews. Paul the Jew joins the Jews he is talking to in a complacent tirade against the Gentiles: "We shall agree that the Gentiles are under God's wrath!" It would be a *captatio benevolentiae* addressed to a Jewish audience, and the basis of a subsequent *tu quoque.*

This is done in stages; Rom. 1:32 serves as a transition. The principle is laid down that guilt is found in doing something with the "knowledge" (*epignontes*; cf. *epignōsis,* 3:20) that it is wrong. In 2:1-16 the ground is prepared for a direct address to the Jew. It is already in the second person addressed to someone who judges others but does the same things himself. This section introduces the distinction between Jews and Gentiles and establishes that the principle of 1:32 entails equal treatment for Jews and Gentiles before God. "Knowledge" is more clearly spelled out as "law." In other words, 1:32-2:16 prepares for Paul's argumentative goal, which is to lead the Jew, who has the law and who judges on its basis, to admit that he is in the same predicament as the Gentile before the judgment. The Jew addressed in 1:17 can draw his own conclusions, in fact. Though Paul soon turns to obvious objections drawn from the privileged position of the Jews (which is not denied, as 3:1 shows), his argument stands, for in terms of the wrath of God the Jews, with the law, are not better off.

In other words, 1:18-3:20 does affirm that all men are under sin (3:9) but it is the Jew who has to be convinced of this fact, to whom the argument is directed throughout. This argument can be summed up in the formula: "not only the Gentiles but also the Jews are under sin." Of course the argument does not stop here and cannot be separated from the next section, 3:21-4:25, which was anticipated by 1:18-3:20. Equality in sin calls for equality in justification. Before we reflect on the role of the Jews at this stage of the argument, we must pursue it to its natural conclusion.

3:21-4:25: Not Only the Jews but Also the Gentiles Are Now In

Here, as in the previous section, something is affirmed of all human beings, namely, justification for all who believe, through the action of God in Jesus Christ. But, inasmuch as there is something to prove, the argument is directed to Jews. The emphatically placed "without the law" in verse 21 suggests that much from the very beginning. The phrase "all who believe" of verse 22 is related to "all have sinned" of verse 23, a phrase that reflects the discussion of the preceding chapters. The point is that this way of salvation (by faith, without the law) is for all (not only Gentiles but also Jews) because all have sinned (not only Gentiles but Jews as well).

That the section 3:27-4:25 is an argument for Jews hardly requires a demonstration. "Is God of the Jews only?" (verse 29) and "Abraham, our father according to the flesh" (4:1), taken together, signal that much. The argument is about justification without the works of the law (3:28; 4:1-8) and the entry of the nations into the fold of Abraham, both a consequence and the original goal of justification by faith. "It is by faith, in order to be according to grace, so that the promise will be validated that applied to all of his seed [Abraham's], not only to the part which is from the law but to that part which is from the faith of Abraham, who is the father of us all" (4:16).

The Rhetorical Function of the Jews in 1:18-4:25

The first part of Romans speaks of justification. But it is argued in front of a Jewish audience characterized not only by its *de facto* possession of the law, but also by the traditional understanding that the law (and obviously its practice) is what qualifies one before God. Paul affirms that the same God, who is also the God of the Gentiles, now has provided in Jesus Christ a way of righteousness that is without the law but through faith, a way that allows the Gentiles to be justified as well. And he argues that this makes sense by the Jewish standards of the Law and the Prophets (cf. 3:21, 31 and 1:2) and by such axioms as the one in 3:29, that God is also the God of the Gentiles.

We are faced, then, with the interesting fact that Paul, in a discourse whose goal is to strengthen the Gentiles in the gospel, provides them with the arguments by which he would make his understanding of the gospel and its consequences credible to Jews. It is not simply that the theological categories used by Paul are Jewish (what other theological framework could we expect Paul to use?), but that it is important for the Gentiles that their position be credible in the eyes of Jews. Their experience of salvation is certainly not dependent on these arguments, but at this point it seems necessary for them to have a theology of their experience that relates them to Israel. The fact that the argument is meant to bring a Jew to understand their position reveals the weight of Judaism. Why would they care whether a Jew will accept them and their salvation if it is not because they are (through Paul) claiming entry into a story which belongs to the Jews from old?

The Jew fictitiously addressed here is not just asked to accept the Gentiles. He is asked to accept a view of justification which conflicts with his own view but which Paul claims as authentic by the standards of Scripture. He is asked to accept also Paul's interpretation of the Christ event on which the justification by faith is based. He is not asked to surrender being a Jew, but to become a different kind of Jew. To maintain the credibility of Pauline Christianity means simultaneously to adopt a certain definition of Judaism. Paul the Jew is no longer the Jew he was before he became a Christian. Again, Paul does not say that the position on the law held by the Jew addressed in the first chapters defines Judaism so that, by renouncing it, he would cease to be a Jew. Paul's ambiguity towards Judaism in Romans derives from the conflict between the claim on Judaism made by Paul and Paul's own recognition that that claim has been rejected by the majority of Jews.

5:1-8:30: The Way to Salvation

The Jews have disappeared from these chapters. Paul presupposes that the previous argument has won the day for his audience. He takes justification by faith for granted ("justified, then, out of faith . . ." 5:1). He is still arguing, however, and meeting the objections which come from trust in the law. He shows how those who claim justification without the law can hope ultimately to be saved. His positive argument is from the nature of the Christ event, which, by way of a *qal-va-homer* argument, is shown to carry for the justified the hope of their ultimate salvation (chapter 5). He shows in chapter 6 how freedom from the law does not mean sin, in chapter 7 why the law itself is not discredited, the reason for its weakness being in the flesh, and in chapter 8 how the Spirit replaces it (8:1-14). Chapter 8 concludes on the hope of glory in the present condition.

This is no place for a more detailed analysis of the argument in chapters 5 to 8. We only want to show how it can be understood in relation to Paul's rhetorical goal. Comforting or strengthening his Gentile audience in the gospel, after having made his point about their justification (1-4), he goes on to show how the gap is bridged between justification and salvation (cf. 1:16, "a power of God towards salvation"). What is remarkable, however, is that he constantly meets the objections coming from the law or, more precisely, from the assumption that the law deals with sin. How can you be saved—or be acceptable to God—without the law? The answer, of course, is the Spirit, and that answer includes the exhortations found in chapters 6 and 8. "Those who walk according to the Spirit" fulfill the *dikaiōma* of the law (8:4). The statement calls for the exhortation to let oneself be led by the Spirit (8:13), the warning that those who are in the flesh cannot please God (8:7), and the judgment that whoever does not have the Spirit of Christ does not belong to him (8:9).

We discern, then, in chapters 5 to 8, Paul's concern, summed up in 15:16, to present the Gentiles as an offering acceptable to God, sanctified in the Holy Spirit. The arguments about the law in chapters 6 to 8 presuppose the principle of holiness as characteristic of those who belong to God. The case for the acceptability of the law-less Gentiles among God's people with the law demands a discussion about the law, with which holiness was previously associated.

Thus even chapters 5 to 8 can be seen as part of Paul's effort to present his understanding of the gospel, and those who live from it, as legitimate by Jewish standards. He argues essentially that, with the law, the Gentiles can meet the demands of the law and can be holy and acceptable to God.

8:31-39: Temporary Conclusion

These verses (8:31-39) conclude the argument of the first section of Romans. They affirm, on the basis of what precedes ("what shall we say after this?"), that Paul and his audience ("we") are indeed in God's election and love (these two go together in 1:6-7; 9:12-13, 25; 11:29). "After all that has been said," says Paul, "here is where we stand." This position, however, is reached over against opposition: "who is against us," "who will accuse," "who shall separate us from God's or Christ's love?" Rather than seeing in this implicit opposition an abstract quantity like evil in general or cosmic forces, it is more natural to assume, as I have argued elsewhere,[7] that the opposition is the one implicit in the argumentation of the previous chapters, namely, Jews. They are the ones who would accuse the Gentiles, deny their inheritance as sons of Abraham, their being chosen and loved.

It is at this point in the letter, when the argument is concluded, that for the first time Paul and his audience appear as a body facing the rejection of those before whom their position has been argued. The argument itself has produced division. The affirmation of the one group over the rejection of the other produced separation. It should be noted that Paul does not claim for his own that they are *the* elect, but that they are among the elect (in 8:33 *eklektōn theou* has no article and should be translated "people whom God has chosen," not "the elect of God"). He does not use the word "church" either, as we have observed earlier. Paul has not separated the Gentiles but claimed that God has chosen them in his love. The rejection of this claim constitutes them as a separate entity. The Gentile Christians are rejected by the group to which, Paul has claimed, they belong, and which Paul now calls Israel.

9:1-11:36: The Parenthesis of Israel's Unbelief

The absence of a transition between chapters 8 and 9 is explainable if the end of chapter 8 is understood in the manner we have suggested. Those over whose opposition Paul has claimed the victory of his argument about the chosen status of the Gentiles are obviously Jews. What comes out in the open is that it is the main body of the Jews, Israel.

For one remarkable feature of this new section is the appearance of the name "Israel" for the first time in the epistle and the practical disappearance of the term "Jew" (with the exception of two passages, 9:24 and 10:12, which are about the call to Jews and Gentiles). Paul does not call the body of unbelieving Jews "the Jews." The reason is obvious: there are Christian Jews. Jews are not yet defined as non-Christians.

7 D. Fraikin, "Romains 8:31-39. La position des églises de la gentilité," (Th.D. dissertation, Harvard Divinity School, 1974).

The discussion, then, is over "Israel," by which term must be meant the corporate body of the Jews as distinct from the other nations (9:30-31), the people addressed by the prophets in the past (9:27; 10:21), the people of God.[8]

The unbelief of Israel is one of the presuppositions of these chapters. It deserves some comment. What is presupposed is not simply that a great number of Jews, or even the majority, have not accepted the gospel yet, but that Israel, the people of God, has not accepted the gospel. "Israel" is more than all individual Jews. Somehow, at some point, the rejection of the gospel by individual Jews or synagogues has led to the theological conclusion that Israel has rejected the gospel. It remained only to explain the "fact." The fact, of course, is the result of an interpretation. When it came about, and who is responsibile for it, are difficult questions to answer, but that it should be considered a major theological event is clear. If Romans, for instance, had not included chapters 9 to 11, all we would have is a discourse persuading Jews that the gospel makes sense. The Jew would remain a candidate for persuasion. Once Paul begins to explain the unbelief of Israel, Israel is classified as unbelieving. Paul might not be the one who created the theological fact but by using it he sealed it. While many have spent time trying to understand how he deals with the fact, few, if any, have thought of refusing the "fact" itself, so difficult is it to recognize it as a construct.

What, then, is the function of these chapters in a discourse aimed at strengthening the Gentile Christians in Rome? Why could Paul not stop after chapter 8? There are many answers to this question because it is still a challenge to scholars. The following is one more answer. It implies a change in perspective. The underlying problem of these chapters is not that Israel has rejected the gospel but that those who have adopted the gospel have been rejected by Israel. What is at stake is the credibility of a community that claimed to be in God's grand design entrusted to Israel, but is rejected by Israel itself. Because of our modern individualistic view of religion it is easy for us to forget that the Gentiles approached by the apostles, including Paul, came to the God of Israel, a people and a religion with prestige. Jesus was presented as the Messiah of the Jews, and conversion for a Gentile was a "coming in" (cf. 11:25). The early Christian movement must have drawn much of its credibility from its being a Jewish movement. The rejection of the gospel and of Christians by Israel is a blow to the credibility of the movement, and is a special threat to the Gentile Christians.

The whole of Romans can be seen as Paul's answer to this problem. It consists in arguing for the credibility of Paul's gospel by acceptable Jewish theological standards (chapters 1 to 8), in affirming his personal

8 For a contrary view see P. Richardson, *Israel in the Apostolic Church* (Cambridge: Cambridge University, 1969), 126-47, especially 133-36, 146-47.

faithfulness to his people (9:1-5), and explaining the rejection of the gospel by Israel in various ways. Essentially Paul, without rejecting Israel, declares Israel in the wrong. Not rejecting means not only affirming his commitment to Israel (9:1-5; 10:1; 11:1, 14) and warning the Gentiles against pride (11:18), but affirming God's commitment to his people and expressing his hope—not just his wish—that all Israel—not just a remnant (11:5-7)—will be saved (11:11-36).

In other words, Paul, although he has to affirm his stand over against the opposition of his people, refuses to write Israel off from his missionary aims (11:14), from the Gentiles' concern, and most decisively, from God's love. He does not speak of a new Israel either. In fact there is no word for the Christians as a group, except perhaps "the saints" (1:7; 15:25, 26, 32).

12:1-16:23: Exhortation and Conclusion

There is not much to say about 12:1-15:13 from our point of view, since the Jews are no longer directly in the picture, only perhaps that the paraenesis is not an unexpected feature in an epideictic discourse, as Wuellner has shown.[9] To confirm the Gentile Christians in Rome in the gospel is also to show them the ways to be an acceptable offering to God (15:16). The conclusion of this section (15:8-13) is heavily oriented towards the Gentiles, as is to be expected, although in verse 8 the priority of the Jews is discreetly maintained.

In the *peroratio* (15:14 to the end) Paul talks about the danger he faces in Judaea on the part of the unbelievers. It is not surprising, but worth noting, that he does not call them "the Jews." Nor, however, does he call the believers there "the church," but "the saints." The word *ekklēsia* ("church") seems to have its simple meaning of assembly: it is not the opposite of "Israel."

Conclusions

We have placed Romans in the epideictic genre of rhetoric. Paul shares with his audience some of the essential values they have in common. To be more precise, we have concluded that the Apostle to the Gentiles is here writing to Gentile Christians and providing them with the grounds for their *kauchēsis* in the "hope of God's glory" (5:2), for the confidence which finds its expression in 8:32-39, and for their reasons to praise God.

The definition of the Gentiles, quite naturally, is reached within Paul's Jewish frame of reference. But this does not mean simply the use of theological vocabulary or categories of thought. What Paul is pre-

9 Wuellner, "Paul's Rhetoric," 346-49.

senting are the arguments for the entry of the Gentiles into God's plan of salvation which originated in Israel. In "both Jews and Gentiles" there is a priority of the Jews which is a presupposition of the argument.

We have argued that in the chapters on justification by faith (1:18-4:25) Paul presents to the Gentiles the kind of argument he would have with another Jew when arguing for a gospel of justification by faith that would allow for the entry of the Gentiles. He shows how justification by faith and not by works of the law makes sense by recognized Jewish standards of judgment. The argument presupposes faith in God's intervention in Jesus Christ. It is essentially a theological justification of the Christian faith and experience *post factum.* But it shows how important it was for Paul to provide the Gentiles with the rationale of their position in Jewish terms, even if, or precisely because, they were rejected by Israel.

From the way the argumentation is conducted in the first chapters, then, Romans could not appear more pro-Jewish. Paul the Jew is talking to another Jew and finding the arguments to justify his position. It is an intra-Jewish discussion. The Jew addressed by Paul, however, is asked to surrender a position characterized by the importance of the law, for one characterized by faith. Inasmuch as the first position is held by the majority of the Jews and is allowed to stand as a definition of Judaism, Paul is actually proposing a redefinition of Judaism. Paul's argument for the legitimacy of his position in Jewish terms stands only by *his* definition of Judaism, determined by his faith in Jesus Christ. It is also by his definition that the majority of the Jews, Israel, will be declared unfaithful or disobedient.

As the argument reaches a climax in 8:31-39, it appears that the position reached and there proclaimed has been won over against an opposition. Chapters 9 to 11 bring into the open the idea that the position attributed to the Jew in the first part of the epistle is that of the majority of the Jews, which Paul calls Israel. In terms of majorities, of groups, the one whose election Paul defends is that of the Gentiles. The rejection of the gospel by Israel is considered a fact which requires explanation. We note that Paul submits himself to the empirical value of words when he reserves the word Israel for the visible majority of his fellow-Jews, even though he argues that not all who are from Israel (Jacob) are Israel (9:6).

In the end, then, Paul preaches a gospel that would open the people of God to the Gentiles on the basis of a new way to be righteous before God, but he is left with the Gentiles only. The situation is that of a reform movement which fails to win the majority. Its values and social credibility derive from the main body, the truth of which it claims to represent. As the new movement meets with the resistance of the old, there comes a point when it has to conclude that the mother body will not follow. Inasmuch as its identity and credibility is still attached to the latter, the reform group has to reinforce its claims to the truth in that original tradition, protest its fidelity, and explain in its own terms the failure of the others to join. At a later stage, which probably requires more social visibility and success, the new group will claim to itself the name and all the values of the other. Romans reflects the intermediate stage of such a process. Paul argues for the validity of his gospel inside Israel over against its resistance. He protests his innocence in the break which has already occurred, proclaims his continued attachment to his fellow-Jews, and finally explains the failure of Israel without claiming the title "Israel" for the Gentiles. The Gentile Christians who constitute the majority of the new movement are rejected by Israel but are asked not to reject Israel in return. There are theological reasons for this attitude, of course, but they don't exclude the sociological one that Christians derive their social credibility from their roots in Israel.

Is Romans anti-Jewish? The answer can only be complex. Throughout the epistle Paul speaks of the Jew as a first candidate for the gospel and eventually an elder sibling in a new order which fulfills the one in which he is at home. The Jew is not defined as a non-Christian but as a potential Christian. Conversely, the majority of the Jews who rejected the gospel are not called "the Jews." This implies an open definition of Judaism which allows a Jew to accept the gospel without ceasing to be a Jew. It is not the position of the non-Christian Jews, the position of the majority of Jews, which defines what a Jew is. The acceptance of the gospel makes an authentic Jew, and its rejection a disobedient one, but both are Jews. All this makes it very difficult to determine what Paul's attitude to the Jews might be in modern terms. His disapproval of those Jews who reject the gospel cannot be read as a negative valuation of Jews or Judaism. Only when the position in Judaism he rejects as unfaithful is allowed to become the very definition of Judaism can that negative valuation be carried on to all Jews.

As time went by it was inevitable that the majority of the Jews, who were non-Christian, would provide the definition of what a Jew is. When that happened, however, Judaism was defined among Christians not on its terms but by a position on the law that Paul himself had refused to make into a definition of Judaism.

Paul does acknowledge that the majority of the Jews, which he still calls Israel, have not accepted the gospel. As we suggested above, this is a drastic move. In some respects it might be seen as a positive one. Just as recognizing the failure of a marriage and deciding to separate is sometimes better than continuing to maintain at all costs the illusion of unity, the decision to recognize that Israel would not accept the gospel and to try to make sense of the situation could be seen as a courageous and positive one. One will never know, of course, if the decision to give up on Israel (for the present) could have been avoided or delayed for some time, but the decision was made.

Paul's attitude to non-Christian Israel remains a positive one. He does not give up his hope for them nor his love. He does not deny to the majority of the Jews the use of the name Israel, with all the theological values attached to it. To use the analogy of divorce again, imperfect as it is, Paul does not deny Israel its title to the house to which he claims the Gentiles have been admitted, nor does he transfer the title to the Gentiles. One could of course argue that he had no choice but to submit to the reality that the majority of the Jews cannot be disposessed from its name by theological fiat, but his reserve seems to be theologically grounded. Considering that from Paul's point of view, it is Israel who rejected the Christians, and not the reverse, his attitude towards Israel, conveyed to the Gentile Christians, is a positive one. It could even be thought providential that the problem of Israel's resistance to the gospel received its New Testament formulation, not from a Gentile but from one who was still so profoundly a Jew.

7

The Trial of Jesus as Jewish-Christian Polarization: Blasphemy and Polemic in Mark's Gospel

Charles P. Anderson

The exchange of the historicizing approach to the gospels for the redactional and the literary not only calls attention to the literary and theological dynamics of individual narratives and the gospels as wholes; it also raises new questions about the evangelists' perceptions of and responses to events contemporary with them. It is now widely recognized that the gospel figure of Jesus is at least sometimes a champion of the evangelist's views. One thing is certain—Jesus and the evangelist never disagree![1] J. Louis Martyn may not be far from the truth when he daringly suggests (at least it was daring in 1968) the concept of "doubling"; in some texts in the Fourth Gospel "Jesus" represents both Jesus of Nazareth and the contemporary Christian preacher.[2] This insight probably applies more or less to each of the gospels. In Mark's case, considerable attention has been given to the literary aspects of the gospel as story, particularly to its main characters, identified by T.J. Weeden as Jesus, the Jewish "Establishment," the disciples, and the crowds.[3] Such studies have emphasized what may be called intramural polemics, demonstrating how Mark's Jesus corrects the disciples' misunderstanding by teaching a passion Christology and its corollary of appropriate discipleship.

---

1 Robert C. Tannehill, "The Disciples in Mark: The Function of a Narrative Role," *JR* 57 (1977), 386-405.

2 J.L. Martyn, *History and Theology in the Fourth Gospel* (New York: Harper, 1968), 7-10.

3 T.J. Weeden, *Mark—Traditions in Conflict* (Philadelphia: Fortress, 1971); see also Tannehill, "Disciples"; Ernest Best, "The Role of the Disciples in Mark," *NTS* 23 (1977), 377-401; David J. Hawkin, "The Incomprehension of the Disciples in the Marcan Redaction," *JBL* 91 (1972), 491-500.

In this paper, I shall concentrate on Mark's extra-mural polemic as it is expressed in the narrative of Jesus' trial by the Jewish court. Two points will be emphasized and a question raised. The points are these: (1) The blasphemy charge is of basic importance for Mark's gospel. Not only is it the core of the trial narrative, but it serves a further literary purpose in relating the trial, the climax of Jewish rejection of Jesus' teaching, to the beginnings of Jewish opposition. (2) The "blasphemy against the Holy Spirit" is not the key to Mark's blasphemy motif. On the contrary, it stands apart from all other blasphemy texts in Mark and must be interpreted accordingly. The question is, to what extent does the Jewish trial in Mark reflect events in which Christians found themselves caught up in Mark's own time?

Mark's Understanding of the Blasphemy Charge

The Two Charges

Mark's account of Jesus' trial by the Jewish court contains two charges. The first arises out of testimony concerning a temple saying attributed to Jesus: "And some stood up and bore false witness against him, saying, 'We heard him say, I will destroy this temple that is made with hands, and in three days I will build another, not made with hands'" (14:57-58). No law is alleged to have been broken, nor does Mark have any such law in mind. That misses the point. Kilpatrick is on the wrong track when he connects this saying to the following blasphemy charge, taking his cue from Acts 6:11-14.[4] The key to the passage, as Lloyd Gaston has correctly seen,[5] is in what at first reading seems curious: that as an example of false testimony Mark utilizes a saying which he himself regards as authentic. Apparently, Matthew also found it curious and by clever modifications transformed the false witnesses into true witnesses and their testimony into a validation of his own Christology.[6] In Matthew the saying is not about destroying and building temples, but about the power or authority of Jesus. It is christological rather than ecclesiological.

Mark also, however, has transformed the saying. Gaston is probably correct in maintaining that this saying has come to Mark by way of anti-Christian polemic—as it also has to John and Luke—and that

4 G.D. Kilpatrick, *The Trial of Jesus* (London: Friends of Dr. William's Library, 1953), 9-10.

5 L. Gaston, *No Stone on Another* (Leiden: Brill, 1970), 65-74.

6 Matthew achieves this by changing Mark's *katalysō* into *dynamai katalysai* (see also Matthew's modification of Mark 6:5 in Matt. 13:58), creating a break between this saying and the concept of bearing false witness by eliminating Mark's *epseudomartyroun*, by substituting the number "two" for the Markan "some," thereby suggesting the legitimacy of the witnesses, and finally by omitting the Markan comment that the witnesses did not agree even on this saying.

Mark has put this negative charge to positive use. Mark's major change was the addition of the word pair *cheiropoiētos/acheiropoiētos* (made with hands/not made with hands), a well-known motif in early Christian teaching concerning the temple theme.[7] A corollary of this addition is the Christian distinction between temples—between the one in Jerusalem and the eschatological community. The form of the saying in 15:29, placed on the lips of mockers, "You destroyer and three-day rebuilder of the temple," shows that Mark is aware that in anti-Christian polemic this distinction is not made. The same is true in John 2:20. Both Mark and John naturally consider the anti-Christian interpretation a misunderstanding. To accuse Jesus on the basis of a misunderstanding of one of his sayings could certainly be regarded by Mark as bearing false witness.[8]

However, it is not the temple saying that proves decisive in Jesus' trial, but the other charge: "And the high priest tore his mantle, and said, 'Why do we still need witnesses? You have heard his blasphemy. What is your decision?' And they all condemned him as deserving death" (14:63-64). On the grounds that Jesus has blasphemed during the trial itself, the court convicts and sentences him. Matthew makes only stylistic changes to this passage; in essence he agrees with Mark. On the other hand, neither Luke nor John mentions either charge in their respective narratives, though both charges or reasonable facsimiles surface elsewhere in their writings.[9]

Blasphemy in Mark

The term "blasphemy" appears seven times in Mark, four in verbal and three in substantive form.[10] Three instances are in the pericope of the unforgivable sin (3:28-30). Another belongs to a list of defilements arising out of the heart of man (7:22; translated "slander" in *RSV* and *NEB*). The fifth refers to taunts directed at Jesus on the cross (15:29; they "derided" him, *RSV*). In the remaining two examples, the word is applied by Jewish leaders to statements of Jesus, to his forgiveness of the paralytic's sins (2:7), and to his confession of his own identity during the trial (14:64). Among these texts, blasphemy has an ex-

7 Gaston, *No Stone*, 63.

8 John Donahue traces the false witness motif to a "pre-Markan tradition of the suffering Just One, directly influenced by the psalms: 'for unjust witnesses have risen against me and their injustice is false' (Ps. 27:12);'Unjust witnesses rise up; they ask me of things that I know not' (Ps. 35:11)." See "Temple, Trial and Royal Christology," in Werner H. Kelber, ed., *The Passion in Mark, Studies in Mark 14-16* (Philadelphia: Fortress, 1976), 51-79, especially 67. Donahue sees this saying as a culmination of "the anti-Jerusalem and anti-Temple polemic which runs through the Gospel."

9 Acts 6:11-14; John 2:19-21; 10:33-36.

10 Verbal: 2:7; 3:28; 3:29; 15:29; Substantive: 3:28; 7:22; 14:64. Mark does not indicate any conceptual distinction between the two forms.

pressed object in only two cases. In 3:29 it is the Holy Sprit; in 15:29 it is Jesus. It is obvious that in 2:7 and 14:64 the implied object is God. The three remaining cases seem to be of a different order. Even if "God" or "divine things" is still the implied object, and that is not certain, the seriousness of the offence is much less than in 2:7, 3:29, and 14:64. That is certainly the case with the two usages in 3:28, where "blasphemies" stands in contrast to the unforgivable blasphemy against the Holy Spirit. The same is true in 7:22 where "blasphemy" is one vice among others which vulgarize (*koinounta*) man, or render him impure. These two passages (3:28; 7:22) may therefore be set aside as not directly relevant to the present inquiry. The important texts are those where either God, the Holy Spirit, or Jesus is the object of blasphemy and where blasphemy is taken with utmost seriousness.[11]

(1) Jesus' Forgiveness of the Paralytic's Sins (2:1-12)

The significance of this pericope in the collection of conflict stories culminating in the determination of Jesus' enemies to destroy him is well known. Perhaps less widely recognized is its importance in introducing the blasphemy motif in Mark and, in turn, Mark's artful integration of that motif with the beginning and the climax of Jewish polemic against Jesus' teaching. In 1:14-3:6, following the prologue, Mark sets the stage for the rest of his gospel. In chapter 1 he tells of Jesus' mission to Galilee, his healings, exorcisms, and teaching. With the understandable exception of the unclean spirits, everyone's response is positive. The first disciples abandon vocational and kinship commitments to follow Jesus. His *didachē*, unlike that of the scribes, is recognized as authoritative in the Capernaum synagogue. People come seeking him from "everywhere" (1:37, 45). But in chapter 2 a new note is introduced: the positive response, while continued, is now joined by a negative one on the part of the scribes and Pharisees and Herodians (2:6-7; 16, 24; 3:2, 6). The community is now shown to be divided in its assessment of Jesus' *didachē*. Thus, early in the gospel, Mark exhibits opposing responses to Jesus. The one leads to the formation of a body of disciples authorized to preach and to exorcise in his name (6:7-13).[12] The other leads to Jesus' death. Mark has no interest in demonstrating a chronological relationship between the opposing responses but simply that the two exist.

Growing out of the negative response to Jesus is a conspiracy motif, which emerges fully in 3:1-6. Noteworthy are the following points: (1) Prior to any word or act of Jesus, his opponents are watching

11 For a broader treatment of blasphemy, see Beyer's article in *TDNT* 1, 621ff.

12 It is true that the disciples are a more complex set of characters than is here suggested; my point is only that they are representatives of those who follow Jesus. Their dullness and faithlessness are other matters. See Robert C. Tannehill, "Disciples." See also Thomas L. Budesheim, "Jesus and the Disciples in Conflict with Judaism," *ZNW* 62 (1971), 190-209.

him, or even lying in wait for him,[13] to see if he will violate the Sabbath by healing a withered hand.[14] (2) Their purpose is to "accuse him," i.e., in a court of law (*katēgorēsōsin autou*).[15] Despite the fact that Mark does not mention Sabbath healing in Jesus' trial, it is clear that this passage points forward to the trial narrative. In the Fourth Gospel also, breaking the Sabbath, like the blasphemy of making Jesus equal with God, is cause for seeking Jesus' death (5:18; 10:33, 36). (3) Those who oppose Jesus have hardened hearts. Mark may think of their hardness of heart as explaining why they reject one who brings good news and who heals, thereby denying themselves his benefits.[16] (4) Pharisees who had been present plot with the Herodians against Jesus, with the intention of killing him (*auton apolesōsin*).

Having established his conspiracy motif, Mark does not return to it until 8:31. From then on it is never far from the surface (10:33-34; 11:18; 12:13; 14:1, 10-11, 43-45) and leads directly to the Sanhedrin trial and beyond it to the trial before Pilate and on to the crucifixion. Mark leaves no doubt that Jesus' death was due to a plot by the Jewish leaders, who were involved at every stage of opposition to Jesus.

Now, to return to the blasphemy motif. Blasphemy is the first charge (though as yet unspoken) made against Jesus by his opponents in Mark. Such an emphatic position is hardly fortuitous. Further, as the first member of the conflict stories, it stands in special relation to the last member, where Jesus' death is plotted. The association of blasphemy and conspiracy is thus established in that early portion of the gospel where the opposing responses to Jesus are also laid out. What is forgiveness of sins to the one is blasphemy to the other. Finally, the series—opposition, charge of blasphemy, conspiracy to kill Jesus—points forward to the trial, where once again, in concert, they prove to be the decisive motifs. From a thematic perspective, therefore, the blasphemy motif introduced in 2:7 is not only significant; in Mark's gospel it is indispensable. It ties together other essential motifs in Mark and provides the author with a conceptual tool which will later be employed skillfully and powerfully as he brings to a climax his treatment of anti-Christian polemic.

(2) The Blasphemy Against the Holy Spirit (3:29-30)

The second mention of blasphemy in Mark is also found in a polemical context. In response to the scribes' accusation that he exorcises by the power of Beelzebul, by whom he is possessed, Mark has Jesus first question the logic involved with three sayings concerning divisions—a

---

13 For this meaning of *paratēreō*, see BAG, *ad loc.*

14 Whether in fact healing by word on the Sabbath was not permitted is another matter. See David Flusser, *Jesus* (New York: Herder and Herder, 1969), 50.

15 BAG, *ad loc.*

16 A similar motif is found in 6:1-6a. See E. Graesser, "Jesus in Nazareth (Mark vi. 1-61): Notes on the Redaction and Theology of St. Mark," *NTS* 16 (1969-70), 1-23.

divided kingdom cannot stand, nor a divided house, nor, obviously, a divided Satan. Mark places next the saying about plundering the strong man's house, which presupposes a different logic from the preceding sayings, but which Mark sees as applicable to the fall of Satan's kingdom. Finally, the logion involving the unforgivable sin caps the series, ending with Mark's pointer back to the beginning accusation: "Truly I say to you, all sins will be forgiven the sons of men, and whatever blasphemies they utter; but whoever blasphemes against the Holy Spirit never has forgiveness, but is guilty of an eternal sin—for they had said, 'He has an unclean spirit'" (3:28-30).

The importance of this saying to Mark is indicated by the introductory asseveration, *Amēn legō hymin*.[17] The subject, as in our first pericope, 2:7, is the forgiveness of sins, but in this case concentrates on a particular type of sin.

Mark's rough Greek (*hosa*, neuter, properly refers to *hamartēmata*, not *blasphēmiai*, feminine)[18] need not detain us,[19] nor deflect our attention from the main issue, which is the one exception to the rule of universal forgiveness of sins. An interpretation of this text must take into account the Q version of the saying in which a sharp distinction is drawn between a word spoken against the Son of Man and blasphemy against the Holy Spirit (Matt. 12:32; Luke 12:10). In all three gospels a two-part form is employed in which the second part is a contrast to the first. In Luke, the first part of the saying affirms forgiveness of anyone who speaks against the Son of Man; the second denies it to one who blasphemes the Spirit. Luke makes no reference to the Markan sins and blasphemies which will be forgiven the sons of men. In Matthew, both points are made, each in a two part form: "Therefore, I tell you, every sin and blasphemy will be forgiven men, but the blasphemy against the Spirit will not be forgiven. And whoever says a word against the Son of man will be forgiven; but whoever speaks against the Holy Spirit will not be forgiven, either in this age or in the age to come" (12:31-32). Only Mark directly relates the saying to the Beelzebul pericope (v. 30; cf. v. 22), though in order he is followed by Matthew. Luke indicates no connection at all between the unforgivable sin and Beelzebul.

The question is, does Mark agree or disagree with the position taken by Matthew and Luke? Does he believe that verbal abuse of the Son of Man is forgivable? According to Burkill, "In St. Mark's view any hostile expression of *apistia*—disbelief in Jesus as Messiah, the Son of God and the Son of Man—constitutes an instance of *blasphēmia*."[20]

---

17 V. Taylor, *The Gospel According to Mark* (London: Macmillan, 1959), 242.

18 *Hamartia* in 2:5; *hamartēmata* in 3:28.

19 Taylor, *Mark*, 242ff.

20 T.A. Burkill, "Blasphemy: St. Mark's Gospel as Damnation History," in Jacob Neusner, ed., *Christianity, Judaism and Other Greco-Roman Cults: Studies for Morton Smith at Sixty*, Part 1 (Leiden: Brill, 1975), 55-74, here 55-56. Donald Juel, *Messiah and Temple* (Missoula: Scholars Press, 1977), 103, takes much the same line.

Since Jesus possesses the Spirit (1:10), to speak a word against Jesus is to blaspheme the Spirit. Burkill's theory of reciprocity holds that, in Mark's view, to accuse Jesus of blasphemy is to blaspheme, not in the weaker sense of 7:22, but in the stronger sense of 3:29. Thus Burkill interprets the trial and the paralytic pericopes in the light of his understanding of 3:29, and concludes that Mark's gospel is really bad news for the Jewish leaders. In attributing blasphemy to Jesus, they unwittingly commit the unpardonable sin.

Burkill's interpretation might be more convincing if he had explained how Matthew and Luke, who share and intensify Mark's conception of the close relationship between the Spirit and Jesus (e.g., Matt. 1:18, 20; 3:16; Luke 1:35; 3:22; 23:46), nevertheless explicitly deny that a word against Jesus is the blasphemy against the Spirit. To assume a simple identification between the Spirit and Jesus in Mark is unwarranted, and I suggest that Mark does not disagree with the other synoptists on this point. Mark's silence regarding the consequences for salvation of verbal attacks against Jesus is hardly evidence in itself for one position or the other. However, that very silence may well have precipitated the need for both Matthew and Luke to include the clarifying saying of Q.

There are two separate issues here—the meaning of the logion in itself[21] and the use made of it by Mark. The point of the logion derives from an attack on the Holy Spirit. But the saying does not indicate what constitutes such an attack, except that it must be something quite extraordinary since it is different from all other "blasphemies and sins." By assigning it the Beelzebul setting Mark indicates his interpretation of the saying, which seems to be along these lines: the unforgivable sin is the confusion or reversal of the symbols of good and evil.[22] To identify the Holy Spirit as Beelzebul or the prince of demons is to commit an unparalleled error regarding ultimate matters. It demonstrates the lack of the valuating and ordering ability necessary to recognize right and wrong, truth and error, good and evil. It shows that one's true end is lost to view. This is much more serious than losing the way. A path can be found again, but if the goal has become a non-goal, or a non-goal the goal, no path is sufficient. To blaspheme Jesus shows that one is not on the right path. But to blaspheme the Spirit indicates that most fearsome, pathological, and destructive of all human conditions where the goal itself is confused. For Mark, that condition stands apart from all others.

My conclusion, therefore, is that the paralytic pericope and the unforgivable sin pericope deal with different issues. The latter goes beyond the Jewish-Christian controversy, even though the two may

21 M. Eugene Boring argues that the saying is a prophetic oracle directed at detractors of Christian prophets. "How May We Identify Oracles of Christian Prophets in the Synoptic Tradition? Mark 3:28-29 as a Test Case," *JBL* 91 (1972), 501-21.

22 T.W. Manson, *The Sayings of Jesus* (London: SCM, 1949), 110.

intersect at points. The typical Jewish anti-Christian polemic is expressed in 2:7. It would be academic to ask whether Mark thought that blasphemy there was forgivable, since it is Jesus who is accused, and that falsely. Nevertheless, I think it likely that if asked whether the accusation itself is forgivable, Mark would reply, "Of course it is forgivable. See my book on this, e.g., 3:28 and 7:22."

(3) The Sanhedrin Trial (14:61-64)

The accusation found in 1:7 is repeated in the trial. Here, however, it is portrayed unmistakably as the official or normative Jewish assessment, not just of Jesus' claim to forgive sins, but of his identity. I say "official or normative" not only because of the broad representation in the trial of Jewish leadership,[23] but also because of the trial format itself. Whereas John and Luke envisage what is best called a preliminary hearing (see Appendix), there can be no doubt that Mark and, following him, Matthew intend their readers to conceive of a trial in a Jewish court. Mark calls it a sanhedrin,[24] portrays the High Priest as its presiding officer, includes witnesses and their testimony, has a decision called for and a judgment delivered. How better to demonstrate the decisive issue between Jews and Christian than to bring them into a trial, indeed to make them emerge as the core of the trial?

It is also important to recognize the basis of this normative assessment. Together, the High Priest's question and Jesus' affirmative reply constitute a Christological confession,[25] containing the two basic Christological titles in Mark: Christ and Son of the Blessed, i.e., Son of God. The interpretive Son of Man, used by Mark in the passion predictions to give a correct view of the title "Christ," has that same function here.[26] Further, the reply contains other Christian affirmations concerning Jesus' enthronement and parousia. The *egō eimi* has nothing to do with Exod. 3:14, as Haenchen recognizes (against Stauffer),[27] but is simply a

23 High Priest, chief priests, elders, scribes. But why are the Pharisees (and Herodians) not included? On this see Michael J. Cook, *Mark's Treatment of the Jewish Leaders,* (Leiden: Brill, 1978), who finds the solution in Mark's sources.

24 See Ellis Rivkin, "Beth Din, Boule, Sanhedrin: A Tragedy of Errors," *HUCA* 46 (1975), 181-99. Rivkin convincingly argues that sanhedrins were called by the high priests as required to deal with matters of political concern. These sanhedrins, as political instruments of the Romans, were designed to facilitate Roman rule. They are quite distinct from the Beth Din which was an instrument of dual-law Judaism. A contributing factor to the confusion of the two is the misleading title given to Mishna Sanhedrin which is about the Beth Din, not sanhedrins under the prefects or procurators and high priests.

25 See Vernon H. Neufeld, *The Earliest Christian Confessions* (Leiden: Brill, 1963), 113-17. Neufeld concludes that "the basic *homologia* in the synoptic gospels is *Iēsous estin ho Christos,* followed by *Iēsous estin ho huios tou theou*" (117). The first was applied during Jesus' lifetime, the second by the early church (142-43).

26 Norman Perrin, "The Christology of Mark; A Study in Methodology," *JR* 51 (1971), 173-87, see 179, n. 12.

27 Ernst Haenchen, *Der Weg Jesu* (Berlin: Topelmann, 1966), 511. John R. Donahue, *Are You the Christ?* (Missoula: Scholars Press, 1973), 92-93, may be correct in finding here a "formula of revelation or identification" (cf. Mark 6:50; 13:6).

natural part of the dialogue with the High Priest, so that out of it emerges a model Christian confession. One could almost find here the core of a baptismal liturgy in which the candidate is asked, "Do you believe in Jesus, the Son of God?" and answers, "I do." The following Son of Man saying is not part of the formula, but is placed in conjunction with it, and derived ultimately from Dan. 7:13 and Ps. 110:1.[28]

A further point of interest is the paradigmatic nature of Jesus' confession, especially in the context of a gospel where discipleship is urged in terms strongly suggesting imitation (8:34-38; 10:43-44). Jesus now practises what he preached in 13:9-11, where he told his disciples that they would be delivered up to councils (*synedria*) and would stand before governors and kings to bear witness before them (or, against them).[29] In Jesus as confessor, Mark presents a model for disciples to follow. Thus are welded into a single unit the christological and discipleship themes which are found in close conjunction in the three passion predictions (8:31-9:1; 9:30-37; 10:32-45).[30] In making his confession, Jesus is both teacher and disciple. This text is the high point of instruction for Christian discipleship.

The difference in type between the temple saying charge and the blasphemy charge should not be overlooked. While the first relates primarily to an act of Jesus, albeit future, the second concerns not a deed but Jesus' identity. That is, from Mark's point of view, Jesus is accused, convicted, and sentenced for being who he is. Taken as an accurate statement of fact, this passage has posed insuperable problems.[31] But taken as a dramatic creation it makes eminent sense. Jesus' confession is a necessary element in the trial as determined by Mark's purpose. It expresses the *Christian* normative statement regarding Jesus. Likewise, the court's judgment represents the *Jewish* normative statement regarding Jesus, or rather, regarding the Christian confession of Jesus as Christ and Son of God. In this way Mark makes clear the major issues dividing the normative Jewish and Christian teachings and attitudes. For him, the typical response of Jewish authorities toward the gospel is to brand its basic premise blasphemous.

In his article, "Good News is No News," Jonathan Smith draws on Morton Smith's notion that in Graeco-Roman aretalogies, the terms magician, divine man, and son of God relate to a single figure, but from three different perspectives, that of the enemies, the "sceptical but

---

28 See Norman Perrin, *Rediscovering the Teaching of Jesus* (London: SCM, 1967), 173ff.; Barnabas Lindars, *New Testament Apologetic* (London: SCM, 1961), 48-49.

29 Neufeld, *Confessions*, 31, sees a close relation between Pilate's question and that of the High Priest; in responding to both, Jesus makes the "good confession" (cf. 1 Tim. 6:13).

30 As Perrin points out, in those three texts "Mark is presenting his own passion-oriented Christology, using Son of Man, and then drawing out the consequences for Christian discipleship. . . ." "Christology," 179.

31 See Juel, *Messiah*, 2ff., 59ff.

reverent admirers," and the believers.[32] Even though the terminology does not apply to Mark, and the concept of the "sceptical but reverent believers" must be substantially modified,[33] the pattern has some significance for Mark, particularly when one considers the overlap between magic and blasphemy. Both transgress well recognized limits of human activity and in fact were considered illegal in their respective settings and could entail the death sentence.[34] Both involve speech which is deemed capable of unleashing dangerous power on the community. The concept of magician could almost be substituted for that of blasphemer in the Markan trial narrative. However, that would greatly weaken the contrast Mark wishes to make, and very likely would not strike the same responsive note in his community. The term blasphemy belongs to the Jewish anti-Christian polemical tradition, just as the temple saying does, and Mark is not free to exchange either for something else, given his goals.

Before summarizing this section of the paper, we shall briefly consider the only passage in Mark where Jesus is the object of blasphemy, 15:29.

(4) The Derision of Jesus on the Cross (15:29)

In 15:29, some unidentified observers of the crucified Jesus blaspheme him. Translators generally if not universally understand the verb here in its weaker sense, "They derided him." That puts this text together with 3:28 and 7:22 and sets it apart from 2:7; 3:29; 14:64. Blasphemy here is not a rejection of God or the Holy Spirit, but a ridiculing of a person. The following verse supports this view: "In a similar way the chief priests and scribes made fun of [him] . . . ." Further, within verse 29 itself, Mark demonstrates this weaker meaning by the epexegetical "wagging their heads" and "Aha, the destroyer of the sanctuary and the three-day builder." Their blasphemy consists in this action and these words. Like the following *empaizontes*, blasphemy here signifies mockery or making fun of Jesus.

Summary and Conclusions

In Mark's gospel, blasphemy has at least two significantly distinct nuances. The one points to what for Mark is the most hopeless religious

32 In Neusner, *Christianity, Judaism,* 21-38. See also Morton Smith, *Clement of Alexandria and a Secret Gospel of Mark* (Cambridge: Harvard University Press, 1973), 220-21. Smith sees in Mark 3:28f. evidence that Jesus was considered a magician in his own lifetime, and that his followers have since answered that charge by identifying the spirit by which he heals as the Holy Spirit (339).

33 On this see Weeden, *Traditions*; also "The Heresy that Necessitated Mark's Gospel," *ZNW* 59 (1968), 145-58; Tannehill; Hawkin.

34 On the illegality of magic, see Morton Smith, *Clement,* 220.

perspective possible in which good and evil are wrongly identified. The unforgivable sin is to make the spirit of God into the spirit of Satan. There exists no path to salvation for those who cannot even identify the goal. The other obvious meaning of blasphemy in Mark's gospel does not presuppose that confusion of the symbols of good and evil. Here the object may be persons, such as Jesus in 15:29, or perhaps even God in 3:28 and 7:22. But there is no attack on the traditional symbol system itself.[35] Even though they are not treated with due respect by word and action, the ultimate religious symbols remain intact along with their meanings and their inter-relationships. There is no question but that these blasphemies are forgivable in Mark's view, just as they are in Matthew's and Luke's.

To which category do 2:7 and 14:64 belong? Perhaps they constitute a separate class, since they alone are applied to Jesus as subject. However, in Mark's perspective, the world view from which they spring is that of the Jewish "establishment." How does Mark think this differs from the Christian? Apart from practical aspects such as the Sabbath and purity laws, the fundamental distinction concerns the evaluation of Jesus. In this, Mark and John are not far apart. For both, the issue has crystalized around the term "Son of God" and its implications. This is fairly clear in John, whose only use of the term "blasphemy" is in connection with Jesus' proclamation "I and the Father are one" (10:30; cf. 10:33, 36). In Jewish eyes, the status attributed to Jesus by the Christians was indistinguishable from that of God himself. Therefore the Christian confession was perceived as a breach of the basic Jewish premise of monotheism. What to one is the wisdom of God is to the other blasphemy against God.[36] In this context, blasphemy has something of *hybris* in it—it points to human transgression against divine rights. But it presupposes the one God of Judaism whose rights are being violated. This has nothing to do either with cursing God or with blaspheming against the Holy Spirit.[37] To my knowledge, cursing God

35 D.R.A. Hare, *The Theme of Jewish Persecution in the Gospel According to St. Matthew* (Cambridge: Cambridge University Press, 1967), slightly confuses the issue when he writes, "Jewish symbols of the first rank were Torah, Temple and Holy City; not far behind were the purity and food laws, circumcision and Sabbath .... Christians subordinated all symbols to the central symbol of their faith, the Christ" (4-5). What is not considered here is the fact that above all these symbols in both Judaism and Christianity is the supreme symbol or concept, "God." The Torah, Temple, Holy City, and Christ all derive their symbolic power from a meaning complex shared by both religions. The Jewish/Christian conflict thus concerns the relation of these secondary symbols to the primary symbol. Mark 3:22-30 raises this issue, but the pericope itself is concerned with an attack on the primary symbol.

36 Paul states the issue somewhat differently: "We preach Christ crucified, a stumbling block to Jews and folly to Gentiles" (1 Cor. 1:23).

37 Despite Lev. 24:10-12, Rabbinic Judaism distinguishes between using abusive language against God and cursing God, according to Solomon Zeitlin, *Who Crucified Jesus?* (New York: Bloch, 1964), 53. He refers there to Talmud Keritot 7 (a man cannot be executed for using abusive language against God, though God may cause his premature death) and, in contrast, to *Sanh.* 7:5 ("cursing God by the name of God" made one liable to capital punishment).

never appears as a Jewish accusation against Christians, while blasphemy against the Holy Spirit is, I suspect, exclusively a Christian, not a Jewish formulation, as is the cursing of Jesus (1 Cor. 12:3).[38] The issue in Mark 2:7 and 14:64 is *Jewish* reaction to Christian preaching. In 3:29 it is *Christian* reaction to a confusion of the symbols of good and evil. The two issues are quite different.

Blasphemy, therefore, expresses both Jewish and Christian viewpoints in Mark. The Jews (erroneously, for Mark) employ the term against Christians for proclaiming forgiveness of sins in Jesus, the Son of God. The Jews understandably think the Christians are denying the oneness of God. Blasphemy also identifies the unforgivable sin. But there is no warrant for confusing these two usages in Mark's gospel. Mark neither explicitly nor implicitly accuses the Jews of the unforgivable sin for rejecting Jesus. Indeed, despite the fact that the disciples and the Jewish leaders represent those who follow and those who consciously choose not to follow Jesus but rather to oppose him, their difference is one of degree. They are not appropriate symbols of good and evil. Both exhibit *apistia.*

My conclusion, therefore, is that in 2:7 and 14:64 we find a third and distinctive use of blasphemy. Here Mark employs it to represent his understanding of Jewish assessment of Christian missionary preaching. By introducing Jewish hostility to Jesus with this concept and again employing it as the key charge in the trial narrative, Mark binds these two passages together. What was begun in 2:7 reaches its climax in 14:64. At first unspoken, at the end it becomes the proclaimed unanimous verdict of Jewish officials. While the Roman trial and the crucifixion remain to be narrated, Jesus' fate is definitively decided by the Jewish court. The Roman trial, as far as factors normally constituting a trial are concerned, is hardly a trial at all. Pilate does not arrive at a valid decision on the basis of evidence, but merely carries out the will of the Jewish court. The decisive judgment takes place in the Jewish trial narrative.

The Trials of Jesus and Other Christians

We have now dealt with the blasphemy accusation as Mark's characterization of Jewish anti-Christian polemic. The remaining question is whether Mark's trial narrative is concerned only with the *idea* of Jewish rejection of the Christian way or if there is a further dimension to be discovered in it.

The proper exploration of this question involves inquiring about the functions of and the reasons for trial stories in early Christian literature. Space permits only a brief treatment here.

38 According to Origen, cursing Jesus was an initiatory or admission requirement among the Ophites. *Contra Celsum* 6:28; *Catena fragm.47 in 1 Cor. 12:3* (ref. in Henry Chadwick's translation of *Contra Celsum,* 344 n. 2).

It seems probable that trial stories made their appearance at a particular stage in the development of early Christianity. Paul nowhere reveals knowledge of a narrative of a trial either of Jesus or of Christians, nor of the charges mentioned in either the Jewish or the Roman trials in any of the gospels. Why then are such stories involving both Jesus and Christian missionaries found in the gospels and Acts, and why are they well integrated into their literary contexts? Why was the church not content to follow the path taken by Paul of concentrating on preaching the crucified and resurrected Messiah? Even an emphasis on Jesus' teaching, his healings and other wonders of revelation and salvation does not necessitate trial stories. What did they contribute to early Christian life?

That Mark has created the Jewish trial scene is supported by overwhelming evidence.[39] Various motifs have been blended into this narrative, some distinctively Markan,[40] some not. The latter are shared with John, who works these motifs into non-trial but still polemical scenes, and with Luke, who works them into the trial of Stephen, but not into his passion narrative. It seems that here as elsewhere in the gospels and Acts the motifs were more important than the settings. All this points to a large measure of literary freedom in the early church concerning the Jewish trial of Jesus. Even if we assume a "tradition" of an actual trial or hearing behind Mark's narrative, we still have to ask why Mark has chosen to include that "tradition" and work it into his gospel in the particular way that he has. The obvious answer is that Christians were now facing trials themselves.

That explanation, which is hardly novel, nevertheless may help to place in proper perspective several factors relating to the trial narrative in Mark. We have already observed the essential place given it in this gospel, especially in relation to the charge of blasphemy. Jesus' trial and death have hovered behind the scenes since the first conflict stories, emerging at important points into explicit expression. The importance of the trial is due not just to the fact that it polarizes the Christian and the Jewish ways and illustrates Jewish rejection of the gospel.[41] Mark also makes plain that the trial and its consequences are the result of Jewish hostility to Christian missionizing.[42] The trial is part of a larger

39 See Donahue, "Temple," and Juel, *Messiah*.

40 Norman Perrin, "Towards an Interpretation of the Gospel of Mark," in Hans Dieter Betz, ed., *Christology and a Modern Pilgrimage, A Discussion with Norman Perrin* (Claremont, 1971), 1-52. Perrin identifies these as "the Messianic secret, the reinterpretation of the Son of God Christology, and the misunderstanding of the disciples . . . ." (32).

41 Juel, *Messiah,* correctly emphasizes the rejection motif (and its counterpart, vindication) in the trial narrative (56-57, 67 and elsewhere), but I cannot agree when he claims "the trial has no causal relationship to the trial before Pilate" (67). In general, however, his study is one of the better treatments to date of the Markan trial.

42 As Burkill points out in "Blasphemy," 57-58, Mark has more than one causational theory. The death of Jesus has both divine and human causes. See also his book, *New Light on the Earliest Gospel* (Ithaca: Cornell University Press, 1972), 177.

pattern: Christian preaching and healing, positive response to them as illustrated in the gathering of disciples, negative response as evidenced in hostility and conspiracy, Jewish trial, Roman trial, and Roman punishment. Every element in the series is necessary in Mark's gospel, but without the Jewish trial, Roman involvement is unexplained and the earlier negative response is of no consequence. To take the Jewish trial out of Mark's gospel therefore would remove the one element which explains all the antagonism facing the Christian mission, and would leave the community in peace.

Second, the statement put in Jesus' mouth by Mark can only be understood as a Christian confession. The scene created by Mark surely reflects his conception of events prophesied in 13:9 and being fulfilled in his own time. The accused Jesus is put in a position where he must openly declare himself regarding the Christian *homologia.* Other charges do not require an answer and, in fulfilment of Isa. 53:7 and Ps. 38:13-16, the accused is silent. No evidence of wrong-doing is turned up by the court—this point is reiterated by Pilate in the Roman trial (15:14). But the accused cannot remain unresponsive to the question, "Do you believe that Jesus is the Christ, the Son of God?" There is no way out; the accused must either deny the confession as Peter explicitly does (14:68-72), making himself vulnerable to the Son of Man's denial of himself at the final judgment (8:38), or he must "hold fast the confession" (Heb. 4:14), risking his life now but saving it for eternity. Naturally, in Mark's narrative Jesus makes "the good confession" (1 Tim. 5:12-13). The Jewish authorities are now certain that the accused is guilty of being a Christian. Mark's Jewish trial narrative therefore plays a role similar to John 9:1-34 in identifying Christians.[43] There is a difference, however. In John the narrative ends in the prospective Christian's excommunication from the synagogue and in his confession of faith. In Mark the trial leads to the Roman court.

Third, as just indicated, the Jewish trial is a bridge to the Roman trial. It stands between the missionary activity of Jesus and his disciples and the Roman trial and execution of Jesus. It is in the Roman court where final decisions are made by those with power to execute. All four gospels make this point. Further, they all portray Jewish leaders as accusers in the Roman court and the accusations as unrelated (with the minor exception of Luke 23:2, "saying that he himself is Christ a king") to the previous trial or hearing. In Mark's case, a clear distinction is made between the two trials. The first serves positively to identify the individual as a Christian, the second to secure a condemnation by the proper authorities.

Fourth, Mark's account of the Roman trial of Jesus is at least as consistent with what little is known of later Christian trials as with what little is known of Jesus' trial. Consider Mark's picture of the legal basis

43 Martyn, *History and Theology.*

of Jesus' conviction. It is true that it can be explained in terms of the latitude allowed to proconsuls, legates, and prefects or procurators within the well-recognized principles of *cognitio* and *coercitio.*[44] However, while Mark apparently knows that Jesus in fact was executed for a political crime (15:26), in the trial scene itself Pilate does not find Jesus guilty of that or any other crime. The sole factors in Pilate's decision against Jesus are the influence of his accusers and the public hostility which they have stirred up (15:15). That pattern of accusers plus public hostility is well known from accounts of later Roman persecutions of Christians.[45] This feature of the Roman trial may reflect events contemporary to Mark or in the recent past. Tradition has been thoroughly reworked into a "relevant" narrative.

Fifth, some of Mark's injunctions to secrecy may be best understood in relation to a setting of persecution.[46] Public identification of Christian teachers and healers was all too easy and special precautions were necessary in the troubled times in which Mark writes. Of course, secrecy was not to be confused with denial. If betrayed and called to account, every Christian was required to make an open confession of his faith. However, while its shadow falls over this whole gospel (e.g., see 4:17b; 8:34), martyrdom is not a cultic requirement or even an ideal for Mark. Therefore, one should not take unnecessary risks.

Finally, it is well established that the passion narratives reveal increasingly a shift of blame for Jesus' death from the Romans to the Jews, and that this movement is to be seen already in Mark.[47] Suggested motives for the shift include the necessity of not antagonizing the Romans and the worsening of relations between Jews and Christians. Both points are probably true as far as they go. But we need to divest ourselves even more from presuppositions stemming from seeing these accounts primarily as dealing with the trial of Jesus, and see them also—perhaps especially—in relation to the conditions faced by Christians vis-à-vis their neighbours and the Roman government. At present, redactional analysis of Mark's trial stories is mostly concerned

44 See A.N. Sherwin-White, *Roman Society and Roman Law in the New Testament* (Oxford, 1963), 1-23.

45 Leon Hardy Canfield, *The Early Persecutions of Christians* (New York: Columbia University Press, 1913); W.H.C. Frend, *Martyrdom and Persecution in the Early Church* (New York: New York University Press, 1967).

46 Especially those injunctions directed at people who are exorcized of demons (or the demons themselves, 1:34; 3:12). Perhaps these are considered unstable people who might unintentionally betray the Christian healer. However, see 5:1-20, where the demoniac himself becomes a missionary—under command of the Lord. In 1:44 the leper is told not to speak to anyone—but the leper disobeys (see also 7:36) and as a result the healer has to avoid the urban areas. Those who witness the raising of the 12 year old are also warned not to speak of it (5:43). There are other indications in Mark of the missionary-healer's desire for a low profile (e.g., 7:24; 8:26), though some of these may be explained as withdrawal for rest (6:31; 7:24; 9:30). See Howard Clark Kee, *Community of the New Age, Studies in Mark's Gospel* (Philadelphia: Westminster, 1977), 169-71.

47 Paul Winter, *On the Trial of Jesus* (Berlin: de Gruyter, 1961).

with theological questions. What is now needed is a full-scale examination of the trial narratives and other relevant portions of early Christian literature in relation to the social conditions in which Christians found themselves.[48] We need to construct a much fuller picture of Mark's—and the other evangelists'—understanding of Christian-Roman relations. Mark is not concerned just with the true believers, the heretics, and the Jewish critics. He is fighting not on two but on three fronts, even though the third of necessity must be treated with some delicacy.

Related to the question of the historical setting of Mark's gospel is his portrait of Jesus. Mark's Jesus has a dual character, but the reason is not that Mark unsuccessfully tries to combine the post-resurrection proclamation with the traditions of an historical Jesus, as Wrede thought. Rather, it is to be found in the fact that Jesus has to play two different roles in Mark's gospel: one as the redeemer and Lord of the community and another as its model of discipleship. Jesus represents both the one who "gives his life as a ransom for many" (10:45) and those who stand before governors and kings and are brought to trial (13:9). Whereas Luke finds his heroes among the first generation of Christians (Peter, Stephen, Paul), Mark unequivocally looks to Jesus. None of the disciples is displayed as an example of faith, though I agree with Best and Tannehill[49] that they are not as negatively presented as Weeden thinks. While they are not models of faith, still there is hope for their salvation.

Since Jesus has two roles to play, it is not surprising that in the Jewish trial scene features of both the redemptive and the heroic appear in the persecuted Messiah/Son of God/Son of Man. Jesus' confession, however, is strictly heroic. This is obvious not only from its content but also from its relation to the Petrine denial, into which the trial scene is sandwiched. Thus Mark presents in the closest possible relationship two ways of facing persecution. Peter's way calls to mind the interpretation of the parable of the sower: "And these in like manner are the ones sown upon rocky ground, who, when they hear the word, immediately receive it with joy; and they have no root in themselves, but endure for awhile; then, when tribulation or persecution arises on account of the word, immediately they fall away" (4:16-17). Peter is the prime example in Mark's gospel of the disciple who falls away. While all the disciples desert Jesus, it is only Peter who actually verbally denies Jesus. Yet he is at the same time one of the first two to follow Jesus (1:16-17). Is it mere chance that in the interpretation of the parable, the seed which springs up so rapidly falls *epi ta petrōdē,* "upon

48 Kee makes an admirable beginning in this direction, as far as the gospel as a whole is concerned, though his concern is not particularly with the conditions imposed by persecution, nor does his book deal in detail with the trial narratives. See also Ernest Best, *The Temptation and the Passion* (Cambridge: Cambridge University Press, 1965), chap. 8.

49 See notes 1 and 3 above.

rocky ground," i.e., upon "Petrine soil"? Does Mark perceive a pun here on Peter's name? Mark apparently does not understand *Petros* as Matthew does, in the sense of a solid foundation for a building (Matt. 16:18) but rather as indicating shallowness of fertile soil. This interpretation is consistent with Peter's confession and its sequel in 8:29-33 where Peter's enthusiasm once again is shown to lack depth.

However that may be, at the very time that Peter denies acquaintance with Jesus, Jesus makes his Christian confession. Mark's Jesus perseveres to the end (13:13). Knowing that the rejection of the gospel by the powerful will lead to their rejection of him, he nevertheless prays, "Not what I will but what you will" (14:36). Mark's Jesus is not only the Messiah, the Son of God, and the Son of Man who inspires awe—he is also Mark's ideal Christian disciple. Who else could say, "If any man would come after me, let him deny himself and take up his cross and follow me" (8:34), and then lead the way?

Does all this necessitate the conclusion that members of Mark's community were facing trials in Roman courts and that they were blaming local leaders of the Jewish community for it?[50] Perhaps not, but that interpretation seems consistent with the evidence. It is possible that Mark is led both by his sources[51] and the requirements of his story to cast the Jewish leaders of Jesus' time in the antagonist's role, and that therefore further inferences should not be drawn about them nor from the trial account. Jesus' confession, however, which can only be seen as belonging to the time of the church, together with his portrayal as the ideal Christian facing persecution, and of Peter as the one who apostatizes under pressure, points to Mark's present situation. Mark's redactional hand is to be seen in his moulding of the tradition so that it thematizes the world of his community. An important aspect of the world is what they perceive as persecution. Mark's gospel is shaped not just by the kerygma of the early church, but by its understanding of the kerygma plus the kerygma's reception and rejection and the implications of both for believers.

Appendix

Mark's trial narrative is distinctive in its selection and representation of events. A brief comparison of it with the relevant accounts in the other gospels will demonstrate this point.

---

50 Whether Mark's view is justified or based on suspicion and rumour cannot at present be answered. See Origen's well known comments in which he blames Jews for spreading rumours about Christians which touched off the persecutions in Rome (*Contra Celsum* 6:27). See also Albert Heinrichs, "Pagan Ritual and the Alleged Crimes of the Early Christians: A Reconsideration," in Patrick Granfield and Josef A. Jungmann, eds., *Kyriakon, Festschrift Johannes Quasten* (Munster: Aschendorff, 1970), 1:18-35.

51 Cook, *Jewish Leaders,* 52ff.

Matthew clearly stands in the Markan tradition. Although he introduces some modifications into both charges (see note 6), the essential features of Mark's account are retained.

Luke, however, presents quite a different scene. The event takes place in two locations, first at night in the High Priest's house (22:54-65), where Jesus is mistreated, commanded to prophesy (v. 64; cf. Mark 14:65), and blasphemed (v. 65; cf. Mark 15:29), and, second, in the morning in an unnamed place of assembly (*eis to synedrion*) where the *presbytērion tou laou* composed of chief priest and scribes (22:66-71) meets. There is no reference to a temple saying or to witnesses or, consequently, to Jesus' silence (Mark 14:61). The whole assembly, not just the High Priest, whose presence is unmentioned, questions Jesus. The Markan question, "Are you the Christ, the Son of the Blessed?" is here found as two separate questions (Luke, like Matthew, has "Son of God"). The return of the Son of Man is lacking, putting stress on his enthronement, as might be expected of Luke. Finally, Jesus' confession is considerably more ambiguous, perhaps even enigmatic, than in Mark, and it is not labelled blasphemous by the assembly. Their response (v. 71) is not part of a legal judgment, but prompts them to take Jesus immediately to Pilate. Luke therefore does not envisage a Jewish trial of Jesus, but an assembly which on the basis of hearing Jesus confess himself as Son of God initiates proceedings before the Roman court. Whether or not Luke's narrative (22:66-71) is more "historical" than Mark's, it exhibits too many distinctive features to doubt seriously its independence of Mark. (See David Catchpole, "The Problems of the Historicity of the Sanhedrin Trial," in E. Bammel, ed., *The Trial of Jesus* [London: SCM, 1970], 47-65.)

John presents a different picture again. Jesus is taken to Annas and questioned privately about his disciples and his *didachē* (18:12-14, 19-23). Jesus replies that he has never taught secretly, but in "synagogues and in the temple, where all Jews come together" (v. 20). Jesus is struck for his apparent insolence, sent to Caiaphas, and in the morning sent on to Pilate. He never appears before a Jewish assembly at all. There are no witnesses (Jesus invites Annas to seek them), no charges, no confession, no decision, and certainly no trial. John stands at the opposite end of the spectrum from Mark and Matthew, with Luke somewhere between them. Only Mark and Matthew convey the impression of a trial. In John, the counterpart is a private, inconclusive hearing, and in Luke it is a public but conclusive hearing. We should not speak of a Jewish trial narrative in Luke or John, but perhaps of a hearing narrative.

What is especially significant is that both Luke and John utilize both the blasphemy and temple saying motifs elsewhere. John locates the temple saying, logically enough, immediately following the cleansing of the Temple (2:14-22). The temple, however, is Jesus' body, and it is not Jesus but the Jews who will destroy it, though Jesus will raise it (not build it) in three days. The Jews misunderstand. As in Mark 15:29, they interpret the saying literally, though here that extends to both parts of the saying, while in Mark the misunderstanding is confined to the second part. The blasphemy charge in John 10 has no literary or thematic connection with the hearing before Annas or with the Roman trial.

Luke's employment of these charges is found not in his gospel but in Acts. It is not Jesus but Stephen who is accused (again, by false witnesses, 6:11) of "speaking blasphemous words against Moses and God" (6:11) and "this holy place" (6:13). It is less clear that behind 6:14, "we heard him say that this Jesus the *Nazaraios* will destroy this place" is something akin to the temple saying of Mark 14. In any case, the charges of preaching the Temple's destruction and of blasphemous words are brought by witnesses before a Jewish assembly. In contrast to Jesus' hearing, this one is presided over by the High Priest who, like the one in Mark's trial, asks questions. Further, as in Mark, false witnesses attempt to make out a case against the accused. What is lacking is the Markan christological formula. But we should not expect it, since Luke has already employed it in his hearing narrative. We see, then, that the two charges in the Markan trial narrative are located by Luke in Stephen's trial and are found in non-trial contexts in John. This not only points to the paramount importance of the motifs over the settings, but also that even by the time of the composition of all four canonical gospels, there was no authoritative account of a Jewish trial of Jesus. More important, it was not even agreed that there had been a trial. This makes it imperative to sort out the factors motivating the composition of the first trial narrative.

All this suggests that Mark has constructed his trial scene around basic issues in the early church regarding Jewish response to Christian missionary preaching, issues which find other expressions in Luke and John. The temple saying is one such issue, but for Mark it has been blown out of proportion by Jewish critics and in any case has been misunderstood. The blasphemy charge, however, penetrates to the heart of the matter. It *is* based on the actual Christian confession of Jesus and it represents in the clearest possible manner Jewish rejection of that confession.

8

Anti-Judaism and the Passion Narrative in Luke and Acts

Lloyd Gaston

"Who killed Jesus Christ?" is the question raised by the controversial film produced by TVOntario called *The Jesus Trial.* "The Jews did," answers a Good Friday liturgy with a dramatic reading of the passion according to St. John. It is in the light of experiencing both of these that the following is being written. We can speak of anti-Judaism in the passion narratives if responsibility for the death of Jesus is assigned to "the Jews" without qualification and if as a consequence "the Jews" are seen to be finally rejected by God with no possibility of repentance. Is that the case with Luke's narrative?

Luke's is in many ways the most complex of the gospels. On the one hand, he is unsystematic enough as a theologian and author that no statement about his work can stand without qualification. On the other hand, he is creative enough as a theologian and author to be able to assert contradictory motifs simultaneously and throughout the course of his two-volume work. Although it seems to be obvious that Luke has used sources other than Mark, no attempt to reconstruct them has won general assent, for he has imposed his own concepts and style fairly consistently on all his material. We may then not be able to give a clear answer to the question as posed.

Luke is the only gospel to be followed by a history of the church. Whereas Matthew and John operate on two levels in their gospels, that of the Jesus of the past and that of their own community in the present, Luke deals with the two levels sequentially. If we are to compare the gospels, it might be helpful to put Acts on top of the gospel of Luke as a kind of overlay. For example, in John "the Jews" without qualification are enemies of Jesus; not so in Luke, but in the second half of Acts "the Jews" without qualification are the enemies of Paul. Matthew has "all the people" cry out, "His blood be upon us and on our children"; not so in Luke, but in Acts 18:6 Paul shakes out his garments on the Jews, saying, "Your blood be upon your heads; I am innocent" (cf. also Acts 5:28). Before coming to the Lukan passion narrative as such, then, we shall first survey the book of Acts,[1] seeking to identify the friends and enemies of Jesus and the church.

The Jerusalem Church in Acts

When a community-forming story is told, the hearers naturally identify with those characters who help them form their own self-understanding. The identification of friends and enemies of those characters is equally helpful. The enemies are those who define us negatively, what we should not be like, and also help us to perceive contemporary threats to our identity. The sympathetic friends not only lend legitimacy to our movement but are those to whom we can appeal to join it. Keeping such considerations in mind, let us first give a synopsis of significant elements in the six mission speeches to Jewish audiences.

Responsibility for the Death of Jesus in the Mission Speeches to Jews

(1) Men of Israel, hear these words: Jesus the Nazoraean, . . . delivered up according to the definite plan and foreknowledge of God, you crucified and killed by the hands of lawless men . . . . Let all the house of Israel therefore know assuredly that God has made him both Lord and Christ, this Jesus whom you crucified . . . . Repent and be baptized every one of you in the name of Jesus Christ for the forgiveness of your sins . . . . For the promise is to you and your children. (Acts 2:14-39)

(2) Men of Israel . . . [God glorified] Jesus whom you delivered up and denied in the presence of Pilate, when he had given judgment to release him. But you denied the Holy and Righteous One, and asked for a murderer to be granted to you, and killed the Author of Life . . . . And now, brethren, I know that you acted in ignorance, as did also your rulers. But what God foretold by the mouth of all the prophets, that his Christ should suffer, he thus fulfilled. Repent therefore . . . . Every soul that does not listen to that prophet shall be destroyed from the people . . . . You are the sons of the prophets and of the convenant. (Acts 3:12-26)

(3) Rulers of the people and elders . . . by the name of Jesus Christ the Nazoraean whom you crucified [this man is healed] . . . . This is the stone which was rejected by you builders. (Acts 4:9-12)

1 At the time this paper was first written, I had not seen S.G. Wilson's paper on Acts. In spite of the length, I have let the sections on Acts remain with the hope that our two contributions will complement one another. In any case, with present developments in the redaction criticism of Luke-Acts it is difficult to discuss any part except in the context of the whole.

(4) [To the high priest and the council:] God . . . raised Jesus whom you killed by hanging him on a tree. God exalted him . . . to give repentance to Israel and forgiveness of sins. (Acts 5:29-32)

(5) We are witnesses to all that he did both in the country of the Jews and in Jerusalem. They put him to death by hanging him on a tree . . . . Every one who believes in him receives forgiveness of sins. (Acts 10:34-44)

(6) Those who live in Jerusalem and their rulers, because they did not recognize him nor understand the utterances of the prophets which are read every sabbath, fulfilled these by condemning him. Though they could charge him with nothing deserving death, yet they asked Pilate to have him killed. And when they had fulfilled all that was written of him, they [sic!] took him down from the tree and laid him in a tomb . . . . Let it be known to you therefore, brethren, that through this man forgiveness of sins is proclaimed to you. (Acts 13:16-41)

To these mission speeches to Jews we can add three other passages in a Jerusalem setting which deal with responsibility for Jesus' death. They are: a statement by the Emmaus disciples, a prayer of the disciples after their release from arrest, and the last words of Stephen, which will also be considered in another context.

(7) Our chief priests and rulers delivered him [Jesus] up to be condemned to death and [they] crucified him. (Luke 24:20)

(8) There were gathered together against thy holy servant Jesus . . . both Herod and Pontius Pilate, with the Gentiles and the people (*laoi*) of Israel, to do whatever thy hand and thy plan had determined to take place. (Acts 4:27-28)

(9) The Righteous One, . . . you have now betrayed and murdered, you who received the law as delivered by angels and did not keep it . . . . Lord, do not hold this sin against them. (Acts 7:52-53, 60)

It could not be stated more explicitly than in these addresses in Acts that the Jews killed Jesus. Contrary both to what is historically probable and to the Markan passion narrative, the Jews as such are not only morally responsible for the death of Jesus but often the actual agents of the crucifixion (1, 2, 5, 6, 9). That Luke thinks of *all* Jews and not just *some* Jews is shown by many of the addresses: men of Israel (1, 2), sons of the prophets, sons of the covenant (2) , you who received the law (9). More specifically, it can be said that it was the rulers of the people who murdered Jesus (3, 4, 7). Although the concept of Jesus being delivered into the hands of the Romans[2] can stand alongside the charge that the Jews did it, with no sense of contradiction (1, 2, 6, 7, and perhaps 9), the Roman authorities are never held responsible for Jesus'

---

2 H. Conzelmann, *Die Mitte der Zeit* (3d edition, Tübingen: Mohr, 1960), 83-84, goes too far when he would interpret Acts 2:33, "through the hand of lawless ones," as *Jews* disobedient to the Torah; or Luke 24:7, "the Son of Man must be delivered into the hands of sinful men," as referring to sinful *Jews.* Nevertheless, Conzelmann is on the right track.

death. Pilate found Jesus innocent (2, 6), and while he gave judgment (*krinein*) that Jesus was to be released (2) , the Jews gave judgment (*krinein*) that he was to be killed (6). Jesus is said to have hung on the tree (4, 5, 6), which *may* stem from an apologetic sense of Deut. 21:22-23 LXX (cf. Gal. 3:13) and say that Jesus was cursed by the Torah of Israel.[3] The reference to "the stone rejected by the builders" (3) *could* be connected with a "passion apologetic" in which the builders in turn are rejected.[4] In any case, nowhere in the NT is the place of the Jews in the crucifixion of Jesus so strongly stressed as in Acts.

Although Jews may be held responsible for the death of Jesus in these selections, there are three factors which mitigate any implication of guilt. In the first place, they acted out of ignorance (2, and to a lesser extent in 6). Second, what happened was in accordance with God's will (1, 2, 6, 8).[5] Finally and most important, the speeches end with a call to repentance and the offer of forgiveness (1, 2, 4, 5, 6, and perhaps 9).

Selection 7 is an exception to the generalization we just have made, for here responsibility seems to be equally divided, in order to make the situation correspond to Psalm 2. But as a part of the correspondence, Herod must be a king,[6] Pilate must be a ruler,[7] and Israel must be the *laoi*,[8] all unique in Luke. This exception will simply be noted for the time being.

Enemies of the Church in Acts 1-5

The sole enemies of the church in these chapters are all associated with the Temple, as can be seen by a simple listing:

the priests and the captains of the Temple and the Sadducees (4:1)

their rulers and elders and scribes . . . with Annas the High Priest and Caiaphas and John and Alexander, and all who were of the high priestly family (4:5-6)

rulers of the people and elders (4:8)

the council (4:15)

the chief priests and the elders (4:23)

3 It is much more likely, however, that the phrase is a Semitism for the word "to crucify" and has nothing at all to do with the "curse" of Deut. 21:22-23. Cf. J.M. Baumgarten, "Does *tlh* in the Temple Scroll Refer to Crucifixion?" *JBL* 91 (1972), 472-81. Cf. also Luke 23:39, where "hanged" is used for "crucified."

4 It should be noted, however, that in Luke, differing from Mark, the parable of the wicked tenants is told *to* the people *about* the leaders (Luke 20:9, 19).

5 For the *dei* of Divine necessity, cf. in addition to these passages also Luke 9:27; 13:33; 17:25; 24:7, 26, 46; Acts 17:3.

6 Luke knows that Herod Antipas was not a king (Luke 9:7; contrast Mark 6:14).

7 The rulers (*archontes*) in Luke-Acts are otherwise consistently Jewish rulers.

8 Only in Luke 2:31 does the plural otherwise appear, in reference to the Gentile peoples.

the High Priest and all who were with him, that is, the party of the Sadducees (5:17)

the High Priest and those who were with him . . . the council and all the senate (*gerousia*) of Israel (5:21)

the officers (*hypēretai* 5:22)

the captain of the Temple and the chief priests (5:24)

the captain with the officers (5:26)

the council and the High Priest (5:27)

the council (5:34, 41)

Here and elsewhere Luke has no concept of who elders and scribes might be, and they accompany other groups seemingly at random. Whatever the council might be, whether a "constitutional" institution advising the High Priest or a more informal gathering, it has nothing to do with the rabbinic *Beth Din.*[9]

We can add to the list those said in the speeches to have been enemies of Jesus: rulers (Acts 3:17; 13:27; Luke 24:20) and chief priests (Luke 24:20). Only in Acts 3:17 are the rulers excused by ignorance and in that sense not enemies.

Friends of the Church in Acts 1-5

The first summary statement in Acts states that the church was "having favour with all the people" (2:47), and this is characteristic of the use of *laos* in these chapters (3:9, 11, 12, 23; 4:1, 2, 10, 17, 21; 5:12, 13, 20, 25, 26, 34).[10] The people in Jerusalem not only hear the preaching of the apostles gladly, but also respond to it in ever-increasing numbers: 3000 (2:41), 5000 (4:4), multitudes (5:14), greatly multiplied numbers, including priests (6:7), tens of thousands (21:20). Especially significant are those passages where the people are aligned with the disciples over against the Temple authorities.

Sadducees . . . annoyed because they were teaching the people and proclaiming in Jesus the resurrection from the dead. (4:1-2)

[The rulers ensure] that it may spread no further among the people. (4:17)

[They let them go] finding no way to punish them because of the people. (4:21)

None of the rest dared join [the apostles] but the people held them in high honour. (5:13)

9 For the distinction between *a* council and *the* Beth Din, see the important article by E. Rivkin, "Beth Din, Boulé, Sanhedrin: A Tragedy of Errors," *HUCA* 46 (1975), 181-99.

10 The word also appears in more neutral phrases in 4:8, 25, 27; 5:37.

The captain with the officers went and brought them, but without violence, for they were afraid of being stoned by the people. (5:26)

The most surprising and most important friend of the church in these chapters is "a Pharisee in the council named Gamaliel, a teacher of the law, held in honour by all the people" (5:34). He not only defends the apostles against persecution by the council and the priests, but he says in effect that "this plan (and) this undertaking . . . is of God," since in fact from a later perspective the priests were not "able to overthrow them," and unlike the followers of Theudas and Judas the Galilean, the Christian movement did not "come to nothing."

In spite of the exaggerated way in which the Jewish people are held accountable for the death of Jesus, Acts 1 to 5 can in no sense be called anti-Judaic. On the contrary, this motif appears in the context of a call to repentance that is an attempt to stand on the side of the people and to win them for the cause. The response of the people is also exaggerated, thereby increasing the appeal of the gospel to popular opinion: the very success of the preaching of the gospel testifies to its truth. Also the Pharisees, presented as greatly respected by all the people, give powerful testimony for the church. The church is on the side of the people and the Pharisees, and this is further emphasized by underscoring their common enemies: the Temple establishment. The Romans appear only on the periphery, neither friends nor enemies but irrelevant. There are modern analogues and R. Scroggs[11] speaks of "The Earliest Christian Communities as Sectarian Movement," an accurate way of describing the tenor of these chapters.

As a presentation of the general attitude of the Jerusalem church, Acts 1 to 5 is also in broad outline true to history. The wealthy, the Sadducees, the High Priest, and the Temple aristocracy were in fact seen by the populace as the oppressing establishment. Although the nature of the Pharisaic movement is currently in dispute, I would argue that it was in fact both popular and anti-cultic.[12] The early Christian movement shared with the Pharisees (and the Essenes) not only an opposition to the aristocracy but also a strong anti-Temple sentiment. That the line-up of forces in Acts is not unreasonable can perhaps be demonstrated by the account of James's death in Josephus, *Ant.* 20: 197-203: when the High Priest Ananus kills James, the Pharisees pro-

11 In J. Neusner, ed., *Christianity, Judaism and Other Greco-Roman Cults*, Vol. 2 (Leiden: Brill, 1975), 1-23. However, when he puts the Pharisees on the side of the Establishment, that is true neither to these chapters nor, I believe, to the history of the Jerusalem church.

12 On this issue I would then side with E. Rivkin, *A Hidden Revolution* (Nashville: Abingdon, 1978), against M. Smith, "Palestinian Judaism in the First Century," in M. Davis, ed., *Israel: Its Role in Civilization* (New York: Harper, 1956), 67-81, and J. Neusner, *The Rabbinic Traditions about the Pharisees Before 70*, Vol. 3 (Leiden: Brill, 1971), 320-68, and *From Politics to Piety* (Englewood Cliffs: Prentice-Hall, 1973). Cf. also J. Bowker, *Jesus and the Pharisees* (Cambridge: Cambridge University Press, 1973).

test so much that James is deposed; Josephus presents this as a popular action. Whatever the success or failure of the Christian movement in Jerusalem, it did in fact understand itself to be on the side of the people and the Pharisees, allied with them against the High Priest.

Transition: The Passions of Stephen and James

"Stephen, full of grace and power, did great wonders and signs among the people" (Acts 6:8), is the last time that the *laos* appears in Acts on the side of the church. Those of the synagogues of the Diaspora "stirred up the *people* and the elders and the scribes" and they seized Stephen and brought him before the council. The charge of speaking against the Temple and the law are more like the charges later brought against Paul than charges made against Jesus in the gospel. The speech ends with the motif of the killing of the prophets and the rejection of Israel.[13] If the story begins with the semblance of a trial before a council, at the end it is the whole people of Israel who lynch Stephen. They are addressed as: "you stiff-necked ones, uncircumcised in heart and ears . . . as your fathers did so do you . . . you who received the law as delivered by angels and did not keep it." It is "they" who become enraged and stone Stephen. His last three words are parallel to sayings in the passion narrative in Luke's gospel: 7:56 (= Luke 22:69); 7:59 (= Luke 23:46); and 7:60 (= Luke 23:34). The last statement, "Lord do not hold this sin against them," is problematic, since there is no call to repentance and no mention of forgiveness being offered, but only the motif of the rejection of an utterly apostate Israel.[14]

When King Herod persecuted the church and killed James, "he saw that it pleased the Jews" (12:3). When Peter escapes from prison he thanks God, who has "rescued me from the hand of Herod and the whole expectation of the people (*laos*) of the Jews" (12:11). It has often been noted that Luke uses the word *laos* to mean *the* people of Israel.[15] In that sense it is equivalent to "the Jews." The people, the Jews, were favourably disposed toward the church in Acts 1 to 5. The martyrdom of Stephen represents a transition, in that the people and the Jews are seen as enemies at and beyond this point. Whether or not this corresponds to an actual bitterness of the church because of the relative failure of the Jewish mission, it is an important transition in the theology of Acts.

---

13 On this see O.H. Steck, *Israel und das gewaltsame Geschick der Propheten* (Neukirchen: Neukirchener Verlag, 1967), 265-69.

14 The significance of the Stephen episode as the rejection of the Jews of Jerusalem in Luke's outline is especially emphasized by J.C. O'Neill, *The Theology of Acts in its Historical Setting* (London: SPCK, 1961), 71-93.

15 Two exceptions in Acts 15:14 and 18:10 apply to Gentiles, the beginning of a movement which will apply the honourable title of Israel to the church and deny it to the Jews. Cf. P. Richardson, *Israel in the Apostolic Church* (Cambridge: Cambridge University Press, 1969).

The Passion of Paul

Enemies Among Jewish Leaders

In general, Paul's accusers in Acts 22 to 26 are the same as those who harassed the church in Acts 1 to 5. We hear about meetings of the council (*synedrion,* 22:30; 23:1, 6, 15, 20, 28; 24:20), but again this has nothing to do with the Pharisaic *Beth Din.* It is probable that the references are to *ad hoc* bodies which advise the High Priest, much as Festus confers with his council (*symboulion,* 25:12, cf. Mark 15:1). In any case, Paul in no sense has a trial before such a body, and its only task in the narrative is to formulate charges against him. The specific leaders mentioned are as follows:

the chief priests and all the council (22:30)

the High Priest Ananias (23:2)

Sadducees and Pharisees (23:6)

scribes of the party of the Pharisees (23:9)

the chief priest and elders (23:14)

the High Priest Ananias with some elders and a spokesman, one Tertullus (24:1)

the chief priests and the principal men (*hoi prōtoi*) of the Jews (25:2)

the chief priests and the elders of the Jews (25:15)

the chief priests (at the time of Paul's persecution of the church, 26:10, 12)

the leaders (*hoi prōtoi*) of the Jews (in Rome, 28:17)

Again Luke has no concrete conception of who the scribes or elders are, and the only constant element is the chief priests, as in Acts 1 to 5. The charges made against Paul are similar to those made against Stephen and are also religious in nature: that he preaches against a) the people, b) the law, and c) the Temple (21:28; cf. 21:21; 25:8; 28:17). If such charges were sustained, then Paul would be the anti-Semite,[16] but Luke has taken great pains in his portrayal of Paul to show that he has not offended against any of the three. Paul defends himself in the speeches of Acts not by responding to the separate charges but by insisting at the top of his voice that he is a Pharisee and the best of the Pharisees. Only once is there a hint of a political charge ("an agitator among all the Jews throughout the world and a ringleader of the sect of the Nazarenes," 24:5; cf. 25:8), and even this can be understood not so

16 Many of the interpreters of the Paul of the letters do so understand him. I believe that in fact Paul is innocent of all the charges, but that cannot be demonstrated here.

much as an offence against the Empire as against Jewish orthodoxy. In any case, all charges against Paul are rejected by the officials.

Friends of Paul

Throughout the account of his career, Paul had been protected and defended by officials of the Roman Empire. This is true of Sergius Paulus, the proconsul in Salamis (13:7-12), the jailer in Philippi (16:29-34), the magistrates in Philippi (16:35, 39), the authorities in Thessalonica (17:8-9), Gallio in Corinth (18:12-17), the Asiarchs (19:31) and town clerk in Ephesus (19:35-41), and now also in Jerusalem: Claudius Lysias, the tribune (21:32-6, 40; 22:24-30; 23:10, 18-31), the governor Felix (24:22-23), the governor Festus (25:1-6, 12), King Herod Agrippa II (26:31-32), Julius, the centurion on the ship (27:3, 43), and Publius of Malta (28:7-10). Not only is Paul protected by these officials from the wrath of the Jews, but the charges of the High Priest are explicitly rejected. Three times Paul is declared innocent:

> [Lysias says] he was accused about questions of their law but charged with nothing deserving death or imprisonment (23:29).
>
> [Festus says] I found that he had done nothing deserving death (25:25).
>
> [The King (Herod Agrippa II) and the governor (Festus) and Bernice say] This man is doing nothing to deserve death or imprisonment (26:31).

Paul is held to be innocent and yet he is not released. Why? The answer is significant. Just as Herod Agrippa I arrested Peter because the death of James "pleased the Jews", so also Felix left Paul in prison "desiring to do the Jews a favour" (24:27), and Festus would have sent Paul back to Jerusalem and his death "wishing to do the Jews a favour" (25:9). It has often been asserted that the positive stance of Roman officials toward Paul is part of a political apologetic in Acts, defending the political respectability of the church in the eyes of Roman readers. On the contrary, I believe that all these officials are character witnesses testifying to Paul's innocence of the charges made against him at his real trial—before the Jewish people.

Before we turn to Paul's real enemies we must look at his most surprising friends in Jerusalem: the Pharisees. In the remarkable scene where Paul stands before the council (23:1-10), the Pharisees come to Paul's defence against the High Priest and the Sadducees.[17] They add to

17 Apart from having been the historical enemies of the Christian movement, the Sadducees function in Luke-Acts more importantly in a theological sense: they are Jews who deny the resurrection. Thus in Acts 4:2 the Sadducees were "annoyed because they were teaching the people and proclaiming in Jesus the resurrection from the dead," and in 5:34-39 the Pharisees defend the church against them. The only other context in which Sadducees appear is Luke 20:27-39, where the Sadducees, "those who deny the resurrection," are opposed by Jesus, who in turn is applauded by a scribe.

the decisions of the Roman officials one more testimony to Paul's innocence: "We find nothing wrong in this man" and add, "What if a spirit or an angel spoke to him?" (23:9). But most important, they testify to the truth of Paul's gospel, for when he says that "with respect to the hope and the resurrection of the dead I am on trial" (23:6), the Pharisees agree and defend the central Christian affirmation of the resurrection. In his defence speeches Paul justifies himself only by the assertion that he too is a Pharisee (23:6; cf. 22:3), while proclaiming the gospel of the resurrection.[18]

The apologetic function of the witness of the Pharisees is clear, and is even more important than the witness of the Roman officials. Luke's predominantly Gentile-Christian community[19] finds its self-understanding called into question by local Jews, who call Paul an apostate from the faith of Israel. Over against them Luke appeals to the great authority of the Pharisees, "the strictest party of [the Jewish] religion" (26:5). In an earlier period they testified to the orthodoxy of Paul and the truth of his message, and even now in Luke's time Paul's Pharisaic life is "known by all the Jews . . . *if* they are willing to testify" (26:45). When we remember that Luke-Acts was probably written at the time when Rabban Gamaliel II had become Nasi at Yavneh and had been recognized by the Roman government as the official spokesman for the Jewish people,[20] it is not insignificant that the only Pharisee named in the NT is his grandfather Rabban Gamaliel I, who was Paul's teacher (22:3) and the defender of the earliest Jerusalem church (5:34-39). Also in the third context in Acts in which Pharisees appear they function in a positive sense. Luke says that it was Christian Pharisees who initiated the discussion at the council in Jerusalem (15:5), in order not to present them as intransigent but to appeal to their authority for the final unanimous decision (15:22) of the church to exempt Gentile Christians from most commandments of the Torah. On this matter too, the authority of the Pharisees is on the side of the Christian movement and against the position of the Jews contemporary with Luke and antagonistic to the church.[21] Just as Josephus can hope to win respect for himself by claiming (falsely)[22] that he has been a Pharisee since his nineteenth year (*Life,* 10-12), so Luke tries to vindicate Paul by claiming that he has been a Pharisee since his youth under Gamaliel and to vindicate Christianity by claiming that on three occa-

18 On the importance of the resurrection kerygma in these speeches, see P. Schubert, "The Final Cycle of Speeches in the Book of Acts," *JBL* 87 (1968), 1-16.

19 Note that Luke must explain to his readers the difference between Pharisees and Sadducees. The very stimulating essays of J. Jervell, *Luke and the People of God* (Minneapolis: Augsburg, 1972), are marred by his strange (and to me inconsistent) assertion (116-17, 175-76, 185-93) that Luke-Acts is addressed primarily to *Jewish*-Christians.

20 Cf. S. Safrai in CRINT 1.1 (Assen: Van Gorcum, 1974), 405-09.

21 A recent (inconclusive) survey of the Pharisees in Luke and Acts is J.A. Ziesler, "Luke and the Pharisees," *NTS* 25 (1979), 146-57.

22 So, probably correctly, J. Neusner, *From Politics to Piety,* 46-47.

sions Pharisees defended the truth of its message. But if the Pharisees are friends of Paul and the Christians, their enemies are simply the Jews.

"The Jews" as Enemies of Paul

If we list the passages which refer to Paul's enemies, "the people"[23] and "the Jews" turn up with a surprising frequency. Any one passage can be understood to mean some Jews of that place (cf. Acts 24:18, "some Jews from Asia"), but the cumulative effect makes inescapable the reference to Jews in general.[24] A listing follows:

The Jews plotted to kill [Paul in Damascus]. (9:23)

The Hellenists... were seeking to kill [Paul in Jerusalem]. (9:29)

When the Jews saw the multitudes [of Jews and Gentiles who believed] they were filled with jealousy... and reviled [Paul in Antioch]. (13:45)

The Jews incited [the leaders in Antioch] and stirred up persecution against Paul and Barnabas and drove them out of their district. (13:50)

The unbelieving Jews stirred up the Gentiles and poisoned their minds against the brethren [in Iconium]. (14:2)

The people (*plēthos*) of the city were divided; some sided with the Jews, and some with the apostles. (14:4)

An attempt was made by both Gentiles and Jews, with their rulers, to molest them and to stone them. (14:5)

The Jews came [to Lystra]... and stoned Paul and dragged him out of the city. (14:19)

[Timothy was circumcised] because of the Jews. (16:3)

The Jews were jealous [and denounced Jason and some of the brethren before the magistrate in Thessalonica]. (17:5-9)

The Jews of Thessalonica ...came there too [Beroea], stirring up and inciting the crowds. (17:13)

The Jews unanimously made an attack on Paul and brought him before the tribunal [in Corinth]. (18:12)

A plot was made against [Paul] by the Jews [in Macedonia]. (20:2)

[Paul speaks in Miletus of the] trials which befell me through the plots of the Jews. (20:19)

23 The word *laos* is also used in a neutral non-hostile sense in 7:17, 34; 10:2, 42; 13:15, 24, 31; 19:4; 23:5; 26:23.

24 "*Hoi Ioudaioi* becomes a *terminus technicus* (as in the fourth gospel) for the opponents of Paul, the bringer of salvation," R.F. Zehnle, *Peter's Pentecost Discourse* (Nashville: Abingdon, 1971), 65.

[Agabus predicts that] the Jews at Jerusalem [will] deliver [Paul] into the hands of the Gentiles. (21:11)

[Paul is accused of teaching] all the Jews who are among the Gentiles to forsake Moses. (21:21)

The Jews from Asia . . . stirred up all the crowd and laid hands on [Paul in Jerusalem]. (21:27)

This is the man [Paul] who is teaching men everywhere against the people and the law and this place. (21:28)

All the city was aroused and the people (*laos*) ran together; they seized Paul. (21:30)

The multitude of the people (*laos*) followed, crying: Away with him. (21:36)

The Jews accused [Paul]. (22:30)

The Jews made a plot and bound themselves by an oath neither to eat nor drink until they had killed Paul. (23:12)

The Jews [ask the tribune to lead Paul into ambush] (23:20-21). [Claudius Lysias writes] This man was seized by the Jews and was about to be killed by them. (23:27)

[Paul is charged with being] a pestilent fellow, an agitator among all the Jews throughout the world. (24:5)

The Jews also joined in the charge [of the High Priest]. (24:9)

[Paul speaks of] some Jews from Asia [as his accusers]. (24:18)

Desiring to do the Jews a favour, Felix left Paul in prison. (24:27)

The Jews who had gone down from Jerusalem stood about him, bringing against him many serious charges. (25:7)

Festus, wishing to do the Jews a favour . . . . (25:9)

[Paul says] to the Jews I have done no wrong. (25:10)

[Festus says] you see this man about whom the whole Jewish people (*to plēthos tōn Ioudaiōn*) petitioned me, both at Jerusalem and here, shouting that he ought not to live any longer. (25:24)

[Paul speaks of] all the accusations of the Jews. (26:2)

I am accused by the Jews. (26:7)

[The risen Christ says to Paul] I will appear to you, delivering you from the people (*laos*) and the Gentiles. (26:17)

The Jews seized me in the temple and tried to kill me. (26:21)

[Paul reports that when the Romans wanted to free him] the Jews objected. (28:19)

This people's (*laos*) heart has grown dull. (28:26-27, quoting Isa. 6:9-10)

Such a lengthy listing seemed to be necessary as a corrective to the well-known and impressive thesis of Jervell that for Luke the Gentile mission presupposes the success of a previous mission to Jews. To be sure, Luke emphasizes that in every city Paul's mission among the Jews was successful: in Antioch (13:43), Iconium (14:1), Thessalonica (17:4), Beroea (17:11-12), Corinth (18:4), Ephesus (19:8-10), and Rome (28:24). But in every case, after saying that *some* Jews believed, Luke goes on to say that *the* Jews were violently opposed to Paul.[25] Both motifs, that of continuity and of discontinuity, must be emphasized, and it is clear which one has the final word.

That the theme of Jewish rejection of the gospel and the consequent rejection of the Jews by God is an important one in Acts has been clear since the time of Overbeck. The Jews of Jerusalem are decisively rejected (Acts 7:51-3), as are progressively the Jews of Asia (13:46), Greece (18:6), and as the final word, in Rome (28:28). Even Jervell[26] says that "Luke has excluded the possibility of a further mission to Jews for the church of his time because the judgment by and on the Jews has been irrevocably passed." Something similar has been said by H. Cadbury, J. Munck, L. Goppelt, E. Haenchen, J. Gnilka, H. Conzelmann, G. Bornkamm, N. Dahl, A. George, J.C. O'Neill, G. Schneider, W. Eltester, S.G. Wilson, and F. Keck.[27]

It is worth emphasizing the near unanimity on this point, because it is what makes Luke-Acts in its final form and as a totality anti-Judaic. Under the dual impact of the fall of Jerusalem and the shift of the church to an almost completely Gentile Christian movement, Luke must deal with some major theological problems. The status of his community as a legitimate people of God is under attack by Jewish neighbours and is questioned in the minds of Christians themselves. Luke overcomes the problem (1) by stressing the continuity of the church with Judaism, by showing its great popularity among Jews and the approval given to it by the Pharisses, and (2) by relegating this

25 This point is forcefully made by E. Haenchen, "Judentum und Christentum in der Apostelgeschichte," *ZNW* 54 (1963), 155-87.

26 Jervell, *Luke and the People of God,* 64; cf. 69, 174.

27 H.J. Cadbury, *The Making of Luke-Acts* (New York: Macmillan, 1927), 256; J. Munck, *Paulus und die Heilsgeschichte* (Aarhus: Universitetsforlaget, 1954), 240-41; L. Goppelt, *Christentum und Judentum* (Gütersloh: Bertelsmann, 1954), 302-03; E. Haenchen, *Die Apostelgeschichte* (12th edition, Göttingen: Vandenhoeck und Ruprecht, 1959), 90-91, 653, et al.; and "Judentum," 185; in Keck and Martyn, eds., *Studies in Luke-Acts* (Nashville: Abingdon, 1966), 278; J. Gnilka, *Die Verstockung Israels* (Munich: Kösel, 1961), 119-54; H. Conzelmann, *Die Apostelgeschichte* (2d edition, Tübingen: Mohr, 1972), 159-60; and in Keck, *Studies,* 308; G. Bornkamm, in Keck, *Studies,* 201; N. Dahl, in Keck, *Studies,* 151; A. George, "Israël dans l'oeuvre de Luc," *RB* 75 (1968), 481-525, 522; J.C. O'Neill, *Theology,* 75, 95; G. Schneider, *Verleugnung, Verspottung und Verhör Jesus nach Lukas 22, 54-71* (Munich: Kösel, 1969), 203; W. Eltester, "Israel im lukanischen Werk," *Jesus in Nazareth* (Berlin: de Gruyter, 1972), 76-147, esp. 111-20; S.G. Wilson, *The Gentiles and the Gentile Mission in Luke-Acts* (Cambridge: Cambridge University Press, 1973), 226; F. Keck, *Die öffentliche Abschiedsrede Jesu in Lk 20, 45-21, 36* (Stuttgart: Katholisches Bibelwerk, 1976), 26.

period of continuity to a generation of the past. It is the great merit of Jervell's studies to emphasize the first point, but the second must not be neglected. Quite different from his presentation of the past, Luke's present is characterized by an implacable enmity between the church and "the Jews" (including also the contemporary Pharisees of Yavneh, although this is not said in Acts). Luke is unable to defend the legitimacy of the (Gentile) Christian movement without declaring the Jews as such to be enemies of the church of God. Adopting the position attacked by Paul in Romans 11, Luke is able to assert the election of the church only by coupling it with the rejection of the Jews. The fronts have shifted significantly in Acts. Whereas the people of Israel, the Jews, were once friends of the church, they now appear on the side of the enemies.

The Gospel of Luke

Friends and Enemies in the Gospel Outside Jerusalem

We continue our rather crude method of asking who is on the side of Jesus and the church and who is on the other side. Before the passion narrative in Luke the answer is clear: the Jews are unanimously and enthusiastically on the side of Jesus and the gospel, and their leaders are just as firmly on the other side. The people of Israel, designated by the words *laos* and *ochlos,* consistently appear as those who seek out Jesus, as the addressees of the gospel, or as those who receive Jesus and the gospel gladly.[28] Jesus and the people stand together over against the wicked leaders, a fact which would serve to commend the gospel even more widely. Popularity is an advocate for the truth.

At the same time, insofar as the gospel contains a tradition of the preaching of the church to Israel, a warning note has to be sounded. In addition to material which serves as teaching to disciples and crowds and as polemic against Jewish leaders, there are sections which can be understood as prophetic warnings to Jerusalem: "unless you repent you shall all likewise perish" (13:3, 5) and Jerusalem will be destroyed (11:49-51; 12:56; 13:34-35; 17:20-37; 19:41-49; 21:5-28). Especially ominous is Luke 21:23: "Great distress will be on the land, and wrath on this people," the first potentially negative use of the word *laos.*

28 *Laos* designates the people of Israel who are presented as friendly toward the gospel in Luke 1:10, 17, 21, 68, 77; 2:10, 32; 3:15, 18; 7:1, 16, 29; 18:43 in Lukan special material, and in 3:21; 6:17; 8:47; 9:13 as additions to Mark. Jesus is popular with the *ochlos* in Luke 3:7, 10; 5:1, 3; 6:19; 7:9, 11, 12, 24; 8:19; 9:11, 12, 16, 18, 37; 11:14, 27, 29; 12:1, 13, 54; 13:14, 17; 14:25; 18:36; 19:3 in Lukan special material, in passages taken from Mark in Luke 5:19; 8:4, 40, 42, 45; 9:38; and as an addition to Mark in Luke 4:42; 5:15 (Luke 5:29; 6:17 use the word in another sense). All passages subsequent to Luke 19:20 will be cited later in the text.

Luke seems to have only a vague idea of *who* the Jewish leaders are. *What* they are is clearer in this gospel than in any other: the rich, the powerful, the oppressors of the people. M.J. Cook[29] has argued plausibly that Mark does not really know who the scribes and elders are who are joined with the high priests in the source of his passion narrative. The same is even truer of Luke. It can be shown that the "scribes" are in every case taken over from Mark,[30] or are added by Luke under the influence of Mark.[31] With the exception of two passages taken from Mark (20:38, 46), they are always attached to other groups.[32] "Elders" come only from Mark or are added conventionally to other groups in Acts.[33] The references to "high priests," while sometimes conventional, are more firmly anchored in the tradition.[34] More significant are the specific Lukan designations of the enemies: rulers (*archontes*),[35] leaders (*prōtoi tou laou*),[36] and captains of the Temple (*stratēgoi*).[37] The leaders in the gospel are vaguely designated or are all associated with the Sadducees and the High Priest, as in Acts 1 to 5, with one significant exception: the Pharisees.

After the clear portrayal of the Pharisees in Acts as friends of the church, it is surprising to see how ambiguous is their appearance in the gospel. The Lukan redaction of Mark shows an increased tendency to portray the Pharisees as the enemies of Jesus. The five controversy stories in Mark 2:1-3:6 mention Pharisees in only two episodes and in the conclusion of the collection. Luke has made every story refer to Pharisees,[38] and they are introduced at the beginning of the collection in a way which generalizes the opposition of *all* Pharisees: "Pharisees (i.e., teachers of the law) were sitting by, who had come from *every* town of Galilee and Judaea and from Jerusalem." On the other hand, the Pharisees are not at all hostile in some of the material peculiar to Luke. Three times Jesus is invited to dine at the house of a Pharisee (7:36-50, 11:37-54, 14:2-24), which is a way of claiming the witness of respected leaders to Jesus' righteousness. They enter into discussion with Jesus

---

29 M.J. Cook, *Mark's Treatment of the Jewish Leaders* (Leiden: Brill, 1978).

30 Luke 5:30; 9:22; 20:1, 46; 22:2.

31 Luke 5:21; 6:7; 11:53; 15:2; 19:49; 20:19, 39; 22:66; 23:10.

32 Cf. also Acts 4:5, 6:12; 23:9.

33 Luke 9:22; 20:1; 22:52; Acts 4:5, 8, 23; 6:12; 23:14; 24:1; 25:15.

34 The *archiereis* are taken from Mark in Luke 9:22; 19:47; 20:1; 22:2, 4, 52, and appear in special Lukan material in 22:66; 23:4, 10, 13; 24:20. They appear in Acts in 4:1, 23; 5:24; 9:14, 21; 22:30; 23:14; 25:2, 15; 26:10, 12. In only a few instances (Luke 19:47; 22:4, 52, 66; 24:20; Acts 5:24) can they be understood as additions to other groups, and in all the rest the story could not be told without them.

35 Luke 23:13, 35; 24:20; Acts 3:17; 4:5, 8, 26; 13:27. The singular is perhaps significant in Luke 18:18, "a ruler" (contrast Mark's *heis*), where Luke omits Mark's "Jesus loved him." There are two rather positive instances of the singular in Luke 8:41 and 14:1.

36 Luke 19:47; Acts 13:50; 25:2; 28:17.

37 Luke 22:7, 52; Acts 4:1; 5:24, 26.

38 They are added to the Markan *Vorlage* in Luke 5:21 and 6:7, and the omission of Mark 2:18 makes the "they" of Luke 5:33 refer to Pharisees.

on halakic (14:1-6) and haggadic matters (17:20b), and they do not disagree with his answers. Pharisees warn Jesus when Herod tries to capture him to kill him (13:31) and, if the reference is not redactional,[39] at the entry into Jerusalem when the action of Jesus' disciples could provoke a reaction by the Romans.[40] The parable of the Pharisee and the tax collector (18:10-12) is like most parables paradoxical: it does not criticize the Pharisee but on the contrary presupposes his righteousness. If the Lukan special material tends to speak favourably of Pharisees as friendly to Jesus and therefore as indirect supporters of the Jesus movement, and if the Lucan redaction of Mark tends to increase Mark's hostility to Pharisees, then we can suspect Lukan redaction of Lukan special material whenever the attitude is hostile. The polemic in Luke 16:14 against the "lovers of money" who "justify themselves" (*hṣṭdq*) was surely originally directed against the Sadducees,[41] and the close parallel of the woes against the Pharisees (11:39-42, 43) to the *Assumption of Moses,* which is clearly directed against the Sadducees,[42] might suggest the same for these Q sayings. Also 15:2 and 19:39 are probably redactional. That makes the remaining two passages surely redactional and especially significant, where Luke contrasts the Pharisees and the people of Israel.

All the people and the tax collectors justified God, having been baptized with the baptism of John, but the Pharisees and the lawyers rejected the purpose of God for themselves, not having been baptized by him. (7:29-30)

The scribes and the Pharisees began to press him hard, and to provoke him to speak of many things, lying in wait for him to catch him at something he might say. In the meantime, when so many tens of thousands [*myriades*, cf. Acts 21:20!] of the multitude had gathered together that they trod upon one another, he began to say to his disciples first: "Beware of the leaven of the Pharisees, which is hypocrisy." (11:53-12:1)

Here and only here the Pharisees[43] appear in the role of the leaders who are contrasted by the people, a role which seems to be very important for the final redaction of Luke but which is otherwise occupied by the Temple authorities.

---

39 The phrase is overfilled: *tines* (a) *tōn pharisaiōn* (b) *apo tou ochlou,* and the following address is to the people, not the Pharisees.

40 So G.B. Caird, *Saint Luke* (Baltimore: Penguin, 1963), 216; F. Keck, *Abschiedsrede,* 26-27. The thesis of H. Cohn, *The Trial and Death of Jesus* (New York: Harper and Row, 1967), can of course not be substantiated with respect to the trial, but that his instincts concerning the Pharisaic attitude to Jesus were basically correct is perhaps shown by Luke 13:31 and 19:39.

41 T.W. Manson, *The Mission and Message of Jesus* (New York: Dutton, 1938), 587-93.

42 *As. Mos.* 7:3-10, where we also have a pun on the name Sadducee, "saying that they are just (*sdyqym*)."

43 The special Lukan word *nomikos* seems to be completely equivalent to Pharisees, with whom they are associated in Luke 7:30; 11:53 (v. l.); and 14:3. Luke 10:25 may originally have referred to a friendly questioner, and the same would have to be said about the "lawyers" in 11:45, 46, 52 as we have said about the Pharisees in that pericope.

Contrast Between People and Leaders in Jerusalem (19:20-22:6)

Contrary to the recent impressive study by F. Keck,[44] I understand Jesus' speeches in Jerusalem to be addressed primarily to the people of Israel and only secondarily to Christians. Like the mission speeches of Acts, they are a call to repentance, here in the light of the coming catastrophe, and an encouragement to repentance by emphasizing that the enemies of Jesus are also the enemies of the people. The speeches have this character not only by virtue of the original address of the special Lukan material (= S) but also by Luke's redaction of Mark. This can be demonstrated here only by looking at the framework of the speeches, especially those passages which show a sharp contrast between people and leaders. In what follows, "people" always represents *laos* and "the multitudes" *ochloi.*

And some [of the Pharisees][45] in the multitude said to him, "Teacher, rebuke your disciples." [Jesus said to them] Would that even today you knew the things that made for peace. (19:39-44, S)

[The chief priests and the scribes sought to destroy him][46] and the leaders of the people (*prōtoi tou laou*) found nothing they could do, for the whole people clung to him listening. (19:47, S)

As he was teaching the people [contrast Mark] in the temple and preaching the gospel, the chief priests and the scribes with the elders came up [and asked a hostile question]. (20:1, Mark)

[The leaders said] all the people [contrast Mark] will stone us; for they are convinced that John was a prophet. (20:6, Mark)

And he began to tell the people [contrast Mark] this parable . . . the scribes and the chief priests[47] tried to lay hands on him at that very hour, but they feared the people [contrast Mark], for they perceived that he had told this parable against them. (20:9-19, Mark)

And they[48] were not able in the presence of the people to catch him by what he said. (20:26, Mark)

---

44 F. Keck, *Abschiedsrede.* That the address is to the people rather than to the disciples is said also by H. Flender, *St. Luke, Theologian of Redemption History* (London: SPCK, 1967), 13, and others.

45 On the possibility that the Pharisees have been added from Mark, see above, note 39. In the present text of Luke this is the only occasion in the gospel where the Pharisees appear in Jerusalem. The following address concerns the multitudes of Jerusalem; they are not yet opposed to Jesus but must be warned of national disaster if they do not repent.

46 As the awkwardness of the Greek sentence shows, this phrase is an insertion from Mark.

47 This phrase is taken from Mark 11:27 and inserted here in order to make a contrast to those to whom the parable of the wicked tenants is told (Luke: "the people"; Mark: "them," viz. the chief priests and the scribes and the elders of 11:27).

48 That is, the "they" who had sent spies (20:20), the scribes and the chief priests of 20:19. Note that Luke here omits Mark's reference to Pharisees in Jerusalem.

There came to him some Sadducees . . . . And some of the scribes[49] answered, "Teacher you have spoken well." (20:27-39, Mark)

And in the hearing of all the people [contrast Mark], he said to his disciples "Beware of the scribes." (20:45-46, Mark)

The rich [contrast Mark] putting their gifts into the treasury [contrast the poor widow]. (21:1-4, Mark)

Some spoke of the temple . . . they asked him, "Teacher . . . ."[50] [as introduction to the apocalyptic fate of Jerusalem]. (21:5-7, S)

And every day he was teaching in the temple . . . and early in the morning all the people came to him in the temple to hear him, [as end to the apocalyptic discourse on the fate of Jerusalem]. (Luke 21:37f, S)

The chief priests and the scribes were seeking how to put him to death, for they feared the people. (22:1-2 Mark)

[Judas] went away and conferred with the chief priests and the captains [contrast Mark] . . . and sought an opportunity to betray him to them in the absence of the multitude [contrast Mark]. (22:3-6, Mark)

There follows a series of incidents in which neither people nor leaders appear, and then Jesus' farewell discourse to his disciples. In the rest of the gospel, the people appear a few more times in contrast with the leaders: Jesus is accused by the leaders of "perverting the nation . . . stirring up the people . . . perverting the people" (23:2, 5, 14), and the Emmaus disciples speak of him as "a prophet mighty in deed and word before God and all the people, [but] our chief priests and rulers delivered him up to be condemned to death and crucified him" (24:19f). But apart from these, the reversal of the role of the people in the passion narrative is astounding.

The Passion Narrative

We come finally to the passion narrative[51] itself; we shall survey it against the background we have sketched in Acts and the rest of the gospel, identifying friends and enemies. Although I believe that there was another source that Luke preferred to Mark in the passion narrative, that will not be taken into consideration here. We shall look at the narrative only in its present form, but also we will try to take into account the context in the whole of Luke-Acts.

49 The approving scribes are taken from Mark 12:32. Since they take the Christian side against the Sadducees on the question of resurrection, Luke perhaps understands them (correctly) to be Pharisees.

50 That the address *didaskale* cannot be by disciples and that therefore the Lukan eschatological discourse was understood as addressed to the people of Jerusalem was argued in L. Gaston, *No Stone on Another* (Leiden: Brill, 1970), 11.

51 A very helpful article is P.W. Walaskay, "The Trial and Death of Jesus in the Gospel of Luke," *JBL* 94 (1975), 81-93.

The Arrest (22:47-53)

A multitude comes to Jesus, led by Judas, and it remains throughout the narrative (23:4, 13). This is not a crowd from the chief priests and the scribes and the elders, as in Mark, but more significantly just a crowd, which in the light of the previous use of *ochlos* seems to mean the people of Israel as such. As in the arrest of Paul, the people are on the other side.[52] "Those who had come out against" Jesus are more specifically defined as "the chief priests and captains of the temple," Jewish soldiers are then involved—the Temple police under the direction of the Segan and the High Priest. They appear only in Luke-Acts, as those with whom Judas conferred (22:4) and as those who arrest the disciples in Jerusalem (Acts 4:1, 5:24, 26). In all references but the last, the chief priests are explicitly named together with them. "This is your hour and the power of darkness," says Jesus to them, raising the drama to a cosmic level. Only in Luke (22:3) and John (13:2, 27) does Satan initiate the events of the passion by entering Judas. Insofar as Satan and the power of darkness are behind the Jews who arrest Jesus, it is perhaps not too fanciful to recall John 8:44: "You are of your father the devil."

Before the Council (22:54a; 22:63-23:1)

There is no question of this scene being in any sense a trial. No witnesses are brought forward, false or otherwise, Jesus does not confess his Messiahship, there is no charge of blasphemy, and there is no decision of condemnation. Even if the trial before the council is a Markan invention and was not in Luke's special material, Luke could have taken it over from Mark had he chosen to do so. There are probably several reasons why he did not. First, Luke knows that the various councils in Acts (4-5; 6; 22-24) were not judicial bodies, and the hearing in the house of the High Priest is therefore not presented as having any official status. Second, Luke is anxious to show Jesus' innocence to the extent that he cannot even be charged with any violation of the Torah let alone be guilty of the charge.[53] Finally and most significantly, Luke thereby is able to suggest that the whole people is responsible for Jesus' death. Paul had no official trial before the council but would have been lynched had Claudius Lysias not intervened. Stephen had no official trial before the council but was lynched by the people. So too Jesus was not tried and condemned but lynched. The mocking of Jesus occurs before he or the council has said a word,

---

52 Cf. Acts 21:30, where Paul is seized by a mob of the people (*syndromē tou laou*).

53 Note how Luke has omitted passages such as Mark 7:1-23 and 10:1-9, where such an interpretation could be possible.

and those who mocked him, "the men who were holding him," are the same as those who arrested him and brought him to the house of the High Priest (22:54a). Those who led him away to "their" council are called "the *presbytērion* of the people" (alongside the conventional Markan chief priests and scribes), which allows for a broader representation. Finally we hear that "the whole company (*plēthos*) of them" brought Jesus to Pilate, a deliberate vagueness that will be exploited in what follows.

Before Pilate (23:2-5)

It is not the chief priests as in Mark who accuse Jesus before Pilate but "they" (23:2), namely "the chief priests and the multitudes" (23:4). This is not a crowd summoned by the chief priests to demand the release of Barabbas as in Mark, but they are present from the very beginning before Pilate, as indeed they have been ever since the arrest and implicitly during the council. At that time Jesus had refused to answer a question about his Messiahship but affirmed rather that he is the Son of God (22:70), a claim with no judicial import either in Jewish or Roman law. The charge that is now made against Jesus is seen to be a blatant lie.[54] On all three counts the reader knows that Jesus is innocent, but the reader also knows that Jesus' accusers have no basis for their accusation. Quite apart from the possible historical accuracy of the charge, it is significant that in Luke it is purely political. Lest we miss the point, Jesus is accused a second time of being a Zealot, beginning like Judas the Galilean also from Galilee (23:5). It is then not parallel to the religious charges against Stephen and Paul, again probably to show that Jesus cannot even be charged with an offence against Israel and the Torah. A parallel to the charge against Jesus is found in Acts 17:6-7, but Luke is less interested in showing that Jesus is innocent of political subversion against the Empire than he is in discussing the Jewish apologetic. Pilate does not for a moment contemplate the seriousness of the political charges but rather declares Jesus innocent. Since such charges probably were in fact responsible for Jesus' death at the hands of the Romans, it is incredible that Pilate should so summarily dismiss them. The point is, as we can see from the passion of Paul in our overlay of Acts and the gospel, that Jesus' real trial is before the Jewish people as part of Luke's apologetic against the Jews of his own day. It is not with respect to the trumped-up political charge (22:67-68; 23:2, 5) but with respect to the religious charge of Luke's time (claiming to be Son of God, 22:70-71), that Pilate declares Jesus to be innocent. That the

54 The point of the questions about Messiahship (denied in 22:67-68) and Divine Sonship (affirmed in 22:70-71), coupled two verses later with a detailed accusation to Pilate concerning *only the first*, is to emphasize the deliberate duplicity and culpability of the Jews as is emphasized by Walaskay, "Trial and Death," 82-84.

charge of perverting or stirring up the people does for a moment again ally Jesus with the people over against the priests and Romans is an inconsistency that Luke has had to let stand.

There is no trial before Pilate,[55] just as Paul had hearings but never a trial before Felix and Festus and Agrippa. Just as Paul was declared innocent by three different people, Lysias, Festus, and Agrippa, so Pilate three times declares Jesus to be innocent:[56] "I find no crime in this man" (23:4), "Behold nothing deserving death has been done by him" (23:15), "I have found in him no crime deserving death" (23:22).

Later Jesus will be declared innocent also by one of his fellow victims (23:41) and by the centurion under the cross (23:47). This is clearly a major motif in the Lukan passion narrative, and one can say indeed that it is the chief function of Pilate. He does not interrogate, he does not condemn, he does not execute; he only declares Jesus innocent.

Before Herod (23:6-12)

This incident has puzzled many interpreters. It is unlikely to be spun out of Psalm 2 via Acts 4:24-28, as Dibelius and Bultmann suggested, because in the Acts Herod and Pilate are enemies while here they are friends. While it is possible that it is a pre-Lukan tradition, even V. Taylor[57] now says that it has been heavily edited. It is even difficult to understand how the story functions in the total narrative, which is seemingly not advanced at all by this digression. One could guess at the source of many of the details. That Herod wanted to see Jesus could be derived from Luke 9:9 and 13:31; that Jesus "made no answer", from Mark 15:5; that "the chief priests and scribes . . . accused him" from Mark 15:4; and that the soldiers mocked him, from Mark 15:16-20. This last transfer gives something of a clue. Thereby Luke is able to eliminate Mark's account of Jesus' mocking by Roman soldiers, with major consequences as we shall see, and he can once more (cf. 22:63-65) have Jesus mocked by Jewish soldiers.[58] There is a certain tension

55 Or perhaps only the semblance of one in the brief exchange of 22:3, taken over from Mark.

56 The same is true of John 18:38; 19:4-6, but this may well be a coincidence. Parallels between the Lukan and Johnannine narratives have often been noted, but they are unlikely to be caused by John's use of Luke (as asserted by, e.g., C.K. Barrett, *The Gospel According to St. John* (London: SPCK, 1955) and J.A. Bailey, *The Traditions Common to the Gospels of Luke and John* (Leiden: Brill, 1963). An impressive attempt to understand the parallels in the context of a *traditionsgeschichtliche* analysis of the passion narrative as this is expressed in the Markan, special Lukan, and the Johannine versions is found in H. Klein, "Die lukanisch-johanneische Passionstradition," *ZNW* 67 (1976), 155-86.

57 V. Taylor, *The Passion Narrative of St. Luke* (Cambridge: Cambridge University Press, 1972), 87.

58 Herod's soldiers are here called *strateuma*; the soldiers of Herod Agrippa I are called *stratiōtai*, Acts 12:4, 6, 18.

between 23:10 where the chief priests go with Jesus to Herod and 23:13 where they stay with Pilate, but this episode provides the necessary background for 23:13-16, where their real point is found. Paul was found innocent not only by the Roman governors Felix and Festus but also by King Herod Agrippa II.[59] It seems likely that Luke wanted a similar testimony with respect to Jesus and has therefore created or edited the account of Jesus before Herod for just that purpose.

Before the People (23:13-25)

Only here in the Lukan passion narrative can we speak of even the semblance of a trial, and it is a trial before the people, who are both judge and executioner. Pilate (and to a lesser degree Herod) appears in the role of a defence attorney desperately trying to dissuade the people from their undertakings. Verses 13 to 16 and 25 are among those which most clearly represent Lukan composition based on no tradition whatsoever, and they are responsible for the present character of the whole passion narrative. "Pilate called together the chief priests and the rulers and the people" (v. 13) and it is they who provide the subjects for all of the impersonal verbs which follow.[60] Because of the rearrangement of the Barabbas material, it is they, and not a crowd stirred up by the chief priests, who cry out "Away with this man," (v. 18) just as the people had cried out "Away with" Paul (Acts 21:36; 22:22). In Luke, unlike Mark, there is no point to the story of the release of Barabbas, for there is no mention of an amnesty custom (however improbable this may be in itself), and hence no trade-off of one prisoner for another, no reason for the release of Barabbas, and no connection between that release and the death of Jesus. Pilate pleads with the people, telling them of his desire (*thelōn*) to release Jesus (v. 20), but they shouted all the more their desire for Jesus to be crucified. Pilate wants to chastise[61] Jesus and release him, but over against his wish stands their demand (*aitoumenoi*), that Jesus be crucified. We hear the ominous outcome of the matter: "their voices prevailed" (v. 23). In the light of this situation, Pilate finally yields, and decides[62] that their demand (*aitēma*) should be heeded; *he* delivered up Jesus to *their* will (*thelēma*, vv. 24-25). In the

59 That this is the source of the story of Jesus before Herod Antipas has been suggested by Walaskay, "Trial and Death," 88-89, and by S. Sandmel, *Anti-Semitism in the New Testament* (Philadelphia: Fortress, 1978), 73, 99.

60 The shift of the people to the side of the rulers is so astounding and runs so counter to the use of the concept *laos* to this point that G. Rau, "Das Volk in der lukanischen Passionsgeschichte; eine Konjektur zu Lk 23, 13," *ZNW* 56 (1965), 41-51, even proposed emending the text from *kai ton laon* to *tou laou*. While there is no justification for this, Rau's observation does point out the extreme tension between Luke and his special source.

61 That is, give him a light beating, as happened to the apostles (Acts 5:30) and almost to Paul (22:24), and not the flagellation prior to execution as in Mark 15:15.

62 *Epikrinō*, not "gave judgment," which would be *krinō* or *katakrinō*.

light of Luke's use of the verb deliver up (*paradidōmi*) in other places as part of "the passion apologetic of earliest Palestinian Christianity,"[63] the reversal of subject and object is striking. Not: Jesus "will be delivered up to the Gentiles" (Luke 18:32, contrast Mark) but Pilate "delivers him up to the will" of the Jews. It is not only in John (19:16) where this happens. Luke gives no motivation for Pilate's action but suggests one elsewhere. Herod Agrippa acted "when he saw that it pleased the Jews" (Acts 12:3), Felix and Festus acted desiring "to do the Jews a favour" (24:27; 25:9). Pilate consistently maintains Jesus' innocence but yields to their demand and so the "trial" turns into a lynching.

The Crucifixion (23:26-56)

"They" led Jesus away, "they" seized Simon of Cyrene, "they" came to the place called Skull, "they" crucified him. By the ommision of the mocking of the Roman soldiers, the antecedent of all these verbs is "their" will of verse 25 and ultimately the "chief priests and the rulers and the people" of verse 13. Nothing in the story is inconsistent with this deliberate impression. Soldiers under the cross mock Jesus (v. 26) but they use words ascribed to Jews in Mark's account (15:30, 31-32), and there is nothing to indicate that they are Roman soldiers. Indeed the only soldiers mentioned heretofore were all Jewish soldiers (22:4, 52; 23:11). The centurion "saw" what had happened, not caused it to happen, and gave once more the Roman verdict: "Certainly this man was innocent." When Joseph of Arimathea asks for Jesus' body, Luke eliminates all reference to Pilate's giving him permission: since Pilate was not responsible for the execution he was also not in charge of the body. Joseph is described as being "from the Jewish town of Arimathea," and when he is called "good and righteous," it is in implied contrast to the other Jews. Joseph had not consented to "their" will and deed, i.e., the crucifixion. (That Joseph, as a member of the *boulē* = *Beth-Din,* and not the *synedrion* = council of the High Priest, was a Pharisee was probably not known to Luke.)

Peculiar to Luke is the presence of the people at the scene of the cross. "The great crowd of the people (*laos*) and of women" (23:28) who bewailed and lamented Jesus did so because they surmised their fate. "Weep for your children," says Jesus to the daughters of Jerusalem. When Luke writes these words he is aware of the destruction of Jerusalem, and they are no longer a warning but an *ex eventu* prediction. "Blessed are the barren" (23:29) is equivalent to "Alas for those who are with child . . . in those days" (21:23). The sense of the mourning of the people is given by the Gospel of Peter. "The Jews and the

63 N. Perrin, *Christology and a Modern Pilgrimage* (Claremont: New Testament Colloquium, 1971), 24. Luke uses the verb in this sense in Luke 9:44; 18:32; 20:20; 22:4, 6, 21, 22, 48; Acts 3:13; 21:11; 28:17.

elders and the priests, perceiving what great evil they had done to themselves, began to lament and to say, 'Woe on our sins, the judgment and the end of Jerusalem is drawn nigh'" (7:25). If in Luke 23:35 the echo from Ps. 22:7 (LXX 21:8) is intended then the watching and the mocking go together and the contrast between people and rulers in the *RSV* is incorrect: "The people (*laos*) who stood by watching mocked him, and also the rulers . . . ." By putting together the darkness and the rending of the Temple curtain, Luke makes the reference to the sealing of the fate of the Temple even clearer than in Mark. Finally, after Jesus' death (in contrast to the friends and women who also saw), "the multitudes" (*ochloi*) who had done this work and witnessed Jesus' death went sadly home to their punishment, beating their breasts (23:48-49).

It is very difficult to reach a decision with respect to the textual variant in 23:34a. "Father, forgive them, for they know not what they do." On MS evidence alone it was not part of Luke's text, and many textual critics and interpreters have come to this conclusion. I believe it is authentic for the following reasons: (1) There is a recognized motive for its omission in the anti-Judaism of the later scribes;[64] (2) it is deliberately echoed in Acts 7:60; and, most important, (3) it is the *lectio difficilior.*[65] It completely contradicts the tenor of the Lukan passion narrative, where responsibility for Jesus' death is put on the people of Israel as a whole. It contradicts all of the predictions throughout the gospel of the fall of Jerusalem which Luke knows to have occurred. It contradicts the end of Acts, where the Jewish people have finally been rejected. It is one of the many problematic contradictions and tensions in the Lukan passion narratives and Luke-Acts as a whole which cry out for explanation.

Conclusion

Is the Lukan passion narrative anti-Judaic? In its present form of course it is. We saw how in Acts the Jewish people shifted from the status of being friends of the Jerusalem church to being enemies of Paul. The same pattern can be seen in the gospel, presumably for the same reason, although the shift does not come until the passion narrative itself. Here the Jews as such, without qualification, are held responsible for Jesus' death, and as a result are punished by the fall of Jerusalem. What earlier in the gospel was a warning coupled with a call to repentance has in the passion narrative become a prediction, and no repentance is possible.[66] Although it is expressed very subtly in the

64 Cf. E.J. Epp, *The Theological Tendency of Codex Bezae Cantabrigiensis in Acts* (Cambridge: Cambridge University Press, 1966), 45.

65 On its genuineness cf. G. Schneider, *Verleugnung*, 186.

66 By using material originally formulated as the message of the early church to Israel in the present context of a Genile Christian work ending (Acts 28) in the final

gospel, the Jews as such have been irrevocably rejected. There are three charges made against Paul in Acts 21:28, of teaching against the people and the law and the Temple; Luke is guilty of all three, and particularly of "teaching men everywhere against the people."

And yet how much of this anti-Judaism is simply a matter of perspective! The question of the readers/hearers addressed is important in any discussion of the hermeneutic of anti-Judaism. Thus Galatians is anti-Judaic, attacking the very foundation of Israel in covenant and Torah, whenever it is read by Jews or is understood to be addressed to Jews; but if it is read exclusively in a Gentile Christian context, both exegetically and hermeneutically, it is not. The synoptic tradition, insofar as it was once addressed to Jews and Jewish Christians is not anti-Judaic; when it is read in a Gentile Christian context, speaking not *to* but *about* Jews, it tends to become so. There is also the perspective of time, which is particularly important in the case of Luke. The special Lukan material contains many warnings of a possible national disaster for Israel which call the people to repentance. When this material is read, whether by Luke or by later readers, in the light of what occurred in 66-73 C.E., this threat and warning have turned into mere prediction and become anti-Israel. There is a vital difference between the phenomenon of prophetic warning, in which the prophet at the same time agonizes with his whole being and prays that the threatened disaster for the nation might not occur, and the phenomenon of the self-satisfied assertion that a prophecy has proven true. Determinism is anti-human, but only the past is determined. A prophet or an evangelist may properly speak of judgment, but only if the rider is attached: unless you repent. O.H. Steck, in his important book *Israel und das gewaltsame Geschick der Propheten,* analyzes the motif of the persecution of Israel's prophets in the context of the Deuteronomic concept of judgment within history. He finds that it occurs frequently in early Jewish writings, including Luke-Acts (Luke 6:22-23; 11:47-51; 13:31-33; Acts 7:51-53). Although the motif is harsh, it is never anti-Judaic because of the call to repentance after disaster. It is this element which is missing in the NT. It is the ending of Acts, which relegates all that has been said about the gospel and the people of Israel to the past, now irrevocably sealed as a part of history, which makes Luke-Acts anti-Judaic. When the gospel was still preached *to* Jews with a call to repentance, it may have been false, it may not really have been relevant to the history and hopes of Israel, but it was never anti-Jewish.

The juxtaposition of the "trials" of Paul and Jesus reveals motifs which make a Roman apologetic purpose of Luke-Acts very unlikely. In neither case are the procurators presented as models of Roman

---

rejection of the Jews, Luke has produced an intolerable tension. As F. Schütz puts it, *Der leidende Christus; die angefochtene Gemeinde und das Christuskerygma der lukanischen Schriften* (Stuttgart: Kohlhammer, 1969), 137, "Bussruf, Verheissung und Polemik in einem Atemzug an den gleichen Hörer schlessen sich aus."

justice, nor do the trials exhibit the kind of treatment that Christians would desire if they were ever brought before Roman magistrates. The charges against Paul have their setting in the context of a debate with the synagogue, and the function of the Romans is to declare Paul innocent of Jewish religious charges. The charges against Jesus are political in nature, but they are neither considered nor refuted by Pilate, whose major function is to declare Jesus innocent, in sharp contrast to the people of the Jews who reject him. Luke's polemic has its context in the agonizing relationship of his community with an outside group, but that group is to be found in the synagogue and not in the government. Luke's approach is not to appeal for sympathetic understanding from potential friends but to defend the church in the person of Paul and to attack the theological status of enemies. The legitimacy of his Gentile Christian community has been called radically into question, not only by contemporary Jews but also in its own mind. Radical problems call for radical solutions. It is understandable that Luke's solution should emphasize both an exaggerated continuity of the church with Israel and a radical discontinuity with contemporary Jews, the election of the church as the people of God and the rejection of the Jews as those cut off from that people (Acts 3:23). Luke's solution to the problem is understandable but the consequences for the later relationship between Christians and Jews, once the church acquires a meaure of self-confidence, are deplorable.

The anti-Judaism of the Lukan passion narrative is extreme but on the surface only. The violent wrenching of the *laos* from a positive to a negative position in the passion story is in sharp contrast with the rest of the gospel and the early chapters of Acts. There are tensions and contradictions within the passion narrative itself. Without the redactional 23:13 and 25, the thrust of the story would be quite different, for then the people who appear frequently in the narrative would take up their customary alliance with Jesus against the priests. Many scholars argue for the existence of a non-Markan passion narrative used by Luke as his major source in these chapters. In particular Luke 22 has received extensive attention, by Schürmann (22:7-38), Rehkopf (22:21-3, 47-53), and Schneider (22:54-71).[67] I have argued elsewhere that a strand (source?) of Luke-Acts can be isolated which contains a consistent theology of a Jewish Christian church preaching to Jerusalem.[68] If this is even partly true, it is our most important source, if

67 H. Schürmann, *Quellenkritische Untersuchung des lukanischen Abendmahlberichtes Lk 22, 7-38* (Münster: Aschendorffsche Verlagsbuchhandlung, 1953-1957); F. Rehkopf, *Die lukanische Sonderquelle* (Tübingen: Mohr, 1959); G. Schneider, *Verleugnung.* There are also less specialized but important studies by V. Taylor, *Passion Narrative*; T. Schramm, *Der Markusstoff bei Lukas* (Cambridge: Cambridge University Press, 1971); and J. Jeremias, *Die Sprache des Lukasevangeliums* (Göttingen: Vandenhoeck und Ruprecht, 1980). We still await the completion of the best contemporary commentary on Luke, by H. Schürmann.

68 L. Gaston, *No Stone on Another,* 244-369. Much of what is said there did not take

not our only one, for the theology of that church. Thus Luke's gospel also contains the most pro-Jewish material in all the gospels, at a level near enough to the surface that the contours are clear even if the mining of it is not easy. I believe that it is possible to reconstruct a Lukan passion narrative about which almost exactly the opposite would have to be said from that which emerged from the analysis above, but that was not the task of this paper. I also believe that one can use the special Lukan passion source as an important witness in reconstructing the historical circumstances of the trial and death of Jesus,[69] but that was also not the task of this paper.

One final matter can be considered only in the context of the wildest speculation. Why did Luke, against the tenor of his non-Markan sources but also against the tenor of Acts, shift in his attitude to the Pharisees in the redaction of the gospel? Why is there such a contradiction between the gospel and Acts in this regard? In my analysis of the Lukan passion narrative it seemed easier to understand the passion of Jesus against the background of the passion of Paul than the other way around. If one were to draw a Lukan trajectory on the basis of a shifting and developing attitude to Israel, it might go something like this: earlier version of the gospel (without Mark), Acts, final editing of the gospel (using Mark). At this point that would be only speculation. In any case the paradox remains that Luke-Acts is one of the most pro-Jewish and one of the most anti-Jewish writings in the New Testament.

---

sufficient account of the Lukan redaction of special Lukan material, but I still hold with the general thrust of the argument.

69 Cf. J.B. Tyson, "The Lukan Version of the Trial of Jesus," *NT* 3 (1959), 249-58; P. Winter, *On the Trial of Jesus* (Berlin: de Gruyter, 1961); and D. Catchpole, *The Trial of Jesus* (Leiden: Brill, 1971), even if his arguments about a sanhedrin trial cannot be accepted.

9

The Jews and the Death of Jesus in Acts

S.G. Wilson

The Speeches

The evidence which relates directly to this theme falls almost exclusively in the missionary speeches and in the prayer of the Jerusalem community recorded in Acts 4:24-30. To begin with it is instructive simply to list the relevant material in order to gain a sense of the uniformity and the degree of repetition involved:

Men of Israel, hear these words: Jesus of Nazareth, a man attested to you by God with mighty works and wonders and signs which God did through him in your midst, as you yourselves know—this Jesus, delivered up (*ekdōtos*) according to the definite plan and foreknowledge of God, you crucified (*prospēxantes*) and killed (*aneilate*) by the hands of lawless men. (Acts 2:22-23)

Let all the house of Israel therefore know assuredly that God has made him both Lord and Christ, this Jesus whom you crucified (*estaurōsate*). (Acts 2:23)

The God of Abraham and of Isaac and of Jacob, the God of our fathers, glorified his servant Jesus, whom you delivered up (*paredōkate*) and denied (*ērnēsasthe*) in the presence of Pilate, when he had decided to release him. But you denied (*ērnēsasthe*) the Holy and Righteous One, and asked for a murderer to be granted to you, and killed (*apekteinate*) the Author of Life, whom God raised from the dead .... And now, brethren, I know that you acted in ignorance, as did also your rulers. But what God foretold by the mouth of all the prophets, that his Christ should suffer, he thus fulfilled. (Acts 3:13-18)

Be it known to you all, and to all the people of Israel, that by the name of Jesus Christ of Nazareth, whom you crucified (*estaurōsate*), whom God raised from the dead, by him this man is standing before you well. (Acts 4:10)

For truly there were gathered together in this city against thy holy servant Jesus, whom thou didst anoint, both Herod and Pontius Pilate, with the Gentiles and the peoples of Israel, to do whatever thy hand and thy plan had predestined to take place. (Acts 4:27-28)

The God of our fathers raised Jesus whom you killed (*diecheirisasthe*) by hanging him (*kremasantes*) on a tree. (Acts 5:30)

And they killed those who announced beforehand the coming of the Righteous One, whom you have now betrayed and murdered (*prodotai kai phoneis egenesthe*). (Acts 7:52)

They put him to death by hanging him (*aneilan kremasantes*) on a tree; but God raised him on the third day and made him manifest. (Acts 10:39-40)

For those who live in Jerusalem and their rulers, because they did not recognize him nor understand the utterances of the prophets which are read every sabbath, fulfilled these by condemning (*krinantes*) him. Though they could charge him with nothing deserving death, yet they asked Pilate to have him killed. And when they had fulfilled all that was written of him, they took him down from the tree and laid him in a tomb. But God raised him from the dead. (Acts 13:27-30)

There are several observations which are pertinent to our theme. First and foremost, the insistent refrain of all the speeches is that the Jews were responsible for Jesus' death. Luke describes this in typically varied and colourful language: the Jews delivered (3:13), denied (3:13-14), condemned (13:27), betrayed (7:52), killed (2:23; 10:39; 13:28), murdered (7:52), crucified (2:23; 2:36; 4:10), and hanged (5:30; 10:39) him. This unmistakable and unvarying message is reinforced by other tendencies in the speeches. For example, in the speeches as in Luke's passion narrative the Romans are in general exonerated from responsibility for Jesus' death. It is the Jews who insist on Jesus' death while Pilate finds him innocent and wishes to release him (3:13; 13:28). There are two possible exceptions. The "lawless men" of 2:23 could be Jews, Gentiles, or both, and Conzelmann thus suggests that while originally it referred to Gentiles (cf. Luke 18:31-33; 24:7) in its present context it refers to Jews.[1] More obvious is the interpretation of Ps. 2:1-2 in Acts 4:27-30 where "Herod and Pontius Pilate, the Gentiles and the peoples of Israel" conspire in Jesus' death and thus fulfil God's predestined plan. This apparently runs counter to both the general tenor of the speeches and the Lukan passion narrative where, although the Romans are implicated, they have at most a passive and unwilling role. Wilckens suggests, therefore, that the passion interpretation of Ps. 2:1-2 is pre-Lukan.[2] He finds confirmation of this in the identification of Herod and Pilate with the "kings and rulers" of Psalm 2, since Luke's normal term for Herod is "tetrarch" and the term "rulers" usually refers to Jewish rather than Gentile leaders (especially in the passion narrative). On the other hand, the reference to Herod is suspiciously Lukan and the unusual use of "kings and rulers" may be

1 H. Conzelmann, *The Theology of St. Luke* (London: Faber and Faber, 1961), 90-91.
2 U. Wilckens, *Die Missionsreden der Apostelgeschichte* (3d ed. rev.; Neukirchen-Vluyn: Neukirchener Verlag, 1973), 132-33.

due precisely to their presence in a quotation. Since nothing is said specifically about Jesus' death, it may be that Luke uses Ps. 2:1-2 to confirm only that the whole world conspired against Jesus—either energetically, like the Jews, or reluctantly, like Pilate. At any rate, this brief allusion to the role of Roman officialdom detracts little from the overwhelming impression throughout the speeches of Jewish culpability.

This impression is confirmed by the observation that, whether Pilate is mentioned (3:13-18) or not (as in most cases), it is suggested that the Jews were even responsible for the typically Roman act of crucifixion. A possible exception appears in Acts 13:28 where the Jews ask Pilate "to have him killed" which, if one turns to Luke's passion narrative to see what happened, depends in turn on the ambiguous "as they led him away" in Luke 23:26 which could refer to Jews or Romans (cf. Luke 24:20). There is also the curious reference to the Jews removing Jesus from the cross and burying him (Acts 13:29) which, at least in tone, is not the most natural way to refer to the sympathetic description which Luke gives of the actions of Joseph of Arimathea in his earlier narrative (Luke 23:50-53). Moreover, the actions which the Jews take against Jesus are dramatized by the victim's innocence, which is implicit throughout and explicit in 3:13-15 and 13:28. Their behaviour had neither legal nor moral justification, as is illustrated by their preference for Barabbas the "murderer" to Jesus the "author of life" (3:14-15).

Luke's case against the Jews is bolstered in at least two other ways: on the one hand the forms of address, especially in 3:17 and 13:27, indicate that not only the Jewish leaders but also the people at large were responsible for Jesus' death; on the other hand, what the Jews did to Jesus was the culmination of their disobedience to God and their crimes against the prophets (7:52). And it may be that yet another factor has to be brought into play, namely, that the soteriological significance of Jesus' death is never made explicit in the missionary speeches and is rarely apparent elsewhere in Luke-Acts. The use of the word "servant" (*pais,* 3:13, 26; 4:27, 30) and the references to Jesus "hanging on a tree" (5:30; 10:39; 13:29) may have traditional connotations, but the most that can be said is that "Luke has taken over certain traditions regarding the meaning of the death of Jesus but he has not in any way developed them or drawn attention to them."[3] The longer reading in Luke 22:19-20 and the reference to the church as having been "obtained by his own blood" in Acts 20:28 are not to be overlooked,[4] and a practical *theologia crucis,* understood as a daily bearing of the cross modelled on the careers of Jesus and his apostles, is clearly a matter of some interest to Luke.[5] Yet the failure of Luke to develop the

3 I.H. Marshall, *Luke: Historian and Theologian* (Exeter: Paternoster Press, 1970), 174.

4 G. Lohfink, *Die Sammlung Israels* (Munich: Kösel Verlag, 1975), 89-92, probably inflates the significance of this solitary reference for Lukan ecclesiology.

5 C.K. Barrett, "Theologia Crucis—in Acts?" in C. Andresen and G. Klein, eds.,

positive notion of Jesus' death as an atonement, even though he is aware of it, means that there is little to counterbalance the negative emphasis on Jewish culpability. Of course, this is not necessarily a deliberate move on Luke's part, for it may well be that Paul's concentration on this theme makes him, rather than Luke, the exception in early Christianity,[6] or that the atonement was an inner-church theme and not part of the missionary kerygma.[7] The effect, however, whether intended or not, is that our attention is focused without distraction on the accusations against the Jews.

In the speeches, therefore, the theme of Jewish culpability is not only clearly stated but also reinforced in a variety of ways. In order to get a balanced picture, however, we need to mention several other themes which have a bearing on the question of Jewish guilt. First, the conviction that Jesus' death was the necessary fulfilment of God's predetermined plan, as expressed in the law and the prophets (2:22; 3:18; 4:28; 7:52; 13:27), is no less conspicuous than the assertion of Jewish responsibility for it. This accords with the specifically Lukan passion sayings (Luke 17:25; 24:7, 20, 26, 46), which emphasize the necessity (*dei*) of these events.

Peculiar to Acts, secondly, is the willingness to explain Jewish complicity in Jesus' death by reference to their "ignorance." The first appeal to this notion (3:17) is more conciliatory than the second (13:27) and both are closely connected with the theme of prophetic fulfilment. Perhaps this connection suggests that Luke is aware of a certain tension between the dual emphasis on Jewish culpability and divine determinism and provides a partial resolution of it by referring to their ignorance—although this may well be to ascribe to him a degree of philosophical sophistication and a concern which he did not share. The use of the same argument with respect to the Gentiles (Acts 17:30) suggests rather that it is an expression of magnanimity,[8] a realistic concession that the past is past and cannot be altered. The concession is limited, however, since it is designed not to confirm the status quo but to prepare the way for a call to repentance (Acts 3:19; 17:30). Indeed, each address to the Jerusalem Jews where they are held responsible for

---

Theologia Crucis—Signum Crucis (Festschrift for E. Dinkler; Tübingen: Mohr-Siebeck, 1979), 73-84.

6 Wilckens, *Missionsreden*, 197-98.

7 J. Dupont, "Les Discours missionaires des Actes des Apôtres d'après un ouvrage récent," *RB* 69 (1962), 50.

8 And not accusatory, as Gärtner argues, identifying ignorance with sin. See B. Gärtner, *The Areopagus Speech and Natural Revelation* (Uppsala: ASNU, 1955), 233-40. For the sake of brevity I have omitted discussion of the variant readings here and elsewhere in the Western text. For the view that the Western variants reveal a strong anti-Jewish tendency see E.J. Epp, *The Theological Tendency of Codex Bezae Cantabrigiensis* (Cambridge: Cambridge University Press, 1966); for a more cautious assessment see C.K. Barrett, "Is There a Theological Tendency in Codex Bezae?," in E. Best and R. McI. Wilson, eds., *Text and Interpretation, Studies in Honour of M. Black* (Cambridge: Cambridge University Press, 1979), 15-18.

Jesus' death concludes with a call to repentance and an offer of forgiveness.

Thirdly, Luke clearly distinguishes between the Jews in Jerusalem/Judea and those in the Diaspora. The former are held responsible for Jesus' death but not the latter, as is shown by the change from second (chaps. 2-7) to third (chaps. 10-13) person.[9] The speeches to the Gentiles (chaps. 14, 17) contain no references to the death of Jesus.

Finally, it should be noted that the references to Jesus' death are enclosed occasionally by allusions to the signs and wonders he performed (2:22; 10:38), which the Jews should have recognized as the work of God (2:22; cf. 13:27), and, more importantly, by repeated references to his resurrection. The latter is emphatically the work of God which counteracts and refutes the deeds of men.

The question of Jewish involvement in the death of Jesus, as recorded in the speeches of Acts, is a matter of some complexity and it will be pursued further in the concluding reflections. For the moment, this aspect of the speeches, like the others, invites enquiry about the traditions, if any, which Luke used. Of course, if we find such a tradition, that he used it is scarcely less significant than if he created it himself. It is nevertheless of some interest to consider whether Luke's view has its roots in early tradition. U. Wilckens, who discusses the possibilities with great clarity,[10] expresses a tentative preference for the view that the combination of divine necessity and Jewish culpability has its roots in a form of Hellenistic-Jewish-Christian preaching which, in turn, is based on a well-established Old Testament and Jewish scheme in which Israel is called to repentance from her disobedience and rejection of the prophets (e.g. Neh. 9:26; Ezra 9:10-15; 2 Chron. 36:14-15).[11] This scheme is Christianized by the addition of the death of Jesus as the culmination of Israel's misdeeds and the substitution of a specifically Christian call for repentance. Wilckens argues that Acts 7 is an essentially pre-Lukan version of such early Christian preaching which, in turn, suggests that it goes back to the preaching of the Hellenists. The traditional scheme of Acts 7, moreover, may have been Luke's model for the other missionary speeches in Acts. This is a plausible hypothesis, however, only insofar as the pre-Lukan origin of Acts 7 can be asserted with some confidence. The case can be made, but so can the equally plausible case for the Lukan origin of this speech.[12] This question, like most attempts to divine the traditions or sources

9 Although it is unlikely that this is why chapters 10 and 13 contain no specific call to repentance. So correctly, Wilckens, *Missionsreden,* 240-41.

10 Wilckens, *Missionsreden,* 109-37, 193-240. I am here, as in the preceding section, necessarily indebted to this most thorough discussion of the speeches.

11 Wilckens here follows O.H. Steck, *Israel und das gewaltsame Geschick der Propheten* (Neukirchen-Vluyn: Neukirchener Verlag, 1967).

12 I am thinking particularly of E. Richard, *Acts 6:1-8:4, The Author's Method of Composition* (Missoula: Scholars Press, 1978).

behind Acts, cannot be resolved with any certainty—and not least because the reasoning is of necessity largely circular. Wilckens' conjecture cannot with certainty take us beyond the Lukan narratives.

Much the same problem arises when we turn to the material in Luke's gospel. The passion summaries, some of which presumably are traditional (Luke 9:22 = Mark 8:31; Luke 9:44 = Mark 9:31; Luke 18:31-33 = Mark 10:33-34; Luke 17:25 and 24:26, 46 are in Luke alone), emphasize Jesus' suffering and death, his resurrection, and the fulfilment of scripture. The similarity to the speeches in Acts is clear, but the differences are perhaps more important. Of these the christological changes—in which the "Son of Man" becomes "Christ", as already in Luke 24:26, 46, and in which he no longer "rises" but is "raised" by God—are for our purposes less significant than the introduction of the motif of Jewish responsibility into a tradition which either does not specify the opponents of Jesus or specifically mentions the Gentiles (e.g., Luke 18:31-33). Of course this accords not only with Luke's editorial procedure in the passion narrative where, in comparison with Mark, both Jewish responsibility and Roman innocence are enhanced, but also with the retrospective summary in Luke 24:19-29 in which the "chief priests and rulers" are held responsible for the condemnation and crucifixion of Jesus. Thus the traditional passion summaries are in important ways different from, and the Lukan passion narrative is in general similar to, the kerygmatic summaries of Acts. That the Jews were implicated in the death of Jesus Luke would have learned from Mark, but it must be assumed that the exaggeration of Jewish responsibility is Luke's handiwork—unless he found it in a passion source independent of Mark.

Perhaps the most interesting parallel to the speeches in Acts is to be found in 2 Thess. 2:14-16:

> For you, brethren, became imitators of the churches of God in Christ Jesus which are in Judea; for you suffered the same thing from your own countrymen as they did from the Jews, who killed both the Lord Jesus and the prophets, and drove us out and displease God and oppose all men by hindering us from speaking to the Gentiles that they might be saved—so as always to fill up the measure of their sins. But God's wrath has come upon them at last.

That the Jews killed Jesus, and earlier the prophets, are both themes of Acts. The reference to wrath is ambiguous, but the understanding of the destruction of Jerusalem in the gospel (Luke 19:41-44; 21:20-24) and the theme of continuing Jewish obduracy and the consequent turning to the Gentiles in Acts (cf. especially Acts 28:23-28) may imply a similar judgment on Judaism. The statement is without parallel in Paul and sits uneasily beside his reflections in Romans 9 to 11, so that many consider it to be an interpolation. But the arguments are scarcely persuasive[13] and the passage should be taken as evidence that Paul, in

13 See the article by John C. Hurd in this volume.

some circumstances, could express himself in a vein similar to the missionary speeches in Acts. To be sure, Paul was provoked by an unpleasant situation in Thessalonica and does not return to the theme elsewhere, and what he says to the Thessalonians may not be what early Christian preachers said in Judea. Nevertheless, it remains the most interesting parallel to the speeches in Acts outside the Lukan writings themselves.[14]

Stephen, Paul, and Jesus

The trial of Stephen and the trial of Paul may well be relevant in a variety of ways to Luke's understanding of the death of Jesus. It is commonly observed, for example, that the account of Stephen's fate hovers uncertainly between a formal trial (Acts 6:12-7:1) and a public lynching (Acts 7:54-8:1). Many suppose that Luke conflated two traditions or that he imposed his own view on a traditional account. It has recently been noted, however, that Luke elsewhere narrates events which combine mob rule with law-and-order (Acts 18:12-17; 21:18-40),[15] although it is significant that on these occasions the Romans represent law-and-order and that the outcome is never the death of the accused. Whether Stephen's death was, in Luke's view, a trial or a lynching or a combination of the two, it is clear that he suffers a Jewish punishment (stoning) and that his death is the responsibility of the Jews. We cannot be certain of the status of this narrative as historical evidence for the era prior to 70 C.E., and even less of its relationship to the Mishnaic rules on blasphemy and stoning; but it does indicate that Luke thought that at the time of Jesus or thereabouts the Jews could put a man on trial, the result of which, though perhaps only under pressure from the mob, could be execution. Perhaps in part it is this which allowed Luke, in both the passion narrative and the speeches, to exaggerate the role of the Jews as both the antagonists of Jesus and the agents of his death.

There are remarkable parallels between the trials of Jesus, Stephen, and Paul. Between Stephen and Paul we can note the following: the accusations (Acts 6:11, 13, 14; 21:21, 28); the mixture of mob rule and legal procedure, as noted above; the opening words of the speeches (Acts 7:1; 22:1); and the manner in which both speeches, while different in content, relate only loosely to the accusations which instigate them. Between Stephen and Jesus we can note the following: the Sanhedrin setting, the interrogation and reply, and the violent reaction

14 1 Corinthians 15:3-5 is relevant only insofar as it may suggest that some elements of Luke's kerygmatic scheme have their roots in a traditional scheme such as Paul quotes here. The differences are, however, crucial: Acts emphasizes Jewish culpability and ignores the atonement. See Wilckens, *Missionsreden,* 72-81, 194-200.

15 Richard, *Method,* 278-81.

of the crowds—all of which may be incidental, though the echoes cannot be wholly ignored; the vision of the Son of Man (Acts 7:56, where if *hestōta* refers to location rather than posture, the parallel with Luke 22:69 is particularly close); the prayer for forgiveness (Acts 7:60; Luke 23:34 variant reading) and the dying words (Acts 7:59; Luke 23:46); and, finally, the accusations in Acts 6:ll, 13, 14, which recall Mark 14:55-60 but are missing from Luke's account of Jesus' trial. Parallels between the trials of Jesus and Paul can be found throughout Acts 21 to 28, but are most obvious in Paul's summary in Acts 28:17-20: both are seized by the Jews and "delivered" to the Romans (Acts 28:17, Luke 22:54; 24:20); the Romans find both of them innocent and wish to free them (Acts 28:18; Luke 23:4, 14, 16, 20, 22) but accede to the strenuous protestations of the Jews (Acts 28:19; Luke 23:5, 18, 21, 23); in both cases the guilt of the Jews and the innocence of the Romans are starkly contrasted.[16]

It is clear from these lists that the parallels are not identical in each case; but it is equally clear that there are significant common features in all three. Of these the most important are: the antagonism of the Jews and their active involvement in the three trials; by contrast, in two cases, the innocence of the Romans, their desire to free an innocent man, and the strong opposition to this from the Jews. In addition we can note that the charges against Stephen and Paul, which are virtually identical, are connected with Jesus in Acts 6:14 even though they are absent from his account of Jesus' trial. In fact the wording of Acts 6:14 is altogether puzzling. It is cast in the future tense and seems to refer to what Jesus will do rather than what he has done, and it is at most only indirectly answered in the following speech where, moreover, no further mention is made of *Jesus'* connection with the law and the Temple. The omission from the trial of Jesus of these accusations, in particular the one concerning the Temple, is difficult to explain. Thus, if they were not in accord with the attitude of Luke towards the law and the Temple,[17] or were thought too dangerous to use in Jesus' trial,[18] why are they used in Acts and in connection with Jesus (Acts 6:14)? What was to stop Luke using them and declaring them to be false, as he does in Acts 6:11, 13? It is possible that Luke followed an independent tradition in his passion narrative in which the accusations did not appear; but if not, it is hard to find a convincing explanation in view of Luke's apparent desire to signal the parallels between the trials of Jesus, Stephen, and Paul. However, it is the overall phenomenon of the parallels, and in

16 The parallels between Stephen and Jesus are well known. Those between Stephen and Paul are noted by Richard, *Method,* 258. Those between Jesus and Paul are discussed in detail by W. Radl, *Paulus und Jesus im lukanischen Doppelwerk* (Bern-Frankfurt: Lang, 1975), 154-65. He notes a degree of tension between Acts 28:17-19 and the narratives in Acts 21 to 26.

17 So M. Simon, *St. Stephen and the Hellenists* (London: Longmans, 1956), 23-26.

18 So, for example, E. Haenchen, *The Acts of the Apostles* (Oxford: Basil Blackwell, 1971), 274.

particular the common features noted at the beginning of this paragraph, which interest us most. Is it possible that one trial was the "source" of at least some features in the others, or have they all become conflated in Luke's mind? It might be thought natural to assume that Luke's understanding of the trial of Jesus has affected his description of the trials of Stephen and Paul. But might not the reverse also be true? Could it be that some elements in the trial of Paul, for example, have spilled over into the trial of Jesus—and especially the theme of Jewish culpability, since it is the Jews who are consistently portrayed as the opponents of Paul in Acts? That they are so portrayed probably has as much to do with accusations against Paul in Luke's time as it does with the experiences of the historical Paul. And thus the exaggeration of the role of the Jews in Jesus' death might derive in part from the contentious reputation of Paul at the time Luke wrote.[19]

Conclusions

In Acts, perhaps more emphatically than in any other New Testament writing, the Jews are blamed for the death of Jesus. In this sense there is an unmistakable anti-Judaic strain in Luke's presentation of early Christian preaching. Yet the matter does not rest there. Along with this central accusation Luke is careful to include a number of mitigating factors. The Jews acted out of ignorance, and what they did was a necessary part of the divine plan. Moreover, it is specifically the Jerusalem Jews and no others who are held responsible for Jesus' death—a distinction which later generations of Christians would have done well to remember. In addition, each declaration of Jewish culpability is tied to a call for repentance and an offer of divine forgiveness—an attitude further exemplified in Stephen's prayer for his Jewish persecutors. Any summing up of Luke's presentation of this theme must also bear in mind that the opposite pole of Jewish culpability is Roman innocence. Which of these is prior and in that sense perhaps the cause of the other is difficult to surmise. Yet if there is a political message in Acts—addressed either to the Romans or, more probably, to Christians—this might help to explain, though not necessarily excuse, Luke's excessive concentration on the role of the Jews in Jesus' death.

There is however another, darker side to the coin. While Jewish responsibility for Jesus' death is mitigated in several ways in the speeches, this theme cannot be considered in isolation from the role of the Jews throughout Acts. Clearly, the mission to the Jews met with partial success and occasional support for the Christian movement comes from the Pharisees (Acts 5:33-39; 23:6-9, etc.); but at the same

19 A similar conclusion was reached independently by L. Gaston and is worked out in a somewhat different fashion in his essay in this volume.

time it is "the Jews" who are consistently represented as the instigators of harrassment and persecution of Christians, especially Paul. As in the Fourth Gospel (the only other New Testament text in which the phrase "the Jews" is used with similar regularity and pejorative force) the Jews in Acts seem to be the natural enemies of the church—a theme which becomes increasingly conspicuous as the narrative proceeds. The parallels in the fates of Jesus, Stephen, and Paul reinforce the impression that, while some were converted and a few favourably disposed, the Jews in general hounded and opposed Christians in precisely the same way that they had earlier treated Jesus—and for this Luke offers no excuses and no mitigation.

This leads us to reflect upon the *Sitz im Leben* of Acts. The similarities with the Fourth Gospel might suggest not only a similar geographical locale (Asia Minor?) but also a similar problem with contemporary Judaism. Does Acts, as is probably the case with John, reflect the situation following the introduction of the *Birkath-ha-minim* into the synagogue towards the end of the first century, of which the *Birkath* is but one expression, that colours Luke's whole account (cf. Acts 18:7; 19:9, where Paul separates himself from the synagogue)? We cannot be sure, but at least it seems probable that disputes with Jews contemporaneous with the time of writing, and centring particularly on Paul, not only influenced Luke's presentation of the Jews as the implacable enemies of the church but may also have worked its way into his perception of their role in the trial and death of Jesus. And if Luke wrote for communities that were predominantly Gentile, after the cessation of the Jewish mission and at a time when the enmity of Judaism was a daily reality, this would clearly affect their response to his description of Jewish opposition to the early church and even, despite the mitigating circumstances, to the role of the Jews in Jesus' death.

When all this has been said, and we have allowed that Luke has exaggerated Jewish responsibility for Jesus' death and minimized that of the Romans, and that he has been influenced in a variety of ways by the circumstances of his day, we might still enquire after the historical worth of his presentation. To what degree does his portrait of early Jewish-Christian preaching approximate reality? The problem, of course, is that there is little evidence against which to check Luke outside of his own two volumes. The best supporting evidence comes in a general way from 1 Thess. 2:14-16—and incidentally, contrary to those who would absolve the Jews of any complicity in the trial of Jesus, shows that one Christian writing in the late forties or early fifties believed the Jews *were* primarily responsible for Jesus' death. Presumably any answer we give to this question will be related to what we think took place during the trial of Jesus as well as to what we think the earliest Christians perceived to have taken place. Merely to raise this complex and contentious matter is to be provided with the best possible incentive to draw to a close.

10

Anti-Judaic Sentiments in the Passion Narrative According to Matthew

Erwin Buck

This essay will investigate the passion narrative of Matthew's gospel with the aim of elucidating the attitude toward Judaism which comes to expression in it. In order to establish the specifically Matthean sentiments toward Judaism we will pay special attention to the ways in which Matthew differs from Mark, his primary source. We will attempt to determine the *Sitz im Leben* of the distinctively Matthean features, and consider whether these Matthean peculiarities coalesce to form a cohesive pattern. From the findings we hope to be able to draw certain conclusions for modern-day relations between Christians and Jews.

To keep the study within reasonable limits, we will confine ourselves mainly to the passion narrative in the narrow sense, covering the period between Jesus' betrayal and his burial.[1]

The Jewish Leadership

In the synoptic passion narrative Jesus frequently finds himself face to face with a coalition of various segments within Judaism. Upon closer

1 This essay owes much to recent contributions, though it is not consciously based on any of them. The aim of this paper is quite simply to assemble the pertinent data relating to a small yet significant portion of the First Gospel and to observe the profile which comes into view when this is done. The following more comprehensive studies are highly recommended for further reading: Michael J. Cook, *Mark's Treatment of the Jewish Leaders* (Leiden: Brill, 1978); A.T. Davies, ed., *Antisemitism and the Foundations of Christianity* (New York: Paulist, 1979); Elisabeth Schüssler Fiorenza, ed., *Aspects of Religious Propaganda in Judaism and Early Christianity* (Notre Dame: University of Notre Dame Press, 1976); Douglas R.A. Hare, *The Theme of Jewish Persecution of Christians in the Gospel According to St. Matthew* (Cambridge: Cambridge University Press, 1967); Hans Küng and Walter Kasper, eds., *Christians and Jews,* Concilium N.S. 8.10 (New York: Seabury Press, 1974); Samuel Sandmel, *Anti-Semitism in the New Testament?* (Philadelphia: Fortress Press, 1978).

examination it becomes evident that Matthew saw that coalition in a slightly different light from the way Mark did.

Several incidents in the passion narrative of Matthew shed light on Matthew's appraisal of the responsible parties within the Jewish establishment. For the narration of these incidents Matthew evidently relies entirely on the information available to him from Mark, yet he deviates from Mark in some significant respects. In these divergences one may therefore hope to discover how Matthew modifies the tradition before him and what special concerns motivate him in his writing.[2]

We focus first on the identity of the parties which Mark and Matthew single out for attention. The data can best be presented in parallel columns.[3]

The identity of those plotting against Jesus:

Matt. 26:3	Mark 14:1
the chief priests	the chief priests
and the elders of the people	and the scribes

The identity of those who sent the mob to arrest Jesus:

Matt. 26:47	Mark 14:43
the chief priests	the chief priests
and the elders of the people	and the scribes
	and the elders

The identity of those gathered at the house of Caiaphas:

Matt. 26:57	Mark 14:53
the scribes	all the chief priests
and the elders	and the elders
	and the scribes

The identity of those who handed Jesus over to Pilate:

Matt. 27:1	Mark 15:1
all the chief priests	the chief priests
and the elders of the people	with the elders
	and the scribes
	and the whole council

2 Although insistent voices are again contesting the Markan hypothesis, this study proceeds on the presupposition that Markan priority is still the best working hypothesis for the study of Matthew. If the present essay should discover that the examined deviations of Matthew from Mark are of a rather uniform character and are such that they may be justly called "Matthean," and that compared with Mark these features may fairly be classified as "secondary," this in itself will constitute a further justification for the continued use of the Markan hypothesis.

3 Unless otherwise indicated, the translation is that of the *RSV*.

The identity of the accusers before Pilate:

Matt. 27:12	Mark 15:3
the chief priests and the elders	the chief priests

The identity of those who agitated for the release of Barabbas:

Matt. 27:20	Mark 15:11
the chief priests and the elders	the chief priests

The identity of those who reviled Jesus on the cross:

Matt. 27:41	Mark 15:31
the chief priests with the scribes and the elders	the chief priests with the scribes

Let us now summarize briefly what role Matthew, in distinction from Mark, assigns to the various groups within the Jewish establishment.

The Chief Priests

In all of the above instances except one Matthew preserves Mark's involvement of the chief priests. That one exception (Matt. 26:57), however, may not be significant, and that for two reasons. First, verse 57 is intimately connected with verse 47 in which Matthew does retain the chief priests from the parallel Markan passage. Secondly, although the chief priests are not mentioned as a group in Matt. 26:57, the chief priest, Caiaphas, figures prominently there, so that even in this instance the chief priests in effect constitute the principal antagonists. Nevertheless, here the Markan "all the chief priests" strikes a more emphatic note than that sounded by Matthew.

The Scribes

From the five instances listed above in which Mark names the scribes, Matthew deletes any mention of the scribes. Although the two remaining occurrences (Matt. 26:57; 27:41) do give one pause, there can be little doubt that Matthew reduces, even if he does not eliminate, the role of the scribes in the coalition of Jewish leaders opposing Jesus. This is all the more striking since in the two passion predictions in which Mark lists the scribes (Mark 8:31; 10:33) Matthew did not proceed analogously but reproduced the Markan version virtually verbatim (Matt. 16:21; 20:18), without removing the scribes.[4]

It follows from these observations that, when Matthew tends to delete mention of the scribes in the passion narrative proper, he creates tensions between that narrative on the one hand and the passion predictions on the other. All the more reason, then, to conclude that this almost total elimination of the scribes from the passion narrative itself must be significant for Matthew.

The Elders

While Matthew diminishes the role of the scribes in his passion narrative, he significantly increases the participation of the elders. He introduces the elders in four places where they do not appear in his source (Matt. 26:3; 27:12; 27:20; 27:41), and three times he draws attention to the fact that they function as representatives of the *people* in the passion narrative.[5]

What possible reason could Matthew have for eliminating the scribes from the camp opposing Jesus while introducing the elders (of the people) into the hostile opposition? We do not as yet have a satisfactory explanation for this puzzling state of affairs, but that the altered picture in Matthew is not the result of accident seems clear enough.

The Degree of the Involvement of the Jewish Leadership

Not only does Matthew revise the composition of the forces ranged aagainst Jesus, he also makes their actions more culpable. This effect he achieves in several ways.

In Matthew the High Priest appears more in the lime-light during the trial of Jesus and he acts with greater determination and resolve than is the case in Mark. For one thing, Caiaphas is much more passionate in his interrogation of Jesus. Whereas in Mark the High Priest, almost politely, asks Jesus to declare whether he considers himself to be the Messiah (Mark 14:61), in Matthew he adjures Jesus to do so (Matt. 26:63). More than that, Matthew's High Priest levels a *double* charge of blasphemy against Jesus (Matt. 26:65; cf. Mark 14:64a) so that, in comparison with Mark, the High Priest of Matthew reacts with a good deal more agitation and hostility to Jesus' identification of himself.

In comparison, the other participants in the drama recede more into the background. Whereas in Mark "they all condemn" Jesus (Mark

4 The second passion prediction (Matt. 17:22//Mark 9:31) does not specify any antagonists and can therefore be left out of consideration here.

5 Matthew refers to the elders specifically as "elders of the people" at Matt. 26:3; 26:47; 27:1.

14:64b) in reply to the High Priest's question, in Matthew they simply give an answer, and it is not even clear whether their reply is unanimous (Matt. 26:66). In Matthew's passion narrative the High Priest, it appears, bears the primary responsibility for the condemnation of Jesus.

Not only does the High Priest appear more culpable in Matthew, but also the various groups opposing Jesus tend to act with a greater degree of unanimity and collusion and form more sinister motives than they do in Mark. When the chief priests and the elders of the people decide to hand Jesus over to Pilate, for example, Matthew's formulation of the resolve excludes the possibility that there was even a single dissenting voice when the decision was made.[6] Matthew even employs a special term (*synēchthēsa,* "gathered") to describe the collusion of various parties against Jesus.[7]

The more pronounced evil design of the conspirators against Jesus becomes evident in several ways. For example, the chief priests and the whole Sanhedrin expressly set out to secure false witness against Jesus (Matt. 26:59, *pseudomartyrian*). In Mark too, it must be granted, Jesus has to cope with false witnesses (Mark 14:56-57) but in this instance it is more the result of unhappy circumstances. The Markan officials were looking for legal testimony (Mark 14:55, *martyrian*) against Jesus, and it appears that, when the witnesses fail to agree, this is a cause for regret. Matthew, however, represents the matter differently. He simply passes over the report about the failure of the witnesses to agree in their testimony (Matt. 26:60, 61; cf. Mark 14:56, 59). The Jewish authorities of Matthew know from the start that there is no possibility of finding legitimate evidence; they do not even bother to look for any, but search for persons who are willing to perjure themselves.

In the morning the chief priests and elders of the people hand Jesus over to Pilate with the express purpose of putting Jesus to death.[8] In the Barabbas pericope Matthew's addition of the words "and destroy

6 At this point in the story Mark, too, creates the impression of a concerted action which, furthermore, is carried out by an even larger contingent of participants than is the case in Matthew (Mark 15:1 includes also the scribes and the whole council), but in the absence of the Matthean *pantes* "all," Mark can be read in such a way that a dissenting vote here and there remains a distinct possibility.

7 The decision to arrest Jesus is made by the chief priests and the elders of the people who had "gathered" in the palace of Caiaphas (Matt. 26:3, *synēchthēsan*; cf. Mark 14:1, *ezētoun*, "were seeking"), and the scribes and elders are still "gathered" there when Jesus is led in (Matt. 26:57, *synēchthēsan*; cf. Mark 14:53, *synerchontai,* lit. "were coming together"). This characteristic term is used twice more in passages for which there is no Markan parallel. The request to have Pilate secure the tomb of Jesus is made by the chief priests and the Pharisees who had "gathered" for the purpose (Matt. 27:62, *synēchthēsan*) and the chief priests and the elders "gathered" (Matt. 28:12, *synachthentes, RSV:* "assembled") to bribe the guard to suppress the news of the resurrection.

8 Matt. 27:1, *hōste thanatōsai auton* is a purpose clause; see BDF, 198, 391(3). Mark 15:1 does not contain anything corresponding to this phrase.

Jesus" (Matt. 27:20) makes the chief priests and elders persuade the people not only to request the release of the notorious prisoner, but specifically to engineer the death of Jesus. According to Matthew the leaders act persistently and with evil intention.[9]

When the Jewish authorities revile Jesus on the cross, according to Matthew (27:43) they express their disdain in "biblical" language by perverting a treasured verse from the Psalms (Ps. 22:8). The chief priests and elders appear especially callous in Matthew when they remain totally unmoved by the remorse of Judas and his guilt over having spilt innocent blood (Matt. 27:3-10).

According to Matthew, moreover, it is the chief priests and the members of the Sanhedrin themselves who spit upon Jesus and beat him. In Mark the story reads very differently. The "some" (*tines*) who began to spit on Jesus (Mark 14:65) could indeed refer to chief priests or members of the council (Mark 14:55), but might well refer to some of the many false witnesses (Mark 14:56-57) or even some of the guards (Mark 14:65). In Matthew (26:67-68), on the other hand, there is no indefinite personal pronoun, so that the subjects of the verbs are the chief priests and the members of the council, the very persons who had condemned Jesus to death (Matt. 26:59, 66). In the same pericope, those who beat Jesus are by Mark identified as the guards (Mark 14:65), but again Matthew omits the subject of the verb, so that from the context we gain the impression that Jesus was beaten by none other than the priests and the members of the Sanhedrin themselves.

These seemingly slight yet in fact very weighty grammatical alterations in Matthew's trial before the Sanhedrin also make the words of derision emanate from the chief priests and the members of the council. Not only that, but Matthew transposes their taunts into a more sinister key. Whereas in Mark Jesus is challenged to prophesy (Mark 14:65), in Matthew the challenge deteriorates into an idle game: Jesus is taunted as the Messiah ("you Christ") to guess (blindfolded?) who inflicted the beating (Matt. 26:68).

Finally, it is Matthew alone who tells of a cover-up operation in response to the report of Jesus' resurrection (Matt. 28:11-15). For this deceit the chief priests are made to bear the primary responsibility. They consult with the elders, and together these two groups agree to bribe the guards to spread a lie, and they promise to look after the matter themselves, should the fraud become public knowledge. The chief priests and the Pharisees had even taken precautions, Matthew tells us, to keep "rumours" of a resurrection from arising in the first place (Matt. 27:62-66).

All in all, then, according to Matthew the Jewish leadership is more deeply involved in the trial and condemnation of Jesus, and

9 According to Mark 15:11 the officials "stirred up the crowd" (*aneseisan ton ochlon*); but according to Matthew 27:30 they "persuaded the people" (*epeisan tous ochlous*; note also the plural!).

greater blame attaches to their role than is the case according to the version of Mark.

The Jewish People

Whatever may be the precise significance of the Matthean coalition of the Jewish leadership in their opposition to Jesus, it seems clear that Matthew does not simply intend to shift the responsibility for the suffering of Jesus onto the Jewish leaders and away from the Jewish people. His focus on the elders as "elders *of the people*" is calculated to draw the Jewish *people* into the limelight as well. It is as representatives of the *people* that the elders function in Matthew's passion narrative. Possibly this is also the reason why Matthew diminishes the involvement of the scribes, who constitute a more specialized group in Jewish society and cannot be cast in the role of representatives of the people as easily as the elders.

Matthew, like Mark, certainly regards the leaders as instigators, but he does not wish to imply thereby that the people are free from blame. On the contrary, Matthew points out that the people readily responded to the suggestions of their leaders. The authorities are able to persuade the crowds (Mark 15:11 speaks of the "crowd" in the singular) to clamour for the release of Barabbas (Matt. 27:20), and when Judas comes to the capture of Jesus, he is able to bring with him a *large* crowd (Mark 15:11 refers to the "crowd" without adjective). In Matthew the people even go so far as to pronounce an imprecation upon themselves and their children, and in this way they assume full responsibility for the death of Jesus; moreover they do so in unison (Matt. 27:25).

Matthew conveys similar sentiments when he relates the people's request for the release of Barabbas in his own unique fashion. According to Matthew the people are confronted with clear alternatives. Pilate demands of them (Matt. 27:17): "Barabbas or Jesus?" He presses for a clear verdict (Matt. 27:21): "which of the two?" And the people make a deliberate choice: "Barabbas," they answer, without hesitation (Matt. 27:21). In Mark the people do not voice such a direct preference at this point; it is related only indirectly that the chief priests persuaded the people to choose Barabbas (Mark 15:11). True, in Mark as well, the people request the death of Jesus (Mark 15:13-14), but in Matthew the choice is now a more deliberate one, and it therefore reflects more adversely upon the people. That Matthew wants to place graver responsibility on the shoulders of the people is also indicated by the fact that he has Pilate confront the people *twice* with the identical set of alternatives between which they must, and do, choose (Matt. 27:17, 21).

The Matthean crowd is also more insistent in its demand for the crucifixion of Jesus: Matthew employs the durative or iterative present and imperfect to describe the clamouring of the crowd (Matt. 27:22,

23), where Mark both times uses the aorist (Mark 15:13, 14), and Matthew underlines the unanimity of their request (Matt. 27:22). Furthermore, while in Mark the people demand that Pilate crucify Jesus (Mark 15:13), Matthew has them speak in the passive voice (Matt. 27:22, *staurōthētō*): "let him be crucified," which might be taken to mean: "give *us* authority to crucify him." Again it appears clear that the crowd, as Matthew portrays it, is more blameworthy than Mark's crowd.

Finally, the action of the mob which comes to arrest Jesus appears more violent in Matthew than in Mark. The Markan crowd simply leads Jesus away (Mark 14:53, *apēgagon*), while in Matthew they seize him (Matt. 26:57, *kratēsantes . . . apēgagon*). Matthew has created a scene in which Jesus is forcibly arrested by a mob.

We turn to a closer examination of the Matthean trial scene before the Sanhedrin in the hope that here, if anywhere, we may discover clues for understanding the various dimensions of the antagonism in the Gospel of Matthew.

The Reason for the Opposition Against Jesus

At the heart of the trial scene stands the direct question put to Jesus by the High Priest. Matthew's formulation of that question is taken over almost verbatim from Mark; however, there are some telltale alterations. In Mark's version one of the two christological titles at issue is "Son of the Blessed" (Mark 14:62). Obviously the Markan formulation, avoiding the direct use of the name of God, is carefully constructed so as not to offend Jewish sensibilities. Since Matthew is known for his similarly motivated use of the expression "Kingdom of Heaven" in places where Mark uses the designation "Kingdom of God," one would have expected him to reproduce the title "Son of the Blessed" just as it stands in Mark. Surprisingly, Matthew substituted for it the title "Son of God" (Matt. 26:63). On the lips of the High Priest these words are most unusual.

It is evident that for Matthew the title "Son of God," more than any other, constitutes the point of conflict between Jesus and the Jewish opposition. This is evident from two further observations. When the passers-by revile Jesus on the cross, the derision in the Matthean form contains, in addition to the Markan epithets, the title "Son of God." Twice Matthew brings this title into this context (Matt. 27:40, 43), once even on the lips of the chief priests and elders. The Markan version has no equivalent for this title in either of the two places where it appears in Matthew during the trial scene. Obviously this is an important clue to Matthew's special concerns. It is primarily as Son of God that Jesus evokes Jewish opposition. We shall have to try to determine the place of this title in the [illegible] tradition before we are able to assess the significance of its use by Matthew.

Of similar importance for Matthew is the designation of Jesus as the Christ. Twice this title appears in Matthew on the lips of Pilate (Matt. 27:17, 22) when he offers to release Jesus, and in both instances the people choose *against* Jesus as the Christ. It is of great interest that, according to Mark, Pilate in both places refers to Jesus as the "King of the Jews" (Mark 15:9, 12). Matthew might have been expected to take up this title from Mark, since Matthew himself is not averse to applying the title "King of the Jews" to Jesus elsewhere at crucial junctures (Matt. 2:2; 27:11, 29, 37). When Matthew substitutes the title "Christ" for Mark's "King of the Jews," this alteration must therefore be intentional. It is not as "King of the Jews" but as "Christ" that Jesus, according to Matthew, incurs the further wrath of the Jewish opposition.

Before we can state with some degree of confidence whether Matthew's passion narrative is more blatantly—or less—anti-Judaic than Mark's, it is necessary to determine how Matthew relates incidents which involve segments in society which are not Jewish in the strict sense of the word. In addition, we will want to ask whether the portrait of Jesus himself assumes any characteristic Matthean profile and whether Matthew can offer a particular theological rationale for the opposition to Jesus.

The Gentiles

The Gentiles, including the soldiers, receive on the whole a less harsh treatment at the hands of Matthew than the Jewish elements just discussed. True, the soldiers accept the bribe offered them by the chief priests and elders to cover up the news of the resurrection (Matt. 28:11-15), but by comparison with those who created and financed the cover-up they are much less culpable. True also, the soldiers mock Jesus in Matthew just as they do in Mark, and in Matthew they even hand Jesus a mock sceptre (27:29) which they then use to strike him, but they do not offer him mock worship as they do in Mark (Mark 15:19).

On the other hand, the chief Gentiles, Pilate and his wife, endear themselves to the readers of Matthew when Pilate's wife, perturbed by a dream, begs her husband not to get involved in the condemnation of this righteous man Jesus (Matt. 27:19), and when Pilate washes his hands and dissociates himself from the whole affair (Matt. 27:24).

Not to be forgotten is the centurion who at the foot of the cross comes to acknowledge Jesus as the "Son of God." Of course, the incident is already documented in Mark (Mark 15:39), but for Matthew the Gentile's acknowledgement of Jesus as "Son of God" is doubly significant, since in the First Gospel this is the very title which occasioned such pronounced antagonism on the part of Judaism. What is more, in Matthew this centurion does not stand alone—as he does even in Luke (Luke 23:47)—for an indefinite number of persons share this centurion's experience and subscribe to his confession (Matt. 27:54). Matthew, then, has consciously introduced some nuances into his passion narrative which, from a Christian perspective, make the Gentiles more attractive.

The Disciples

It is common knowledge that the disciples fare better in Matthew than they do in Mark. From the passion narrative we need only cite a few prominent examples. The reaction of the disciples toward the woman who anointed Jesus at Bethany (Matt. 26:9) does not contain the Markan words "and they reproached her" (Mark 14:5). Matt. 26:43 omits the words "and they did not know what to answer him" (Mark 14:40) as a comment on the disciples' aporia when Jesus returned the second time from praying at Gethsemane. Matthew's disciples, although tired, were not "totally out of it."

Even Judas, the disciple turned betrayer, assumes more attractive features through the pen of Matthew. Like the other disciples, he fears that possibly he himself might betray the Lord. He expresses his apprehension directly to Jesus, using the same words as do the other disciples (Matt. 26:25). After the terrible deed is done, he repents and confesses his transgression as sin (Matt. 27:3-4).

Yet Matthew also has his own way of placing the disciples into a less favourable light. In the Matthean version of the Gethsemane pericope Jesus in various ways admonishes his disciples to share his own trials. He comes *with them* to the place (Matt. 26:36), he asks them to watch *with him* (Matt. 26:38), and rebukes them for not being able to watch *with him* (Matt. 26:40). The close link which is thus created between the disciples and Jesus is evidently very significant for Matthew. The disciples are called to participate in Jesus' own experience. Their failure is precisely their inability to live up to their high calling.

Jesus returns *to the disciples* (Matt. 26:40) and his rebuke for their failure to watch *with him,* though addressed to Peter, as it is in Mark (Mark 14:37), really has them all in view, as is clearly indicated by the third person plural (*ischysate*) in place of Mark's first person singular (*ischysas*).

Matthew also goes out of his way to make absolutely clear that it is the *disciples* who flee and leave Jesus alone at the time of his arrest (Matt. 26:56). Mark had left the matter much more indefinite (Mark 14:50). Even at the appearance of the risen Lord (Matt. 28:17) Matthew's disciples are not immune from doubt.

The disciples are by no means perfect even in the First Gospel. Matthew underlines not only the failure of the Jewish leadership and populace, but also the short-comings of the disciples. Yet these two motifs play very different roles. The representatives of Judaism turn against Jesus because they are enemies of Jesus, whereas the disciples fail because of their inability to meet the high standards of loyalty expected of followers of Jesus. By comparison with the rejection which Jesus meets at the hands of the Jews, the failure of the disciples is of a totally different sort. They are weak but they do not take offence at Jesus as Lord, Christ, or Son of God.

The Posture of Jesus

Through all the rejection and disappointment Jesus remains in absolute control of the situation and of himself. This is most clearly demonstrated in Matthew's handling of the Gethsemane pericope. When Jesus goes to pray in Gethsemane he is not distressed, as in Mark, he is grieved (Matt. 26:37; cf. Mark 14:33).

In both Mark and Matthew Jesus leaves and returns to his disciples three times in the garden of Gethsemane. Both evangelists underline the three-fold structure of the drama by introducing the ordinal number *triton* ("third," Matt. 26:44; Mark 14:41), but there is an interesting and significant difference between the two versions. Mark tells us that Jesus three times found the *disciples sleeping* (Mark 14:41) whereas Matthew points out that Jesus three times *went to pray* (Matt. 27:42, 44). The spotlight is not on the disciples but on Jesus and his dialogue with the Father. The words which he addresses to God are most revealing.

Jesus' prayer in all three synoptics is one of ready submission to the will of God (Mark 14:36; Matt. 26:39; Luke 22:42), but Matthew *twice* reports the content of the prayer in direct speech (Matt. 26:39, 42), and on the second occasion has Jesus employ words of the Matthean Lord's Prayer (Matt. 26:42; cf. Matt. 6:10b). Jesus prays, as he has taught his disciples to pray, that the will of the Father might be done, even if that will may ordain suffering, and even death. As one of his last acts Jesus teaches how one ought to pray (cf. Matt. 6:5-8).

The Matthean pericope of the arrest of Jesus demonstrates concretely what will be the consequences of such a filial attitude toward God. To resort to the use of the sword, even if only in self-defence, would mean resisting the Father as he works out his eternal plan (Matt. 26:52-56).

In describing the scene before Pilate, Matthew draws attention to the posture of Jesus who "stood" (*estathē,* 27:11) before the governor, and we can rest assured that by this term Matthew does not just have the physical posture of Jesus in mind. When the chief priests and elders reviled Jesus before Pilate, Matthew points out that Jesus replied "not even to a single charge," so that Pilate wondered "greatly" (Matt. 27:14).

Jesus remains totally in charge. Without flinching he accepts the will of God even when it is the will of God that he drink the cup and endure persecution to the very death.

Persecution and the Will of God

Matthew, even more than the other gospel writers, emphasizes that Jesus' suffering is in keeping with the will of God; in fact, that the passion amounts to a fulfilment of Scripture. Matthew maintains this even when he cannot cite any specific passages from the Law or the Prophets which must be fulfilled by the suffering of the Messiah. All one can say in the final analysis, Matthew is convinced, is that the inexplicable is necessary, because God wills it so (Matt. 26:54, 56; cf. Mark 14:49).

To the "fulfilment-passages" of Mark, Matthew adds a few of his own. The price for the betrayal of Jesus is thirty pieces of silver, in fulfilment of Zech. 11:12-13 (LXX), and by some tortuous exegesis the further use that is made of that money (Matt. 27:9-10) is represented as the fulfilment of "the prophet Jeremiah" (possibly Jer. 39:6-15; 18:2-3). The derision of Jesus on the cross (Matt. 27:43) is couched in the words of Ps. 21:9 (LXX), so that Matthew's readers are encouraged to see even this last indignity heaped upon Jesus as a recapitulation of what the people of God have had to endure throughout history or, more specifically, as an event foreseen by the prophet of old. Such experience does not violate the will of God, then, but can be endured in complete reliance upon the Father.

This theology of suffering is not an invention of Matthew; already Mark had written his passion narrative from such a theological perspective. Matthew shares that conviction of Mark, and, as we have seen, provides it with additional accentuations of his own. In some mysterious way the will of God not only allowed for, but actually preordained, the persecution which the Messiah had to endure. By saying this, Matthew no doubt also wants to caution his own readers not to regard the persecution which they may have to endure "as though something strange were happening" to them (cf. 1. Pet. 4:12).

Matthew's *Sitz im Leben*

We must now attempt to determine the historical situation which is reflected in Matthew's passion narrative, since this may have important implications for understanding the gospel and interpreting its message for today.

Several of the peculiarly Matthean features discussed above are difficult to account for as historical data from the life of the historical Jesus.

That Pilate followed the Jewish custom of washing one's hands as an expression of one's withdrawal from complicity (Matt. 27:24), or that the members of the Jewish establishment deliberately set out to secure false witnesses (Matt. 26:59) and so to break the Decalogue itself, are only two such Matthean assertions which strain historical probability.

It is also hardly conceivable that while Pilate seeks to absolve himself from guilt in the condemnation of Jesus the people who witness this act should collectively pronounce a self-imprecation (Matt. 27:25), thus voluntarily assuming all responsibility for the death of Jesus and passing it on to their descendants like a curse.

No less baffling is Matthew's assertion that the chief priests, the scribes, and the elders mocked Jesus for having trusted in God, and that they are now delighted to discover that his trust had been misplaced (Matt. 27:43). The puzzle becomes all the more enigmatic when we recall that the words of the psalm (Ps. 21:9) which the Jewish leaders employ are words which in their original context are hurled by the non-believers against the righteous one of God who suffers innocently at their hands. This whole situation is just too incongruous.

Finally, the tradition which asserts that the Jewish establishment took precautions against the stealing of the body of Jesus (Matt. 27:62-66) and subsequently bribed the soldiers to suppress the news of the resurrection (Matt. 28:11-15), has all the appearance of an apologetic against the claim that the disciples had feigned a resurrection by stealing the body of Jesus. The charge that the body of Jesus had been stolen would itself have originated in the post-Easter milieu: Matthew indeed hints that the claim is a vestige of a Jewish refutation of the resurrection when he identifies it as a Jewish rumour still current in his own day (Matt. 28:15).

Many of these peculiar Matthean features are less a reflection of the historical situation than the result of a new interpretation of the historical event in retrospect, and from an altered vantage point. These elements in the Matthean passion narrative may have a quite different *Sitz im Leben.*

It makes eminent sense to argue that the claim of Jesus to be the Messiah became the object of ridicule only when a sect continued to believe in him in spite of the fact that Jesus had been put to death as a criminal, just as the messianic claim on behalf of Bar Kokhba became untenable only after he had passed from the scene without bringing about the liberation of Israel.

That the chief priests and the Sanhedrin should have mocked Jesus because of his claim to be the Messiah (Matt. 26:68) is also historically unlikely, for Bar Kokhba was eagerly welcomed as the Messiah by none other than the renowned Rabbi Akiba. To claim to be the Messiah is not a punishable offence in Judaism, in spite of the fact that the direct question by Matthew's High Priest (Matt. 26:63) implies that it is.

But this is not all that is strange in this passage. The title "Son of God" on the lips of the High Priest (Matt. 26:63) does not appear historically accurate. The Markan "Son of the Blessed" (Mark 14:61) would be more credible, although even that term creates difficulties in the present context. The very formulation of the High Priest's question is historically out of place. "Tell us if you are the Christ, the Son of God" (Matt. 26:63) implies that to be Messiah is to be Son of God, and vice versa. While this equation of titles is in complete agreement with later Christian theology (cf. Matt. 16:16), it is very questionable whether the Jewish High Priest would have made such an identification of titles.

The combination of these two titles in fact constitutes the *proprium* of Matthean Christology. The whole Gospel of Matthew centers around the confession of Jesus as both Messiah and Son of God. This is the structure of Matthean theology and the designing of this structure can be credited to the redactor; it represents the *novum* in the history of tradition.[10] To confess Jesus as the Messiah and Son of God or to call such a confession into question is therefore to accept or to reject Matthean theology; it implies little or nothing about one's attitude toward the historical Jesus. The words of the Matthean High Priest, therefore, indicate where official Judaism stands in relation to Matthean Christology; they do not amount to a condemnation of the historical Jesus.

We can only conclude that the contours of the antagonism which Matthew portrays in the trial scene reflect the conflict which has developed between church and Synagogue at the time when Matthean Christology has become the accepted credal expression of the young church. The various pieces of the puzzle are now beginning to fall into place.

It seems best to conclude, then, that most if not all of the characteristically Matthean nuances in his passion narrative are the result not of historical reporting but of theologizing about the present state of the church in Matthew's own day. The opposition which Jesus encounters in the passion narrative is in fact the opposition which the church encounters at the time of Matthew's writing.

This confrontation between the church and the Synagogue becomes nasty when the church keeps insisting on worshipping a crucified Messiah while nevertheless claiming to be the true Israel. It is understandable that such a conflict should arise and it is understandable that as the conflict escalates, the opposing parties should hurl at each other innuendo, ridicule, and accusations which transcend the bounds of discretion. Of course, it is one thing to understand a lamentable set of conditions, it is quite another to perpetuate such conditions indefinitely, even though the circumstances which originated them have ceased to exist.

10 Jack Dean Kingsbury, *Matthew: Structure, Christology, Kingdom* (Philadelphia: Fortress Press, 1975), 40-83, passim.

Hermeneutical and Practical Conclusions

The pronounced anti-Judaism of Matthew is best explained as a reflection of the experience of the Matthean church in its relation to the Synagogue. The church of Matthew is a minority in danger of either being swallowed up by Judaism, or of being deprived of the right to consider itself as a part of the true Israel. Matthew's church is fighting for its very existence, and in such a fight one does not always observe the gentlemanly rules of sport.

And yet it is noteworthy that Matthew discourages the church from resorting to the use of force. Possibly Matthew is motivated by prudence; when a small minority resorts to arms it can expect to be wiped out by force of arms (cf. Matt. 26:52). On the other hand, Matthew may be motivated by theological convictions: if God is truly in control of history, then to try to alter the course of history by force of arms is to resist the working out of God's plan (cf. Matt. 26:54). In any case, Matthew counsels that it is better to suffer wrong than to inflict wrong (cf. Matt. 5:39). His anti-Judaism should therefore be seen as a weapon of defence, not as a weapon of attack.

The theological challenge of Judaism is too threatening to be ignored by the fledgling church. To establish her legitimacy the young church must show that the challengers are wrong and that their attack is not only unwarranted but constitutes an outright violation of the will of God. The pervasiveness of Matthew's anti-Judaism attests to the vigour of the challenge which Judaism brought to bear upon the young church and to the precariousness of the situation of that church.

Matthew, of course, considers himself called upon to defend the faith, the Christology of the church. That at the time of Matthew's writing the battle has been in progress for some time is evident from a reading of Mark. Matthew, however, bears the marks of an escalation of that conflict.

The question now remains whether it would not be more in keeping with the faith which Matthew proclaims to de-escalate the conflict rather than to pour oil on its flames, and whether history has not altered the situation sufficiently for us to effect such a de-escalation.

The church is no longer in her infancy and the attack of Judaism no longer constitutes a threat to her existence. In fact, it is correct to say that now there is no such attack emanating from the side of Judaism at all.

It must therefore be argued that it is no longer legitimate for the church to continue castigating Judaism. Christian preachers, teachers, and laypeople ought to do more, however, than simply desist from casting aspersions upon Judaism. Whenever we read or preach upon texts in which the Matthean anti-Judaic sentiments find expression, it is incumbent upon us to recall and to explain to one another that Matthew's attitude is the result of historical circumstances and that there is no theological warrant for continuing this line of preaching and theologizing today. Matthew himself would not condone it.

It is no easy thing, of course, to break out of the vicious circle which has hypnotized us and is threatening to draw us into its vortex. It will demand conscious effort and assiduous study to develop and maintain a historical perspective in the reading and interpreting of the Christian scriptures, including the words of Jesus in the synoptic gospels.

Such study, we are confident, will lead us to the ever new realization that the conflict between church and Synagogue is the result of regrettable historical and sociological circumstances. Anti-Judaism is not a constituent part of the Christian faith.

11

The Setting of Matthean Anti-Judaism*

Benno Przybylski

A polemic directed against at least some aspects of Jewish life and thought pervades the Gospel of Matthew. This polemic surfaces in Matt. 2:16, 22 where it is stated that various rulers of the Jewish people were intent on Jesus' destruction right from his birth and youth, and it does not come to an end until the final chapter of this gospel, where it is alleged (Matt. 28:11-15) that the Jewish chief priests and elders perpetrated the lie that the disciples of Jesus had secretly removed Jesus' body from its tomb. It should be noted that Matt. 2:16, 22 and 28:11-15 have no parallels in the other New Testament gospels.

In the main body of the Gospel of Matthew the anti-Jewish polemic focuses on a particular segment of the Jewish people, namely the Pharisees.[1] The polemic against the Pharisees commences in what according to Matthew is the first recorded sermon of Jesus: Matt. 5:20 states, "For I tell you, unless your righteousness exceeds that of the scribes and Pharisees, you will never enter the kingdom of heaven." The strongest expression of anti-Pharisaic feeling is found in one of the last Matthean sermons of Jesus—the woes against the Pharisees in Matt. 23:13-36. While these woes are also explicit in Luke 11:39-44 and implicit[2] in Luke 11:45-54 and Mark 12:38-40, the Matthean woes are phrased in more derogatory language. For example, according to Matt. 23:15 the Pharisees are children of hell (Gehenna).

The climax of the whole Matthean anti-Jewish polemic is undoubtedly reached in Matt. 27:25. Here, in the context of the trial of

* I would like to express my appreciation to the participants of the Anti-Judaism in Early Christianity Seminar of the Canadian Society of Biblical Studies for stimulating my research.

1 The Pharisees are often mentioned in conjunction with the scribes, but as will be seen below the main focus in the anti-Jewish polemic is on the Pharisees.

2 In these passages only the scribes are explicitly mentioned.

Jesus, the entire attendant Jewish crowd ("all the people"), in response to Pilate's affirmation of neutrality, is portrayed as answering "His blood be on us and on our children!"

Before dealing with the original meaning and intent of Matthean anti-Judaism, we should outline the main effect which this polemic has had in terms of the relationship between Christians and Jews since New Testament times. Keeping in mind the complexity of Jewish/Christian relations, it can nevertheless be said that especially Matt. 27:25 has been used more than any other New Testament passage to legitimate overt anti-Semitism. Glock and Stark, for example, have shown that "The main theme in religious hostility toward Jews has been that they are under a curse."[3] The curse referred to is the one reported in Matt. 27:25, "And all the people answered, 'His blood be on us and on our children!' " This passage has been taken as proof that the Jews *voluntarily* accepted eternal guilt for the death of Jesus.[4] Christian anti-Semites have felt justified in persecuting Jews even to the point of inflicting death. After all, no punishment could be viewed as being too severe for a people who were tainted with the blood guilt of having committed deicide.

While it is thus clear that Matthean anti-Judaism has been utilized to legitimate overt social anti-Semitism, it is by no means clear that such use of the Gospel of Matthew is justified. The question is to what extent the Gospel of Matthew itself, rather than its later interpreters, is responsible for anti-Jewish thought and behaviour in Christianity?

The question just posed is by no means novel. It has been considered by a number of scholars. For example, in the introduction to Rosemary R. Ruether's book *Faith and Fratricide,*[5] Gregory Baum states that while he used to be "convinced that the anti-Jewish trends in Christianity were peripheral and accidental, not grounded in the New Testament itself but due to later developments . . . "[6] under the influence of Ruether's writings he had to change his mind.

There is no doubt that *Faith and Fratricide* has drawn attention to a number of problems. For example, it cannot be denied that "Christian theology must question the anti-Judaic side of its redemptive language"[7] and that Christianity has been responsible "for the translation

3 C.Y. Glock and R. Stark, *Christian Beliefs and Anti-Semitism* (New York: Harper and Row, 1966), 197.

4 Ibid., 50-51, 197. For similar views as to the importance of Matt. 27:25 in the history of anti-Semitism see J.A. Fitzmyer, "Anti-Semitism and the Cry of 'All the People' (Mt 27:25)," *TS* 26 (1965), 668; F. Herr, *God's First Love: Christians and Jews Over Two Thousand Years* (New York: Weybright and Talley, 1970), 23; Samuel Sandmel, *Anti-Semitism in the New Testament?* (Philadelphia: Fortress Press, 1978), 66; P.E. Grosser and E.G. Halperin, *Anti-Semitism: The Causes and Effects of a Prejudice* (Secaucus, N.J.: Citadel Press, 1979), 72.

5 R.R. Ruether, *Faith and Fratricide* (New York: Seabury Press, 1974).

6 Ibid., 3.

7 Ibid., 259.

of theological anti-Judaism into social anti-Semitism."[8] The role of the New Testament in this process should not, however, be viewed quite as simply as Professor Baum suggests. Before a final word can be said regarding the roots of anti-Jewish trends vis-à-vis the New Testament, much more research must be done in order to uncover the original meaning and intent of alleged anti-Jewish passages in the New Testament. It is within this overall framework that the present article considers the question of the nature of anti-Judaism in the Gospel of Matthew.

The Historical Setting of Matthew

The basic conviction underlying the present study is that the true nature of the anti-Jewish polemic in the Gospel of Matthew can only be ascertained once the question of its historical setting has been settled. One's perception of the meaning and significance of Matthean anti-Judaism varies directly with one's view regarding the setting of this polemic.

When considering the question of historical setting, stages of development within New Testament thought have to be taken into account. The initial stage, of course, is the setting of the actual life of Jesus. Modern research has shown, however, that it is extremely difficult to establish the actual words and deeds of Jesus with historical certainty. For the purpose of the present study it is fortunately not necessary to reconstruct this initial stage, for it is not the initial historical events that have exerted this influence but rather the events as recorded in the New Testament. This is not to prejudge the historical reliability of the New Testament accounts; the question of the initial life-of-Jesus setting can be left open. In this study the emphasis is therefore on the gospel itself—on determining the setting of the final redaction of the Gospel of Matthew.

Unfortunately, there is no scholarly consensus as to the specific nature of the final redaction of the Gospel of Matthew. Until the late 1940s the view of the Gospel of Matthew as exhibiting a Jewish Christian character and being intended for Jewish Christians was widely accepted.[9] With the appearance of an article by K.W. Clark, this view was seriously questioned.[10] The Gentile Christian character of the Gospel of Matthew was also advocated by P. Nepper-Christensen, *Das Matthäusevangelium, ein judenchristliches Evangelium?*[11] However, it was

8 Ibid.

9 There is also no scholarly consensus regarding the definition of Jewish Christianity and Jewish Christians. Here these terms will simply be used with reference to persons who at one time belonged to main-stream Judaism but then accepted at least the minimal teaching that Jesus was the Messiah.

10 K.W. Clark, "The Gentile Bias in Saint Matthew," *JBL* 66 (1947), 165-72.

11 P. Nepper-Christensen, *Das Matthäusevangelium, ein judenchristliches Evangelium?* (Aarhus: Universitetsforlaget, 1958).

not until the publication of studies by Wolfgang Trilling[12] and Georg Strecker[13] in 1959 and 1962, respectively, that the hypothesis stressing a final Gentile Christian redaction of the Gospel of Matthew was systematically worked out.

What implications would a final Jewish Christian as opposed to a Gentile Christian redaction have on the meaning and significance of Matthean anti-Judaism? The full implication of a Jewish Christian setting will be explored later in this article. At this point it must simply be pointed out that if the final redaction has a Jewish Christian setting, then Matthean anti-Judaism must be seen in terms of an *internal* Jewish dispute. A final Gentile Christian redaction, on the other hand, elevates the dispute into the arena of Gentiles *versus* Jews.

Strecker's Gentile Christian Redaction

Let us consider more closely the argument for a final Gentile Christian redaction of the Gospel of Matthew. It will suffice to consider the work of Georg Strecker whose argumentation is perhaps the most comprehensive of all the scholars holding this general view.[14]

Strecker[15] claims that Matthew, as the final redactor, thought strictly in Gentile Christian terms. He was a member of the second generation, i.e., the Gentile Christian generation of his church, which was far removed from contact with the synagogue. The Jewish Christian elements in the Gospel of Matthew date back to an earlier redaction which stems from the first generation of the church, which was strongly Jewish Christian.

It is not always possible to infer from Strecker's study to which of the various levels of redaction the components of the anti-Jewish polemic as described in this paper belong. Nonetheless, the implications of his view for the nature of the Matthean anti-Jewish polemic are clear. If this polemic has its basic setting in the final Gentile Christian redaction then one is forced to conclude that the congregation represented by Matthew was indeed violently anti-Jewish, if not anti-Semitic. After all, in a Gentile Christian context allusions to Jews would be understood as referring to Jews in general. No distinctions would be made as to possible factions among Jews.

12 W. Trilling, *Das Wahre Israel* (3d rev. ed., Munich: Kösel-Verlag, 1964).

13 G. Strecker, *Der Weg der Gerechtigkeit* (3d rev. ed., Göttingen: Vandenhoeck and Ruprecht, 1971).

14 See L. Gaston, "The Messiah of Israel as Teacher of the Gentiles, the Setting of Matthew's Christology," *Int* 25 (1975), esp. 34 n. 24, for a positive treatment of scholars who look at Matthew in Gentile Christian terms. For some comprehensive summaries of the state of Matthean scholarship see Joachim Rohde, *Rediscovering the Teaching of the Evangelists* (London: SCM, 1968), 47-112; D.J. Harrington, "Matthean Studies since Joachim Rohde," *Heythrop Journal* 16 (1975), 375-88; D. Hill, "Some Recent Trends in Matthean Study," *Irish Biblical Studies* 1 (1979), 139-49.

15 Strecker, *Weg*, 34-35.

If, as Strecker might conceivably argue, the anti-Jewish polemic in the Gospel of Matthew does not belong to the final Gentile Christian but rather to a previous Jewish Christian redaction, then the original intent of this polemic would have had a different nature. Thus, while relegating the anti-Jewish polemic to a penultimate redaction may mitigate the actual intent of fostering anti-Semitism, it does not remove it completely. The problem that remains is why Matthew, as the final Gentile Christian redactor, included this polemic in his gospel. This is especially perplexing since the other synoptic gospels, which were primarily intended for Gentile Christians, contain relatively little anti-Jewish material in comparison to the Gospel of Matthew. While the reasons for this state of affairs are by no means self-evident, the possibility that it was occasioned by a concern for preserving or establishing a satisfactory relationship between Gentile Christians and Jews must be taken into account.

Consequently, regardless of whether the anti-Jewish polemic in the Gospel of Matthew was consciously composed by the final Gentile Christian redactor or simply taken over from a previous redaction, the net effect of including such a polemic in a writing redacted by a Gentile Christian and addressed primarily to Gentile Christians was to polarize Gentile Christians and Jews *per se.* Taking account of the components of the Matthean anti-Jewish polemic, such a polarization could easily foster anti-Semitism. Thus, if the final redaction of the Gospel of Matthew has a Gentile Christian character, it must be concluded that not simply later interpreters but the Gospel of Matthew itself bears the responsibility for initiating significant anti-Jewish trends in Christianity.

At this point it must, however, be noted that it is not at all certain that the final redaction of the Gospel of Matthew was Gentile Christian. For example, some of Strecker's alleged Gentile Christian characteristics in the Gospel of Matthew could very well be Jewish Christian after all.

Strecker[16] points out that Matt. 5:43, "You have heard that it was said, 'You shall love your neighbour and hate your enemy,'" is presented by Matthew as a Pharisaic ethical teaching. Such a teaching, however, is foreign to the older rabbinic tradition, Strecker argues, and this shows that Matthew did not know the Jewish tradition.

In my opinion, Matt. 5:43 does not present conclusive evidence for Matthew's lack of knowledge of the Jewish tradition, since this verse could easily reflect teaching similar to that of the Qumran sectarians as expressed in 1QS 1.10 or 9.21.[17]

Strecker claims that the faulty interpretation of Hebrew poetic structure in Matt. 21:1-9 can only be the result of hellenistic thinking.[18]

16 Ibid., 18.
17 Cf. H. Braun, *Qumran und das Neue Testament* (Tübingen: J.C.B. Mohr, 1966), 1:17.
18 Strecker, *Weg,* 19.

In this passage Matthew presents Jesus as riding on an ass *and* a colt while Mark 11:1-10 and Luke 19:28-38 portray Jesus as riding on only one animal. The problem presented by Matt. 21:1-9, however, cannot be solved as easily as Strecker supposes. The fact that Jesus is portrayed as riding on two animals at the same time hardly provides proof for the redactor's detailed knowledge of hellenistic culture. What Strecker's argumentation does suggest is that the redactor was grossly ignorant of both Jewish and hellenistic techniques of riding. This is hard to imagine!

Consequently, it is likely that the so-called faulty interpretation of an Old Testament *parallelismus membrorum* conceals an argument which has eluded many modern interpreters. Rather than misunderstanding repetition in Hebrew poetry, Matthew may have followed a rabbinic mode of exegesis of Scripture which thrived on texts in which repetition was involved. For example, in the Mekilta de-Rabbi Ishmael Shirata 6, on Exod. 15:7, the repetition based on the parallel structure of Hebrew poetry in Ps. 28:5 is interpreted as referring to two ages:

"He will break them down
and not build them up" (Ps. 28:5)—
"He will break them down," in this world;
"and not build them up," in the world to come.[19]

Rather than providing proof for the Gentile Christian identity of Matthew, Matt. 21:1-9 may indeed prove the exact opposite. The use of Jewish principles of exegesis would suggest the Jewish Christian identity of Matthew.

Strecker goes on to claim that Matt. 12:11 contradicts Jewish law.[20] In this verse Jesus is reported as saying, "What man of you, if he has one sheep and it falls into a pit on the sabbath, will not lay hold of it and lift it out?" Strecker argues that according to rabbinic law the owner could feed the animal or even help it to help itself but he could not actually lift it out. Matthew 12:11 thus demonstrates that Matthew was not familiar with this rabbinic rule and consequently he must have been a Gentile rather than Jewish Christian.

This argument once again is not convincing. Although it is true that 12:11 conflicts with the mainstream of rabbinic Judaism, it is possible that Matthew is echoing the minority opinion of a rabbi who favoured a more lenient interpretation of the sabbath law, or that he is simply referring to what was done in practice rather than in theory.[21]

It appears Strecker feels that his strongest proof for the Gentile Christianity of Matthew is based on the argument from language.

19 Translated by J.Z. Lauterbach, *Mekilta de-Rabbi Ishmael* (Philadelphia: Jewish Publication Society of America, 1933-35), 2:47.

20 Strecker, *Weg*, 19.

21 C. Rabin, *The Zadokite Documents* (2d rev. ed.; Oxford: Clarendon, 1958), 57, commenting on CD 11.14 notes that Matt. 12:11 "shows that popular practice was more liberal."

Strecker states that if Matthew were a born Jew this fact should be obvious from his language.[22] On the basis of a study of semitisms, Hebrew loan-words and Old Testament quotations, Strecker arrives at the conclusion that there is no evidence that Matthew knew Hebrew.

Once again it has to be pointed out that Strecker's analysis is not very convincing. As E.P. Sanders[23] has demonstrated, semitisms are a very weak criterion for providing proof of the kind that Strecker wants to derive. In order to arrive at his conclusion Strecker also has to claim that Matthew, as the final redactor, used no other form of the Old Testament than the LXX. Consequently, the *Reflexionszitate* and passages such as Matt. 16:27b; 22:37 and 27:43, 46, which show signs of the use of a Hebrew text of the Old Testament, are all arbitrarily assigned to a pre-Matthean tradition.[24]

Pharisees and Sadducees

Another argument critical for Strecker's overall view is related to the role of the Pharisees and Sadducees in the Gospel of Matthew. Specifically, Strecker argues that Matthew's depiction of the Pharisees and Sadducees does not primarily reflect his contemporary situation vis-à-vis Judaism but rather represents his view as to the probable historical situation in the life of Jesus.[25] In other words, Strecker claims that Matthew views the Pharisees and Sadducees first and foremost as the representatives of Jewish theology who stood in opposition to the proclamation of Jesus. It is only in a very secondary sense that this representation reflects the theological stance of the Matthean church. It must be reiterated that this theological stance, according to Strecker, in no way reflects an actual polemic with contemporary Judaism. The church is far removed from the synagogue.

Let us consider the role of the Pharisees and Sadducees in the Gospel of Matthew more closely. A comparison between Matthew and the other synoptic gospels points to a number of peculiarities in Matthew's treatment of the Pharisees. For example, while Luke shows both the good and bad sides of the Pharisees Matthew concentrates on showing their weaknesses.

There are four pericopes in Luke, including nine references to the Pharisees, which are generally favourable. The setting for Luke 7:36-50, the pericope dealing with the anointing of Jesus, is a meal in the house of Simon, a Pharisee. The parallel pericope in Matt. 26:6-13, on the other hand, takes place "at Bethany in the house of Simon the

22 Strecker, *Weg*, 19.

23 For a discussion of the role of semitisms in the synoptic tradition see E.P. Sanders, *The Tendencies of the Synoptic Tradition* (Cambridge: Cambridge University Press, 1969), 190-255, 297-300.

24 Strecker, *Weg*, 25-28.

25 Ibid., 140-41.

leper" (26.6). Matthew does not mention that Simon is a Pharisee, nor does Jesus get a meal!

In Luke 11:37 it is reported that Jesus accepts the invitation of a Pharisee and dines with him. In the ensuing discussion about the rules of purity Jesus calls the Pharisees fools (Luke 11:40). The fact remains, however, that Jesus dines with a Pharisee. Such an act shows that Jesus views the Pharisees with some favour. It is interesting that while Matt. 23:25 parallels the discussion about purity it does not mention the setting of the discussion, i.e., the meal with the Pharisee.

According to Luke 13:31 some Pharisees even warned Jesus at one time to go away because Herod wanted to kill him. Here the Pharisees are portrayed as friends of Jesus. There is no parallel in Matthew.

The setting for the pericope of the healing of a man with dropsy (Luke 14:1-6) is the house of a ruler who belonged to the Pharisees. Jesus had gone there to dine. This pericope has no parallel in Matthew.

In contrast to Luke, Matthew shows only negative aspects of the Pharisees. There are no exceptions. At first sight the following two passages may seem to give credit to the Pharisees but on closer inspection it becomes evident that they actually do not.

The first passage is found in Matt. 9:11-13. In verse 13 Jesus says, "For I came not to call the righteous, but sinners." From the context arises the implication that the Pharisees are the righteous. However, this implication should not be overemphasized. First of all, it is quite clear from Matt. 9:11-13 that the main topic of discussion is the role of Jesus with respect to sinners. Secondly, we see from Matt. 23:28, a passage where the topic under discussion is the Pharisees, that the Pharisees only "appear righteous to men, but within . . . are full of hypocrisy and iniquity." Hence, it is clear that the term "righteous" in Matt. 9:13 is to be understood in an unfavourable, perhaps even ironic sense.

The second passage is Matt. 23:2-3: "The scribes and the Pharisees sit in Moses' seat; so practise and observe whatever they tell you, but not what they do; for they preach but do not practise." It would appear that the Pharisees are honoured as good teachers. In actual fact, however, the main emphasis in this passage is on their hypocrisy—they preach but do not practise. It is the latter theme which is developed in the following verses. In a sense the alleged knowledge of the Pharisees is set up as a foil to point to their hypocrisy insofar as they preach but do not practise. It should also be noted that this passage serves as the introduction to the woes on the scribes and Pharisees starting in Matt. 23:13.

Not only is the Gospel of Matthew consistent in portraying the Pharisees in a negative manner, but it also expresses this polemic in rather abusive language. This is clearly revealed by the woes against the Pharisees (23:13-36). The woes are not only much more extensive than in Mark and Luke but also more derogatory. In Matthew the Pharisees are consistently called hypocrites. In the gospel as a whole this term occurs 13 times,[26] while it occurs only once in Mark[27] and three times in Luke.[28] In Matt. 23:15 the scribes and Pharisees are even called children of hell; "you make him [the proselyte] twice as much a child of hell as yourselves."

Could such seemingly harsh treatment of a group of people be occasioned simply by a desire for historical accuracy? Is it probable that the polemic against the Pharisees pertains primarily to the life of Jesus as Strecker has claimed? Strecker's conclusion appears doubtful; the polemic against the Pharisees is so deeply imbedded in the redactional structure of the Gospel of Matthew that it is inconceivable that its prime purpose was to describe a phenomenon in the life of Jesus. In Matthew's eyes the significance of the Pharisees goes far beyond such a role. The nature of this role will be outlined further below.

Strecker's argumentation relies more on the Sadducees than on the Pharisees. He stresses that Matthew's portrayal of the Sadducees goes beyond the common synoptic tradition concerning the fact that the Sadducees denied the resurrection (Matt. 22:23, 34; Mark 12:18; Luke 20:27).[29] Strecker argues that all the five remaining Matthean references (Matt. 3:7; 16:1, 6, 11, 12) are redactional. He further notes that in these passages the Sadducees are always linked with the Pharisees. These observations taken in conjunction with the fact that the Sadducees were politically unimportant after the destruction of Jerusalem in 70 C.E. leads Strecker to conclude that Matthew sees the Pharisees and Sadducees first and foremost in a historical perspective as the main representatives of Jewish theology who stood in opposition to the proclamation of Jesus.

How sound is Strecker's argument? Are the five redactional references to the Sadducees in fact so significant as to be a good basis for Strecker's conclusion? When he states that there are five redactional references to the Sadducees in Matthew and draws the conclusion that the Sadducees are therefore mentioned relatively often,[30] it should be noted that Strecker is in fact referring to only two passages, for the four references in Matt. 16:1, 6, 11, 12 all refer to the same context.

Why does Matthew, in comparison to Luke and Mark, have two additional contexts in which he mentions the Sadducees? Would a Gentile Christian audience attach great significance to this? Would such references be significant for Jewish Christians after 70 C.E.? These questions cannot be answered definitively on the basis of the evidence which we possess.

What can be questioned, however, is Strecker's conclusion that the Pharisees/Sadducees as a group are redactionally significant insofar as

---

26 Matt. 6:2, 5, 16; 7:5; 15:7; 22:18; 23:13, 14, 15, 25, 27, 29; 24:51.
27 Mark 7:6.
28 Luke 6:42; 12:56; 13:15.
29 Strecker, *Weg,* 140.
30 Ibid.

they are the significant representatives of Jewish theology in the Gospel of Matthew. It has already been shown that the Matthean redactional activity with respect to the Pharisees is quite extensive and consequently overshadows that with respect to the Sadducees. It will now be demonstrated that if one wants to speak in terms of a group in opposition to Jesus then the combination Pharisees/scribes is much more significant than Pharisees/Sadducees, and it is obvious that the former combination can serve to refer both to the life of Jesus and to the post-70 C.E. period.

The formulaic expression "scribes and Pharisees" occurs eleven times in the Gospel of Matthew (Matt. 5:20; 12:38; 15:1;[31] 23:2, 13, 14, 15, 23, 25, 27, 29). In 5:20, 12:38, and 15:1 this group is seen in opposition to Jesus and in each case the expression "scribes and Pharisees" is probably redactionally significant. Matthew 5:20 has no synoptic parallels. Luke 11:29, the parallel to Matt. 12:38, has "crowds." Mark 7:1, the parallel to Matt. 15:1, has "Now when the Pharisees gathered together to him, with some of the scribes . . . ." Here the scribes only seem to be included incidentally in comparison to Matt. 15.1.

The redactional significance of the formulaic expression "scribes and Pharisees" is most clearly shown by the woes against the scribes and Pharisees in Matthew 23. In this chapter the expression "scribes and Pharisees" occurs eight times. Mark, on the other hand, has only a single reference to "scribes" in his woes (Mark 12:38). Luke, in his woes, has "lawyers" in 11:46 and 52, "Pharisees" in 11:39 and 42, and "scribes" in 20:46. It is only in the summary statement at the end of the woes that Luke uses the expression "scribes and Pharisees" (Luke 11:53).

It should also be noted that while there is only a single case in Matthew where the Sadducees are seen in opposition to Jesus independently of the Pharisees, there are numerous instances where the scribes play such a role (Matt. 9:3; 16:21; 20:18; 21:15; 26:57; 27:41).

The above examples provide ample evidence for the conclusion that if any group can be singled out as appearing to provide the main Jewish opposition it is not the Pharisees/Sadducees but rather the Pharisees/scribes. Strecker's argument thus loses its main pillar of support. This result is especially significant since the relevance of the scribes goes beyond the life of Jesus. References to the scribes have a significant bearing on Matthew's contemporary situation.

The Scribes

An important clue to the redactional significance of the scribes is provided in Matt. 7:29. "For he [Jesus] taught them as one who had

31 In this verse the order is reversed, i.e. "Pharisees and scribes."

authority, and not as their scribes." The *autōn* in this verse is indicative of a polemical theme relevant to Matthew's contemporary situation.

In contrast to Matthew's totally negative treatment of the Pharisees, his portrayal of the scribes is both negative and positive. The negative treatment is especially visible in passages where the scribes are grouped with the Pharisees. Such passages have been discussed above in the treatment of the Pharisees.

Positively in Matt. 8:19 a scribe is portrayed as a potential follower of Jesus, and according to 23:34 some scribes are seen as martyrs in the cause of truth. Both are redactionally significant.

The most positive portrayal of a scribe, however, occurs in Matt. 13:52: "Therefore every scribe who has been trained for the kingdom of heaven is like a householder who brings out of his treasure what is new and what is old." This saying has no parallels in Mark and Luke.

Who are the good scribes? The *autōn* in Matt. 7:29 suggests that there are "their scribes" who are to be distinguished from "our scribes." The latter undoubtedly are the scribes who have "been trained for the kingdom of heaven" (Matt. 13:52). The good scribes are the ones who belong to the Matthean community.

The foregoing discussion shows that, in Matthew's total redactional activity, the references to the Sadducees are not nearly as significant as Strecker supposes. In fact, the redactional activity concerning the Pharisees and scribes greatly overshadows that of the Sadducees and it is clear that the relevance of the former is not restricted to the life of Jesus but pertains also to the contemporary situation of the Matthean community.

Gentile Christian or Jewish Christian Redaction?

Having shown that a number of Strecker's important proofs for the Gentile Christian nature of the final redaction of the Gospel of Matthew are not conclusive in no way denies that there are some important Gentile Christian motifs in the Gospel of Matthew. For example, the many positive references to the nations/Gentiles[32] in the Gospel of Matthew should not be overlooked.[33] The people (those of Galilee of the Gentiles) have seen a great light (Matt. 4:15-16). The disciples are to bear testimony to the Gentiles (10:18). The Gentiles will have hope in the name of Jesus (12:21). The kingdom of God will be taken away from the Jews and given to a Gentile nation (21:43). The disciples are to go and make disciples of all nations (28:19).

On the other hand, having shown that a number of Strecker's important proofs for the Gentile Christian nature of the final redaction

32 For a discussion of the translation equivalents nations/Gentiles see J.P. Meier, "Nations or Gentiles in Matthew 28:29?" *CBQ* 39 (1977), 94-102.

33 At the same time there are also significant negative references; e.g., Matt. 10:5; 20:19, 25; 24:9.

of the Gospel of Matthew are not conclusive does call into question the great significance which Strecker attaches to Gentile Christian motifs in the overall redactional process of the Gospel of Matthew. Rather than assigning Jewish Christian and Gentile Christian characteristics to two distinct successive redactions, with the Gentile Christian redaction as the final one, I suggest that both of these elements are compatible with a single redaction, that is, a predominantly Jewish Christian redaction which is cognizant of Gentile Christianity. Specifically, I suggest that the immediate context of the final redaction of the Gospel of Matthew is the concern of Jewish Christians to define themselves in opposition to the Judaism practised in their immediate environment. While engaged in this activity, the Matthean community is at the same time aware of a larger context, namely, its relationship with Gentile Christianity. While this relationship does not exclude very practical considerations, I suggest that it is primarily based on theoretical considerations, that is, Jewish Christians were concerned with their theological relationship to Gentile Christians.

I do not claim that the Matthean community was exclusively Jewish Christian in membership. A description of the membership of the Matthean church in terms of the alternatives 100 per cent Jewish Christians versus 100 per cent Gentile Christians is quite artificial. In arguing for a predominantly Jewish Christian final redaction of the Gospel of Matthew, I do not rule out the possibility that there could have been a significant Gentile Christian minority within the Matthean community.

The circumstances just outlined should not be surprising. The scholarly consensus appears to be that the final redaction of the Gospel of Matthew took place during the last quarter of the first century.[34] By that time all Jewish Christians must have been aware of the Gentile mission. After all, by the latter part of the first century it is quite likely that Gentile Christians far outnumbered Jewish Christians. While the attempt to come to terms with Gentile Christianity may have been influenced to some extent by the concept of Jewish universalism, it is probable that the greatest impetus came by way of the obvious historical fact of the success of the Gentile mission.

The conclusion that a Jewish Christian community toward the end of the first century would be forced to come to terms with the existence of Gentile Christianity has an important corollary. Because of its relative numerical superiority a Gentile Christian community could afford to ignore the existence of Jewish Christianity. Those advocating a final Gentile Christian redaction for the Gospel of Matthew would be hard-pressed to propose a convincing rationale of why a Gentile Christian redactor would leave so much Jewish Christian material in his gospel.

34 While some earlier dates have been proposed (*c* 40 to 60+) by J.A.T. Robinson, *Redating the New Testament* (London: SCM, 1976), 352, the consensus points to 80 to 100 C.E.

The Church-Synagogue Polemic

Let us now attempt to define the Jewish Christian setting of the Gospel of Matthew more precisely. The analysis of the Pharisees and scribes has already indicated that a polemical relationship existed between the Matthean community and various groups adhering to mainstream Judaism. Such a relationship is further documented, and in my view indeed conclusively demonstrated, by the Matthean church-synagogue polemic. This church-synagogue polemic is principally concerned with the relationship between the members of the synagogue such as the Pharisees and scribes and the members of the Matthean church.

We may begin by analyzing the passages in which the synagogue is explicitly mentioned. The term *synagōgē* occurs nine times (Matt. 4:23; 6:2, 5; 9:35; 10:17; 12:9; 13:54; 23:6, 34). In six of these passages *synagōgē* is modified by a possessive pronoun: by *autōn* in Matt. 4:23; 9:35; 10:17; 12:9; 13:54 and by *hymōn* in 23:34. We will consider the six latter passages first.

In Matt. 23:34 Jesus is reported as saying, "some you will scourge in your synagogues." The "you" and "your" refer back to "you, scribes and Pharisees, hypocrites" (Matt. 23:29). In this case the synagogue is a place where the righteous men are mistreated. Matthew 23:34 has no synoptic parallels.

Matthew 4:23 and 9:35 are both summary statements in which it is stated that Jesus was "teaching in their synagogues." Both of these verses are parallel to Mark 1:39 which has "preaching in their synagogues." The *autōn* in Matt. 4:23 and 9:35 is thus not necessarily redactionally significant.

The expressions "their synagogue/synagogues" in Matt. 10:17, 12:9, and 13:54, on the other hand, may be redactionally significant. In Matt. 10:17 Jesus is reported as saying to his disciples, "Beware of men; for they will deliver you up to councils, and flog you in their synagogues." The parallel passages in Mark 13:9 and Luke 21:12 do not have *autōn.*

In Matt. 12:9 it is reported with respect to Jesus, "And he went on from there, and entered their synagogue." The context clearly indicates that *autōn* includes the Pharisees (Matt. 12:2, 14). In the parallel passages in Mark 3:1 and Luke 6:6 the possessive pronoun *autōn* does not occur.

Matthew 13:54 states, "and coming to his own country he taught them in their synagogue." The parallel in Mark 6:2 does not include *autōn*; Luke has no parallel.

We thus have three instances in which Matthew has "their synagogue/synagogues" but where the parallel passages in Mark and Luke do not include "their." In addition Matt. 23:34, a passage which has no synoptic parallels, has "your synagogues." The "your" is really equivalent to "their", the only difference being that in the your-passage a group is addressed directly, whereas in the their-passage a group is referred to indirectly. Matthew thus has four unique their-passages.

In the Gospel of Luke the expression "their synagogue" is found only in 4:15. This passage has no parallel in Matthew. In the Gospel of Mark the expression "their synagogue" occurs twice (1:23 and 1:39). Mark 1:39 parallels Matt. 4:23 and 9:35. The incident reported in Mark 1:23 has no parallel in Matthew. Consequently, in parallel passages Matthew always has "their" when Mark and Luke have it, while Mark and Luke do not show such parallels in three and two instances respectively.

On the basis of this evidence, it must be concluded that the use of their/your with reference to the synagogue is redactionally significant in Matthew.[35] This does not mean that Matthew coined this expression. After all, it also is part of the synoptic tradition underlying the gospels of Mark and Luke. But it is clear that Matthew applies this terminology more consistently than the other synoptic gospels.

Having established that the use of their/your with respect to the synagogue is redactional in Matthew, we will now examine the significance of this fact, beginning with the three passages in Matthew where the synagogue is mentioned without being modified by possessive pronouns.

Two of the passages are found in Matthew 6. They have no synoptic parallels and are both directed against hypocrites.

> Thus, when you give alms, sound no trumpet before you, as the hypocrites do in the synagogues and in the streets, that they may be praised by men. Truly, I say to you, they have their reward. (Matt. 6:2)

> And when you pray, you must not be like the hypocrites; for they love to stand and pray in the synagogues and at street corners, that they may be seen by men. Truly, I say to you, they have their reward. (Matt. 6:5)

The third passage is found in Matt. 23:6. Here Jesus is reported as saying with respect to the scribes and Pharisees, "they love the place of honour at feasts and the best seats in the synagogues." This saying has parallels in Mark 12:39 and Luke 20:46.

It is striking that all three passages deal with abuses which take place in the synagogue. The synagogue is the place where the hypocrites[36] give alms, pray, and get the best seats in order to appear pious. In other words, the synagogue is portrayed as the place where hypocrisy abounds.

It is against this backdrop that the modifier "their" must be understood. "Their synagogue" refers to a place from which the redactor, Matthew, wants to be dissociated. Although Jesus teaches and heals in a synagogue, the redactor wants to make certain that the synagogue

35 Cf. Gaston, "The Messiah of Israel," 28, esp. n. 10, for Matthew's use of "their."

36 According to Matt. 23 the hypocrites are to be identified with the scribes and Pharisees.

as an institution is not associated too closely with Jesus. All passages clearly show that Jesus is in "their" synagogue.

That Matthew wants to portray the synagogue solely as a place of corruption is not only indicated by the passages which explicitly refer to the synagogue but also by traditions where references to the synagogue have been deleted. The pericope "Jairus's Daughter and a Woman's Faith"[37] is a triple tradition found in Matt. 9:18-26, Mark 5:21-43, and Luke 8:40-56. In this pericope, Jairus, or a ruler as he is called in Matthew, is portrayed as a man who has great faith in Jesus. While in Mark's and Luke's accounts Jairus is associated with the synagogue, in Matthew's account he is not. It appears likely that Matthew's omission of "the synagogue" is not accidental since this pericope would then have been the only one in the Gospel of Matthew to view the synagogue in a positive light, inconsistent with Matthew's overall view.

Matthew, however, does not simply engage in negative criticism, showing the abuses carried on in the synagogue; he also provides a positive criticism insofar as he proposes an alternative to the synagogue. This alternative is the church (*ekklēsia*). The Gospel of Matthew is unique among the synoptic gospels in its use of *ekklēsia.* This term occurs in Matt. 16:18 and twice in 18:17 where its usage is definitely redactional.

In Matt. 18:17 the term *ekklēsia* is used within the context of a discussion of church discipline, showing the institutional character of the *ekklēsia.* Matthew 16:18 shows that the church is an alternative to the synagogue: the church is specifically portrayed as built by Jesus. "My church" (*mou tēn ekklēsian*) is intended to contrast with "their synagogue."

Taking into account Matthew's view of the *ekklēsia,* it becomes even clearer that "their" in conjunction with the term synagogue must be polemical. On the one hand, there is the *ekklēsia* which provides the background for the Matthean community and, on the other hand, there is "their synagogue," the place of the hypocrites, identified in Matthew 23 as the scribes and Pharisees.

Thus, on the basis of a study of the terms *synagōgē* and *ekklēsia,* it is clear that the relationship between the synagogue and the church is one of opposition. Christians do not belong to the synagogue but to the church. The schism between members of the synagogue and church is complete in the Matthean community.

Excommunication?

Although the following argument based on the idea of an official excommunication from the synagogue is not absolutely conclusive, it

37 The incident describing the woman's faith is only included in Mark and Luke, not in Matthew.

should nevertheless be noted since it may provide independent proof of the foregoing conclusion. J. Louis Martyn[38] has presented a convincing case for the view that the idea of an official excommunication of Christians from the synagogue is an important concept underlying the Gospel of John. His main argument is based on the pericope concerning the blind man, John 9:1-40: "His parents said this because they feared the Jews, for the Jews had already agreed that if any one should confess him to be Christ, he was to be put out of the synagogue." (9.22)

On the basis of this verse, Martyn concludes that there must have been "a formal agreement or decision reached by some authoritative Jewish group . . . at some time prior to John's writing"[39] with respect to "Jews who confess Jesus as the expected Messiah."[40] Such Jews were to be excommunicated from the synagogue. While a convincing case can be made with respect to John, Luke 6:22 appears to be the sole passage in the synoptics that reflects such an idea: "Blessed are you when men hate you, and when they exclude you and revile you, and cast out your name as evil, on account of the Son of Man!" Matt. 5:11, the passage parallel to Luke 6:22, states: "Blessed are you when men revile you and persecute you and utter all kinds of evil against you falsely on my account." A comparison of these verses shows that while Luke could possibly be alluding to the practice of excommunicating Christians from the synagogue, Matthew is definitely referring to a more general type of persecution of Christians. In other words, Matt. 5:11 could very well have been redacted to fit a situation which presupposes a split between church and synagogue. Christians have left the synagogue. Exclusion is not a problem. Persecution, on the other hand, is a concern.[41]

On the basis of the foregoing evidence, any simple theory that Matthew's church is closely associated in a positive manner with organized Judaism must therefore be questioned. For example, Bornkamm's view of the close union between Matthew's church and Judaism must be re-examined. Does the pericope concerning the Temple tax in Matt. 17:24-27 really show "that the congregation which Matthew represents is still attached to Judaism"?[42]

In the light of the Matthean polemic against the synagogue and the high regard for the disciplinary measures of the church, the state-

38 J.L. Matryn, *History and Theology in the Fourth Gospel* (New York: Harper and Row, 1968).

39 Ibid., 18.

40 Ibid., 19.

41 For a comprehensive study of the theme of persecution see D.R.A. Hare, *The Theme of Jewish Persecution of Christians in the Gospel According to St. Matthew* (Cambridge: Cambridge University Press, 1967).

42 G. Bornkamm, "End-Expectation and Church in Matthew," in G. Bornkamm, G. Barth, and H.J. Held, *Tradition and Interpretation in Matthew* (London: SCM, 1963), 20.

ment that the Matthean church is "a congregation which still recognizes the general Jewish ruling authority and has still not developed any administration of justice of its own"[43] cannot be substantiated.

Does the following general conclusion by Bornkamm account for all the facts? "Matthew's Gospel confirms throughout that the congregation which he represented had not yet separated from Judaism . . . . The struggle with Israel is still a struggle within its own walls."[44] Such a simple solution stressing a positive union between Matthew's church and organized Judaism does not take account of all the facts. The church-synagogue polemic in the Gospel of Matthew indicates that the struggle had broken the bonds of organized Judaism.

It is apparent, however, that while the Matthean church (*ekklēsia*) is an institution distinct from the synagogue, it is not totally removed from the synagogue in a physical sense. The foregoing analysis points to the conclusion that Matthew represents a predominantly, though not necessarily an exclusively, Jewish Christian church that exists in a Jewish environment. Matthean anti-Judaism is not a theoretical exercise but a practical day-to-day concern. As Stendahl has so aptly put it, the scribes and Pharisees " . . . are the representatives of the synagogue 'across the street' from Matthew's community."[45] Indeed, in order to make the gospel tradition relevant to his own situation, Matthew modifies the roles of specific groups in this tradition.

In comparison to the Pharisees and scribes, the Sadducees play a relatively minor role in the Matthew's redaction. In the light of the fact that the Sadducees were of little importance in Jewish life after the fall of Jerusalem in 70 C.E. Matthew's treatment of them is quite understandable. The Pharisees and scribes, on the other hand, play very significant roles in the Matthean redactional activity. The Pharisees are always portrayed in a negative manner and symbolize the members of the synagogue who are opposed to the members of the Matthean church. The scribes are an intermediate group; they symbolize the members of the synagogue who are potential converts to Christianity. Thus, while those scribes who are still members of the synagogue are often viewed in a negative way, other scribes who have or are about to become members of the *ekklēsia* are viewed in a positive light.

---

43 Ibid., 26.

44 Ibid., 39. It should be noted that in his essay "Der Auferstandene und der Irdische (Mt 28, 16-20)," in E. Dinkler, ed., *Zeit und Geschichte, Dankesgabe an Rudolf Bultmann zum 80. Geburtstag* (Tübingen: J.C.B. Mohr, 1964), 171-91, Bornkamm appears to have softened his stance insofar as there is less stress on the Matthean church's close relationship with organized Judaism.

45 Krister Stendahl, *The School of St. Matthew and its Use of the Old Testament* (2d ed.; Philadelphia: Fortress, 1968), xi; cf. Reinhart Hummel, *Die Auseinandersetzung zwischen Kirche und Judentum im Matthäusevangelium* (Munich: Chr. Kaiser Verlag, 1963), 17, for the view that the Pharisees were actual opponents of Matthew at the time of the final redaction of this gospel.

Matthean Anti-Judaism

If the historical setting of the final redaction of the Gospel of Matthew corresponds to the above description, what implications should be drawn as to the nature of Matthean anti-Judaism? In essence it would have to be viewed in terms of a limited internal Jewish dispute.

Matthean anti-Judaism is limited in several ways. Insofar as the anti-Jewish polemic is redactional in nature it is not likely to reflect an intrinsic element of the initial, founding stage of Christianity. Rather it takes the form of a dispute relevant only to a limited number of Christians at a specific time and place. Even more significantly the polemic is limited in terms of the contestants. From the observation that the Matthean church was predominantly Jewish Christian in character it is evident that the polemic does not pertain to the problem of the relationship between Gentiles and Jews but rather to a dispute between two Jewish factions, that is, between those Jews who had and those who had not accepted Jesus as the Messiah. Any specific Gentile versus Jewish antagonism can therefore not be posited as a part of Matthean anti-Judaism. In a dispute among Jews any implication of overt hatred of Jews in general is precluded.

Let us now look more closely at the observation that Matthean anti-Judaism is an *internal* dispute insofar as it deals primarily with a conflict between two groups of Jews:[46] Jews who have and who have not accepted Jesus as the Messiah. The fact that we are dealing with an *internal* Jewish dispute has a direct bearing on the intensity of the Matthean polemic and its very derogatory language. This should not be taken as direct and irrefutable evidence for overt hatred, but as natural side effects of an *internal* dispute.

Sociological research in the area of conflict can be quite helpful in explaining the dynamics of an internal dispute. Lewis Coser, for example, has made the general observation that "the closer the relationship, the more intense the conflict."[47] Coser does not argue that there is the likelihood of more frequent conflict in closer relationships than in less close ones, simply that if conflict does arise in close relationships, this conflict is likely to be very intense.

The research of G. Simmel is also very relevant to the social reality underlying the Matthean situation. Simmel contends that "Two kinds of commonness may be the bases of particularly intense antagonisms: the common qualities and the common membership in a larger social structure .... People who have many common features often do one another worse or 'wronger' wrong than complete strangers do."[48].

46 Cf. Herr, *God's First Love,* 23, concerning the concept of an internal Jewish dispute.

47 Lewis A. Coser, *The Functions of Social Conflict* (New York: The Free Press, 1964), 67; cf. 67-72.

48 Georg Simmel, *Conflict* (New York: The Free Press, 1955), 43-55.

Simmel also draws particular attention to the fact that the renegade is prone to especially intense expressions of conflict.[49]

On the basis of sociological conflict theory it is not surprising that the Matthean conflict is quite intense. After all, the conflict is between Jews who at one time belonged to a homogeneous group, and even after separation the two groups hold much in common. There was one primary point of disagreement—the messianic role of Jesus in Judaism.[50]

In the Matthean conflict a predominantly Jewish-Christian church was in the process of defining itself in opposition to the contemporaneous Judaism of the synagogue. Matthean anti-Judaism served primarily as a tool in the struggle for identity of the Matthean church. After all, in a Jewish environment distinct lines of demarcation had to be drawn in order to differentiate between Christian Jews and non-Christian Jews. Consequently the members of the synagogue were consistently depicted in a bad light. In this way the feeling of identity of the members of the *ekklēsia* was constantly reinforced and the distinction between the members of the synagogue and Jewish members of the church made absolutely clear in the eyes of prospective Jewish converts to the church.[51] What was at stake was the establishment of an identity of a specific group of Jews within a larger Jewish community, an identity that in turn grew out of confrontation. The Matthean community defined itself over against its opponents, involving intense conflict. The use of abusive language is indicative of the fact that in a Jewish environment extreme measures were needed to establish the identity of members of the *ekklēsia* vis-à-vis those of the synagogue.

Insofar as Matthean anti-Judaism must be characterized as an internal Jewish dispute, it is unwarranted to conclude that it was the intent of the final redaction of the Gospel of Matthew to instil hatred of Jews in general. Rather, Matthean anti-Judaism deals with the problem of the correct interpretation of Judaism. Jewish Christians insist that the acceptance of Jesus as the Messiah is part of true Judaism. What is at stake is this interpretation of what is Jewish, not the wholesale rejection of Judaism and Jews. It cannot be said, therefore, that it is the intention of the final redaction of the Gospel of Matthew to foster anti-Jewish trends. In a Jewish Christian setting the Gospel of Matthew has no anti-Semitic overtones.

Once the Gospel of Matthew was taken out of a Jewish Christian context, however, and placed in a Gentile Christian environment the special nuances involved in an internal Jewish dispute would have been lost. No distinctions would have been made as to various Jewish sub-

---

49 Ibid., 47.

50 Cf. Hummel, *Die Auseinandersetzung,* 109.

51 Ruether, *Faith and Fratricide,* 260, refers to the use of anti-Judaism as a means of establishing the identity of Christianity in general. My argument is that it played a special role in the identity crisis of Jewish Christians.

groups. Gentile Christians would have understood allusions to Jews as referring to Jews *per se*. Taking account of the components of Matthean anti-Judaism, such a polarization between Gentiles and Jews could easily foster anti-Semitism. Thus the historical fact that the Gospel of Matthew has played a major role in providing a rationale for overt anti-Semitism cannot be blamed on the original intention of the final redaction of the Gospel of Matthew. Rather, it rests on a misreading of the Gospel of Matthew by Gentile Christians who were out of touch with Jewish Christian life and thought.

Conclusion

We conclude by applying the insights of this study regarding the historical setting of Matthean anti-Judaism to a specific example, "And all the people answered, 'His blood be on us and on our children!'" (27:25). Taking account of the fact that some Jews had become followers of Jesus, the term "all the people" does not refer to Jews in general but only to Jews who did not accept Jesus as the Messiah. It should be noted, however, that by the use of the word "all" it is indicated that the vast majority of Jews had not accepted Jesus.

"On us" and "on our children" in turn most likely refer to two distinct historical periods. The final redactor of the Gospel of Matthew wants to point out that not only in the time of the life of Jesus (i.e., "on us") but also in his own day (i.e., "on our children") the vast majority of Jews rejected the messianic role of Jesus.

The reference to the blood must not be viewed as referring to perpetual guilt but rather as pointing to the blood of the covenant. In terms of the struggle for identity Matthew depicts Christian Jews as those who accept the blood of the covenant for the forgiveness of sins (Matt. 26:28).[52] Non-Christian Jews are those who reject this blood (Matt. 27:25).

52 It should be noted that the phrase "for the forgiveness of sins" is not found in the parallel passages in Mark 14:24 and Luke 22:20.

12

Anti-Judaism in the Passion Accounts of the Fourth Gospel

David Granskou

Introduction

The anti-Judaism of the Fourth Gospel has long been a subject of discussion. The term "Jew" is used seventy-one times in John as compared with five times in Matthew and Luke, and six times in Mark.[1] This use of "Jew," often in a pejorative sense, together with John's high Christology have singled this gospel out. So in one sense the problem is easy: the Fourth Gospel is anti-Jewish, and most likely its anti-Jewish statements are meant for a Christian audience.

Beyond this kind of statement there are complications. The scope of the passion in the Johannine setting is broad and the use of the term "Jew" is frequent: as a result defining the terms precisely is difficult. The references to the death of Jesus occur throughout the gospel. "The Jews" as a term has a variety of meanings and contextual settings. The term "Jew" in the passion account may not square with other usages in the rest of the gospel, and what is said about the passion throughout the gospel may be somewhat different from the passion account itself. Before we look at the use of the term "Jew" in the passion accounts in the narrow sense we shall look at the overall usage of terms related to Judaism and the Jewish people, and the relation of the whole of the Fourth Gospel to the understanding of Jesus' passion and death.

These investigations have led to a thesis that the Fourth Gospel is caught between two positions in making its case for belief in Jesus. One set of texts suggest that belief in Jesus is tantamount to a spiritual

1 R. Morgenthaler, *Statistik des neutestamentlichen Wortschatzes* (Zurich: Gottheil, 1958), 107.

Judaism, while another set of exclusivistic texts and interpretations suggests that the true believers are part of a new religion already separated from Judaism. The difficulty with the gospel is that it has not clearly chosen one of these two emphases, but rather seems to be moving back and forth in its position. The Jewish and spiritualizing side of the gospel suggests Jesus is the new temple, the giver of the new law, and the essence of the Torah. The more exclusivistic texts put the true believers into an esoteric community separated from Judaism, speak of Jesus as moving on to equality with the Father, and assert that believing in Jesus separates one from the synagogue. The anti-Judaism in the spiritualizing texts is more specific and controlled. In those texts Jesus is against the priests, the Temple, Jerusalem, Judeans, and Pharisees. He is calling for a new Judaism which worships in spirit and truth. The anti-Judaism of the exclusivistic texts seems directed against Judaism as a whole. Moses stands for one thing, Jesus for something quite different, a new religion.

The Jews and Related Terms in the Fourth Gospel

Jesus as Jewish

One of the distinctive features of the Fourth Gospel is its use of expressions such as "the feast of the Jews," or "the passover of the Jews" (see John 2:13; 5:1; 6:4; 7:2; 11:55). Similarly there are the references to the jars of purification (2:6), burial customs (19:40), and the day of preparation (19:42) as being Jewish. Pilate says he is not a Jew (18:35). Jesus speaks to his disciples about the Jews (13:33). The titles King of Israel (12:13) and King of the Jews (18:33; 18:39; 19:3; 19:19; 19:21) are used emphatically in the gospel. Jesus is called a Jew (4:9), and in the same context salvation is said to be from the Jews (4:22). Gutbrod in his article on "Israel" in Kittel notes this usage and suggests a certain remoteness on the part of the author or his audience that requires this type of language.[2] In his conclusion he states, "We may thus discern both a general historical remoteness, at least on the part of the readers, and also a cleavage which is due to the relationship between Christianity and Judaism exemplified in the Gospel."[3]

Does distancing produce an anti-Judaism? We would have to conclude that distancing of itself is neutral. It only becomes anti-Jewish when it is linked with other negative implications. Fortna has pointed out that the reference to the water jars in the wedding at Cana is negative: the Jewish rites of purification needed something more.[4] The

2 W. Gutbord, "*Israel,*" *TDNT* 3:378.
3 Ibid., 379.
4 R.J. Fortna, *The Gospel of Signs* (Cambridge: Cambridge University Press, 1969).

designation of Nicodemus as a ruler of the Jews may be neutral but it too carries a negative undertone. The feasts of the Jews can have the same negative undertone, especially when Jesus falls into difficult circumstances in the context of the feasts. Pilate's question, "Am I a Jew?" (18:35) could be a neutral statement, but again it is difficult to avoid a sense of sarcasm.

It is also important to see the way the evangelist plays so much with the title "King of the Jews." In Johannine usage Jesus is proclaimed King of the Jews in spite of the objections and misunderstandings of the people, producing a potentially anti-Jewish cast. This kind of distancing can be a form of condescension, but is most serious if it can also be shown that the followers of Jesus are in the process of dissociating themselves from Judaism in favour of a spiritualized Judaism or a new and different religion. If this is the case "the King of the Jews" in the Fourth Gospel takes on an especially forceful anti-Jewish ring. The king, ironically, is rejected by the people who have no king but Caesar. Thus the contexts in which these usages exist can suggest either a neutral or a negative meaning. The majority of these passages have something to do with the passion, or events and feasts connected with the passion and Jerusalem.

His Very Own

"His very own" is another expression used infrequently in reference to the Jewish people, occurring in the plural collective form (*ta idia*). We mention it in this study because it is used in connection with the passion accounts in 16:32 and 19:27, and with the prologue in a slightly different form (1:11). In the prologue "his very own" is connected with the world; as Bultmann has noted there is a parallelism between the world which does not know the Logos and his very own (*hoi idioi*) who did not receive him.[5]

The references in 16:32 and 19:27 seem to point more to the identification between "his very own" and the disciples. Those who are scattered in 16:32 do not exclude the Jewish people. In a similar manner, Mary being taken *eis ta idia* (19:27) would not necessarily exclude the Jewish people. Thus this term allows for an unusual association of the disciples and the Jewish people. Everyone deserts Jesus in the trial—both the people and the disciples. The aloneness of Jesus at the cross is what matters. Those "very own" who reject him are not alone in rejecting him; the fourth evangelist sees a pervasive scene of unbelief surrounding Jesus. Thus, when something is said about the Jewish people as "his own" this is not intended to suggest that they are unbelievers in contrast to other peoples who do believe in Jesus. Rather

5 R. Bultmann, *Gospel of John* (Philadelphia: Westminster, 1971).

"his own" are among the general all-pervasive darkness of the human response to Jesus. What gives a special anti-Jewish cast to this problem of unbelief is that the Jewish people are singled out by word frequency. While they are no different from any other group, they in fact receive more mention in the gospel.

The World

One incontestable fact is the frequent occurrence of the term "world" in Johannine usage. There are seventy-eight instances in John's gospel in comparison with three each in Mark and Luke, and eight in Matthew.[6] The overall impact of the term is negative. The Logos comes into the world and the world does not know him (1:10). In the end Jesus overcomes the world in the passion and death (16:33).

Hermann Sasse has argued that "world" means the created universe in Johannine usage. This is seen not just in the prologue but in the whole of the gospel. As he sees it the term cannot mean just "humanity."[7]

Barrett and Bultmann take the other position, that with a few exceptions "world" in Johannine usage means people, or humanity. Humanity's response to the Logos is the world's response.[8] "Rather men are *kosmos* and *skotia* by *virtue* of their being God's creation and the place and object of the saving revelation."[9]

When "world" is related to "his very own" in the prologue the resulting effect is anti-Jewish. Chapters 15 and 16 also seem to suggest that "world" means "Jews." Jesus came to the world, namely his own people, and it persecuted both him and his disciples (15:20). Even clearer is Jesus' answer to the High Priest's question when he says that he spoke "openly to the world," that is in synagogues and in the Temple (18:20) which is "where all the Jews come together." It is also interesting that there is a frequent use of "world" in the farewell discourses and the high priestly prayer in John 17. Oddly enough, with this concentration of the term in the prelude to the passion, there are relatively few instances in the trial account itself. There is heavy usage from chapter 12 through to chapter 18 and then the term is not used from chapter 19 on.

What does this association between "world" and "the Jews" mean for the understanding of the question of anti-Judaism? The association could cut both ways. It could spread the hostility toward Jesus out beyond the Jews, thereby diluting the gospel's anti-Judaism. Or it could

6 Morgenthaler, *Statistik,* 114.
7 H. Sasse, "*Kosmos,*" *TDNT* 3:894.
8 C.K. Barrett, *The Gospel According to St. John* (London: SPCK, 1960), 135; and Bultmann, *John,* 36-37.
9 Bultmann, *John,* 55.

heighten the anti-Judaism by suggesting that the quintessence of the world's unbelief can be seen in Judaism. Perhaps the reading and the rereading of the texts with this association will pull first in the direction of anti-Judaism, and then away from that point of view. The gospel is calling the reader to move beyond a worldly religion to the worship in spirit and truth. As we have noted this could call for a spiritual Judaism, or for a new spiritual religion distinct from Judaism. These texts all call for a spirituality without unequivocally condemning Judaism.

The Jews and Jerusalem

A geographically oriented use of the expression "Jew" can be found in the Fourth Gospel, where distinctions are being made between Jerusalem and Galilee, or between Jews and others such as Samaritans. Generally, Jesus is seen as being allied with Galilee more than Judea and Jerusalem.

While 1:46 states that Jesus is from Nazareth, his homeland is called Judea (4:44); he is seen having a good reception in Galilee (4:46, etc.) but difficulty in Judea and Jerusalem. This is different from the synoptic account where Jesus encountered difficulty in Galilee (Mark 6:1-6), which is also called his homeland.

In chapter 1 Jews out of Jerusalem come to question John the Baptist. While there is nothing negative, there is also no sign of friendliness. In Jesus' first visit to Jerusalem many there believe in him and the signs which he does, but it is also stated that Jesus will not trust himself to these people because he knows what is in the heart of humanity (2:23-25). The making of the water into wine occurs in Galilee, and the results are more positive in Galilee than in Jerusalem. It must be remembered, however, that many in Jerusalem did believe in him. (We will note this later.) In chapter 3 Jesus and his disciples can go into Judea without any problems (3:22).

Later, however, Judea is the place of danger where the Jews are seeking to kill Jesus (7:1; 11:8). But again in both chapters there is also an indication that not everything is negative in Jerusalem and Judea. In 7:3 there is mention of disciples in Judea and in 11:32 people come from Jerusalem to console Mary and Martha. While Jerusalem and Judea usually carry negative implications, instances such as those just cited must then caution us that not all the negative statements against Jews are directed against the whole people.

This centring of hostility to Jesus in Jerusalem, and in the high priesthood can remind us of the gospel's texts which seem to call for a spiritualized Judaism. They may well call for a Judaism in the spiritual sense purged of the negative associations which come from Jerusalem, for what is said about the Temple, the Pharisees, and the high priests goes together.

Jews as Authorities

In many cases "Jews" means Jewish authorities, not the people. In 2:18 Jews question the cleansing of the Temple, and they do not understand Jesus (2:20), but these uncomprehending Jews are contrasted with "many" who believed in his signs (2:23). The Nicodemus story (chap. 3) seems to concentrate on his role as a teacher and authority within Judaism. In 5:10; 5:15; 5:16 the Jews are likely the authorities, but it is not fully clear. In 7:35 "Jew" refers back to Pharisee (7:32). In chapters 8 to 10 the references to Jews are interwoven with references to Pharisees, so again the whole people is not meant. In chapter 11 the reference to the Jews means the authorities and the people around Jerusalem. In the trial and Crucifixion, the references to the Jews point mainly to the authorities such as chief priests (18:12, 14, 31, 36; 19:7, 12, 14, 31).

In some instances the texts state a clear division between the chief priests and Pharisees and the people. In 7:45-52 there is also a division among the Pharisees which implies that Nicodemus and some Galileans were for Jesus. Not all the texts, however, are so clear in their references to the Jews as Pharisees or high priests. The sword can cut both ways, and the impression one gets in reading chapters 7 to 10 and 18 to 19 is blurred. Sometimes when "Jew" is alternated with "Pharisee" or "High Priest" the impression is created that these authorities are speaking for the people, not always against them or apart from them. The unclear interlacing of these authorities and the term "Jew" can lead to a heightened anti-Jewish ring. That this occurs in the passion texts will alert us to potential problems as we move on to study the passion texts themselves.

We might suppose that the passion narrative is taken over from traditional material. If the term "Jew" is introduced into the text by the redactional inclinations of the fourth evangelist we could see this as a generalizing or anti-Judaic tendency. By exchanging "Jew" for "High Priests" in some of the texts he is subtly focussing attention on the whole of the people.

Jews as Either Crowd or Authorities

We have already pointed to the problem of ambiguity. It is sometimes unclear whether the text means authorities or the whole people. Some examples are worth examining. In 3:25 a Jew has a discussion with the disciples of John over purification. We do not know whether he is from the people, or a member of the chief priests or the Pharisees. Chapter 5 is not really clear about who the Jews are, though they are associated with the Temple (5:14).

In chapter 7 there is even more confusion. The term "Jew" can mean Judean (7:1), either the people or the authorities (7:11), the authorities (7:13), or the Jews who believed (7:15), who are puzzled as a crowd, and even divided (7:35). If one also remembers that the same chapter has used expressions like "crowds," "chief priests," and "Pharisees," the confusion increases.

The context of chapter 8 focusses on the Pharisees. There is some difficulty particularly in one instance (8:31) where the text speaks of "Jews who believed in him." We cannot be certain what the term implies in the central section of this chapter. The point of the unclarity is in the movement in the text from questioning and enquiry to unbelief.

Another ambiguous reference is in the account of the Crucifixion where the Jews read the title over the cross (19:20). The expression "fear of the Jews" (19:38; 20:19) serves to underline the ambiguity which we have previously seen. While the major source of the unbelief in the Fourth Gospel is the authorities, the case is not clear-cut.

The Jews and the Crowds

References to Jews also occur in connection with the "crowds." Statistically it should be noted that the Fourth Gospel uses *ochlos* rather than *laos* in all but two cases. *Ochlos* is in itself a more negative term both socially and theologically.[10] The use of "crowd" is concentrated in chapters 6, 7, and 12. It is not clear who the members of the crowds are. The statement in chapter 7 is instructive: "The Pharisees answered them, 'Are you led astray, you also? Have any of the authorities or the Pharisees believed in him? But this crowd, who do not know the law, are accursed'" (7:47-49).

The general pattern in all these chapters is that the crowds come to Jesus and believe, only to have belief give way to debate, division, and unbelief. They can come from the region of Galilee, or even from Jerusalem. The Pharisees and the chief priests can fear them, and also they can fear the authorities. "Jew" can be associated with this group in the chapters cited, especially in chapters 6 and 12. In general the tone is negative and anti-Jewish. While the crowds in the Fourth Gospel are sometimes on the side of Jesus, they are not consistently so.

The Jews and the People

Another term similar to "crowd" (*ochlos*) is "people" (*laos*). Johannine usage is unique in mentioning people (*laos*) only twice, or only once if you consider that the cryptic remark of Caiaphas, the High Priest, is repeated: "It is proper for one man to die for the people" (11:50; repeated in 18:14). The word *laos* traditionally refers in the LXX to the

10 R. Meyer, "*Ochlos*," *TDNT* 5:586-90.

people of God, the nation of Israel.[11] Is the fourth evangelist suggesting that Jesus died for Israel, the people?

There is a double level of meaning or irony involved in the statement. The High Priest is opposed to Jesus, and at the same time he is speaking a prophetic truth for Jesus and for the people, who are probably the Jewish nation. The death of Jesus does not condemn the people but saves them. The people may of course be a remnant of Israel, or the new people, the church. Whatever the precise significance, we have a Jewish High Priest making a prophetic and cryptic statement about the meaning of the death of Jesus in relation to the people of God. The statement is positive, and it is a special mark of the Johannine usage. The evangelist sees some positive role for Israel, a further development of what salvation from the Jews means.

To further complicate the matter the High Priest, who probably symbolizes "the ruler the world," is judged (16:11). Thus the ruler of the world is also the one who proclaims the salvation of the people though the death of Jesus. This is another instance of the complexity of the Johannine stance toward the Jewish nation and religion.

Summary

The Jews can stand for the people, the world, the crowd, the high priests, the Pharisees, high priests and Pharisees, Judeans, residents of Jerusalem, Jewish religion, earthly religion, and so on. Jesus is often defined in terms of Judaism: he is the Messiah, the Lamb of God, he gives the new law, he is related to Moses, etc. In some parts of the gospel there is a hard core of opposition to Jesus. Pharisees, high priests, Judeans and the like form this core of opposition. The fusing of the term "Jews" with these other terms tends to widen the concept of opposition to the Jewish nation and gives the gospel an anti-Jewish tendency. Within the core of Judaism, however, there are interesting examples of prophecy or belief such as Joseph of Arimathea, Nicodemus, and Caiaphas. These look like symbols of a remnant theology. Both the widening and the remnant aspects seem to be part of a special Johannine point of view. The fourth evangelist distances himself from Judaism while still working with the concept of remnant.

Whether these elements are part of the historical reality or are symbolic motifs of the faith and unbelief is not clear. But since the Fourth Gospel is probably written in the post-Jamnian situation (9:22) it is questionable whether the historical situation is the key to the full understanding of the anti-Jewishness of the text. It is more likely that Judaism is a complex symbol-system to the fourth evangelist, or, better, that historical blends into universal and symbolic, and reverses itself. The author does not use historical situations to solve historical ques-

11 H. Strathmann, "*Laos*," *TDNT* 4:34-35.

tions alone. His use of Jews as a symbol-system of unbelief is very dangerous, for the reader can take his affirmations too literally, and can think of Judaism as the symbol for unbelief par excellence. This would be a one-sided viewpoint. It is not the Jews alone who are in the darkness.

We shall see later that everyone deserts Jesus in the Johannine passion account. Even Mary and the beloved disciple leave Jesus' side and fade into the background to their own kind. The Samaritan woman is a believer, but her religion is earthly. Pilate is a type of witness, but he is not a believer, and the Roman structure is seen as subservient to the highest authority connections through Jesus. So Judaism is not set in a rigid darkness-light dichotomy. The Jews are the chosen people. Jesus dies for this people, Jesus is defined for this people, but they are of the world. The fourth evangelist's theological and symbolic concerns see Jesus totally isolated from everyone but the Father. He does not place the Jews over against other religious groups; rather, everything is set against the singular Jesus. In this dualism of world and Jesus the "Jews" occur most frequently as the examples of the unbelieving world.

The Fourth Gospel is anti-Jewish. The author sees the Pharisees and the high priests as the centre of this people. Galileans are better than Judeans, but all eventually turn away from him. Still there is hope for the people because Jesus died for the people. There is also a remnant.

The danger of misreading these texts in the Gospel of John as referring only to the historical group called Judaism is very great. What is worth noting are the accents on a remnant and on salvation for the whole people. How can this ambiguity stand when the evangelist also pictures the followers of Jesus as being rejected from the synagogue? The answer is unclear. One of the dangers in the anti-Jewish stance of the gospel is that the more negative aspects of Judaism seem clearer than the positive. In summary John's gospel is anti-Jewish and the historical side of his material puts the author in opposition to the leaders of Judaism in particular. Beyond that, his anti-Judaism is theological and symbolic rather than historical or concrete.

The Passion in the Fourth Gospel

The Crucifixion Orientation of the Fourth Gospel

Even before turning to the passion account itself, the Fourth Gospel places a heavy emphasis on the passion and crucifixion. It is helpful to list some of the passages involved, because it is so unlike the synoptics.

John 1:11: "He came to his own home, and his own people received him not." The lack of reception may refer to the passion and death of Jesus.

John 1:29: "'Behold the Lamb of God who takes away the sin of the world.'" The title relates directly to the sacrificial death of Jesus.

John 2:13-22: The cleansing of the Temple has been changed to the beginning of the gospel. The reference to destroying his body heightens the orientation to the passion, so that the whole ministry of Jesus is related to the death of Jesus by this alteration in chronology.

John 2:13,23: At the same time the feast of Passover is brought forward in the gospel so there is a more constant passion connection (cf. also 6:4; 12:1).

John 5:18: "This was why the Jews sought all the more to kill him . . . ."

John 6:51: "'[A]nd the bread which I shall give for the life of the world is my flesh.'" This refers to the sacrament of the eucharist and the passion.

John 7:1-2: "After this Jesus went about in Galilee; he would not go about in Judea, because the Jews sought to kill him. Now the Jews' feast of Tabernacles was at hand."

John 7:13: "Yet for fear of the Jews no one spoke openly of him." This implies that the authorities had served notice of his arrest.

John 7:25: "'Is not this the man whom they seek to kill?'" Again, the authorities are implicated, because they know about Jesus (7:26).

John 7:32: "The chief priests and Pharisees sent officers to arrest him."

John 7:44: "Some of them wanted to arrest him, but no one laid hands on him." Here it is part of the crowd who are the opponents.

John 8:37: "'You seek to kill me.'"

John 8:40: "'But now you seek to kill me.'"

John 8:59: "So they took up stone to throw at him." These three passages imply that the Jews who believed (8:31) wanted to kill him.

John 10:15: "'I lay down my life for the sheep.'"

John 10:18: "'I lay it down of my own accord.'" The involvement of others is secondary; Jesus dies according to his purposes.

John 10:31: "The Jews took up stones again to stone him."

John 10:39: "Again they tried to arrest him, but he escaped from their hands." These are Jews in the Temple at the feast of the Dedication (10:22).

John 11:8: "'Rabbi, the Jews were but now seeking to stone you, and are you going there again?'" Here the Jews are Judeans.

John 11:50 "'It is expedient for you that one man should die for the people.'" See above for this special use of people (*laos*).

John 12:1-8: The anointing of Jesus as the prelude to burial.

John 13-17: The whole of the farewell discourses and final prayer are related to the passion and death of Jesus.

This survey of passages reveals a constant interest in the passion and death of Jesus. From the very first chapters the stress is on the word of Jesus, his works, and his death. There is no messianic secret: John the Baptist speaks of the significance of the death of Jesus openly as the Lamb of God whose death bears the sins of the world. In the Fourth Gospel the focus on the death of Jesus is more constant than in the other gospels.

Two features in the chronology of the gospel highlight this: the cleansing of the Temple in the beginning of the ministry, and the four visits to Jerusalem. The timing of the cleansing is more than a chronological change, for it includes specific references to the death of Jesus and his resurrection. Likewise the visits to Jerusalem are not just incidental trips, but centre around appearances at feasts and in the Temple, which point to the theme of Jesus' death at one or more points in the structure of each visit. The authorities of the nation were in opposition to the people in their hatred of Jesus and desire to kill him (7:46-48). We shall see there is a similar theme in the passion accounts.

Three places present a significantly different point of view. In chapters 6, 7, and 8 there is a pattern of hard sayings which seems to turn the crowd of faithful against Jesus. The issues change but the general pattern remains. The crowd which was seeking Jesus out turns against him. In chapters 8 and 10 there is mention of an actual attempt to kill Jesus (8:52; 10:31 and 39). These texts are difficult in the sense that they don't always hold together in the most logical way. In chapter 6 the statements about eating the flesh of Jesus seem to break into the previous logic of the chapter. In 8:31 the Jews who believe in Jesus six verses later (8:37) become opponents seeking to kill him. In 10:19-21 there is a division in the crowds where there is mention of believers as well as opponents; and with little in the form of transition, the crowds turn against Jesus and attempt to stone him (10:31).

Thus the centring of opposition in Judea, Jerusalem, the Temple, the Pharisees, and high priests does not indicate that the people from Galilee, or the crowds in general are totally loyal. Even with a centred opposition there is a collective opposition indicated by the fourth evangelist.

There is no doubt that the Jewish authorities are described as the opposition to Jesus and the agents of his death. The readers of the Fourth Gospel are fully prepared for the passion and death, but the focus on the authorities does not exclude the crowds in the Temple and in Jerusalem at the time of the feasts.

The Jews and the Arrest of Jesus

It is surpising that, in the arrest of Jesus, Romans are involved (18:3; 18:12). In other gospels those who arrest Jesus are exclusively Jewish.

Even within the structure of John, Roman involvement is surprising for previous mention of arrest attempts involved Jewish officials only (7:32; 7:45).

There have been suggestions that the mention of the Roman involvement was due to the sources available to the fourth evangelist, and is more historical. While there may be historical truth in the inclusion of Romans in the arresting detachment, it is hardly the historical motif alone which brings items into the Johannine agenda.

It is more likely that, in the structure of the text, there is a contrast between the forces of darkness and the light of the world. At the pronouncement of the divine"I AM" they fall to the ground (18:6) and remain there while safe passage for the disciples of Jesus is arranged (18:8-9). Roman involvement does not shift blame for the death of Jesus away from the Jews, for there is no contrast to the clear statements of Jewish blame for the death of Jesus in the rest of the gospel.

The Two Jewish Trials and the Jews

The accounts of the Jewish trials of Jesus are very brief and cryptic. Where the other three canonical gospels mention only the one trial before the High Priest, the Johannine version has a double trial: one before Annas, the other before Caiaphas. Appearances before two Jewish high priests creates a more forceful impression; but one might suspect that there is an underlying source in which there is only one trial. The first trial is before Annas, the father-in-law of the High Priest, and in that trial the High Priest does the questioning (18:19), rather than Annas, the father-in-law. Peter's denial, likewise, is stretched over two trials, another mark of editing and expanding a source with one trial into the present form of two. (From the standpoint of the number of trials, the Johannine account might be judged more anti-Jewish.)

In other respects the impression of the Jewish trials in the Fourth Gospel is not forceful. The trial is more private; the High Priest alone convenes and carries the trial forward; the questioning is briefer—in fact, the second trial doesn't even mention any questions being put to Jesus, the only question asked in the second trial was to Peter. The mistreatment of Jesus is also stated in a more subdued fashion and there is a less formal delivery of Jesus to Pilate in the Fourth Gospel. It is almost as though it is Peter who receives more attention in the trials than Jesus. Seven verses are devoted to Peter, four to Jesus. In the strict sense, these are not Jewish trials, but high priestly trials. Up to this point in the gospel the high priests and the Pharisees have all been active in putting questions to Jesus, but now the High Priest alone questions him, a narrowing that does not accord with earlier material found in the gospel which also included Pharisees and crowds as seeking to kill Jesus. This narrowing to the High Priest lessens the anti-Jewish force by making the trials more strictly priestly and more anti-Petrine in nature. The reader's attention is therefore directed away from the Jewish people to other factors in the text.

The Trial Before Pilate and the Jews

The high-priestly role continues in the Roman trial with a significant variation in the language. Throughout the trial the high priests are involved with Jesus and Pilate, but the term "High Priest" is not used consistently as in the Jewish trials. Sometimes "Jew" is substituted for "High Priest." This substitution tends to make the reader think of the people as a whole. It should also be noticed that the Fourth Gospel makes no mention of elders, scribes, or Pharisees in the trial before Pilate. So the role of the high priests is kept in front of the reader and at the same time mention of the Jews is interjected into the text without indicating that the composition of the opponents of Jesus has altered along with the alteration of the terminology.

Thus the historic reference of the text is to "chief priests," but the alternate use of the term "Jews" widens the scope of association to heighten the anti-Jewishness of the trial scene. In addition the term "nation" is inserted in the narrative (18:35). Even though the narrative moves from the high priestly trials to the trial before Pilate without involvement of crowds, the evangelist uses Pilate's statement to fix the reader's attention on high priests and nation. This widening tendency is especially interesting when we remember that later on in the text it is not the people but the high priests in particular who say they have no king but Caesar (19:15). The trial is therefore anti-high priestly, and anti-Jewish.

The most striking feature of the trial before Pilate in the Johannine setting is the curious function of Pilate as a witness (to the problem of truth) and at the same time an outsider to Jewish questions. Pilate is seen as an opponent of the Jews in defence of Jesus. We have noticed that in the high-priestly trials Peter was as much on trial as Jesus. Here the action and the word of Pilate puts the Jews on trial as much as Jesus. It might be well to spell some of this out.

The high priests deliver Jesus to Pilate without entering the praetorium on the Passover, but this should be taken as subtly anti-Jewish. By the trial and the death, the authorities defiled the Passover (18:28), but still kept the appearance of being clean. In the next section, the Jews are seen as admitting that they desire the death of Jesus and that this is not lawful (18:29-32).

The Roman trial is arranged in an episodic manner: 18:33-40; 19:1-6; 19:7-12; 19:13-16. There is a dialogue between Jesus and Pilate, and between Pilate and the high priests. Pilate repeatedly proclaims

Jesus innocent, and King of the Jews, but this in itself does not make Pilate a believer. The chief priests deny the messianic concept by asserting they have no king but Caesar. If we read the trial with 16:11 and 11:49-52 in mind, the weight of the judgment is on Pilate and the chief priests. Pilate hands Jesus over to the high priests, to be crucified. The chief priests defile the Passover. So the guilt centres on the high priests, but also involves the people. The rulers and the nation have been judged guilty, but Jesus dies for the nation and for the scattered children of God. A strange combination of anti-Judaism and soteriology! The fourth evangelist seems to be holding out for some kind of remnant, or spiritual Israel, related positively to the death of Jesus, but in a different way from the gospel of Matthew where the guilt for the death of Jesus is to be on the nation forever.

The Jews and the Crucifixion of Jesus

The initial portion of the Crucifixion text is a problem; because "chief priests" is the antecedent to the verb in 19:15, it appears as though Pilate handed Jesus over to them for crucifixion (19:16-17). In the same section, however, it is Pilate who places the superscription on the cross (19:19), thereby acknowledging that the Jews were not in control of the process. This may suggest that the fourth evangelist had a source in which the Roman soldiers were in charge of the process of crucifixion, and that he altered it to stress priestly involvement. If so, this would be similar to the Lukan account where the crowd crucifies Jesus. However the text reached its present form, Pilate and the high priests are soon in contention over the title "King of the Jews" (19: 19-22). The superscription is given much more importance by attaching a dialogue to it, picturing the chief priests as argumentative. This heightens the anti-priestly feature of the text. On the other hand there is no taunting of Jesus on the cross by either the Jews or the soldiers or the authorities and in that sense the text is less negative toward the Jews. The paradox is that Jesus is identified as King of the Jews by a Roman authority.

Next the beloved disciple and Mary go home. The purpose of the text is to leave Jesus on the cross alone with his followers scattered (16:32). Saying they went to their own (*eis ta idia*; a possible reference to Judaism and the Jewish nation) makes us think of the prologue where the *logos* was not received by his own people (*ta idia*).

The piercing of the side of Jesus, the unknown witness to the water and the blood which flows from the side of Jesus, and the reference to the looking on the one whom they pierced (19:33-37) could be an unknown Jewish witness, or a witness of an unknown disciple of Jesus. If the witness was Jewish then the text would have the ring of a remnant theology—a witness among the Jews believed. They killed Jesus, but in looking on him some came to belief. Whatever the identification, something positive comes out of the Crucifixion.

The Jews and the Burial of Jesus

The tradition of Joseph of Arimathea is common to all four gospels. What is special in the Johannine version is the mention of Nicodemus with Joseph, that they were secret disciples, and that Jesus is buried as a Jew. There is an interesting interweaving of themes in the Fourth Gospel. Joseph is the secret and fearful disciple. Nicodemus is the one who comes at night. This indicates fear or lack of understanding. When we remember the reference to Nicodemus in chapter 7, where he speaks a tentative word for Jesus (7:50-52), it might suggest that he is a believing remnant among the Pharisees. These may be the ones who witnessed the piercing of the side. In any case, they come forward for the body of Jesus and bury Jesus as a Jew.

The anti-Judaism of the Fourth Gospel has this ending. Two from within the opposition to Jesus come forth in faith and witness to the crucified Messiah. Pilate did not understand, the disciples were scattered, the Jews killed Jesus, but some among them came forward in faith at the darkest hour. His death is for the nation and those who are scattered abroad in the world. By removing the taunts of the Jews found in other gospels, and highlighting the role of these two secret disciples, the fourth evangelist is less harsh to the Jews. In the midst of all the anti-Judaism, Jesus is King of the Jews.

Conclusion

When the gospel is judged by practical effects, its use of the term "the Jews" has had the greatest effect in setting in motion a negative point of view toward Judaism. This negative point of view is reinforced by reading early church anti-Judaism back into these passages. It shows how deeply stereotyped expressions hold our attention.

The study has shown that the text of the Fourth Gospel is more complex than has often been recognized, that being anti-Temple or anti-High Priest is not the same as being against Judaism. It is perhaps the gospel's suggestions of a spiritual Israel which need further exploration.

Strict construction of the negative passages cited would show that it is not Judaism in general that is the problem. The high priests crucify Jesus, not the Jewish crowds. The sons of the devil are not the whole nation, but the Jews who believed in Jesus (8:31). The Pharisees' guilt remains (9:41). Judgment is on the ruler of the world, not on Judaism (12:31). Judea is the region which has rejected Jesus. All these themes collectively suggest that the author of the Fourth Gospel understands Jesus to stand against the authorities in Jerusalem and the Temple. This does not make the whole nation apostate; Jesus still dies for the people, and the whole nation will not perish (11:49-51).

The Fourth Gospel clearly states (4:22) that salvation is from the Jews. In the same context it is stated that the Jews are the ones who know God, and also that in the future there will be a worship in spirit and truth which will make the Temple in Jerusalem unimportant. Jesus can be seen as the true temple (2:21), as the new lawgiver (13:34), who works in co-operation with Moses (1:17), and who is now in heaven to be reached through the spirit (chap. 14). He died for the nation of Israel and for all the nations (11:47-53). This new Israel has a new High Priest and a new temple, namely Jesus. There is clearly a mission to others than those of the house of Israel, but there is also a continuation of converts from Judaism to Jesus like Nicodemus and Joseph of Arimathea, so Jesus is drawing disciples out of Judaism as well as from other nations.

It would also be easy to look differently at these same texts. The Jewish roots could be seen in terms of the past, not in the present or the future. The Baptist (as a symbol of Judaism) is on the decrease (3:30). The denial of all kings but Caesar places Judaism outside the sphere of Christianity (19:15). Moses is no longer valid.

The Pharisees are blind and have a guilt which continues (9:41). Jesus did not trust the people in Jerusalem (2:23-25). He condemned the Jewish people as sons of the devil (8:44). The chief priests were the ones who crucified Jesus (19:16). They were also the ones who said they had no king but Caesar (19:15).

The fourth evangelist has distanced himself from Judaism, by widening the reference to chief priests and the like, and by overusing the category Jews, generally with a negative tone. It is difficult to escape the powerful and pervasive negative attitude found in the Fourth Gospel with regard to Judaism.

Two possible interpretations of the data lead us back to the original thesis that the Fourth Gospel has not resolved the direction in which faith in Jesus is to go. On the one hand there are those statements moving toward a spiritual Judaism, and on the other are those statements calling for a new religion. It is one of the tragedies of interpretation that the harsher statements have blotted out the milder and more inclusive ones.

Index Nominorum*

* Indexes prepared by Barry W. Henaut.

Index Locorum

The Hebrew Scriptures

Roman Writings

SR SUPPLEMENTS

1. **FOOTNOTES TO A THEOLOGY**
   The Karl Barth Colloquium of 1972
   Edited and Introduced by Martin Rumscheidt
   1974 / viii + 151 pp.
2. **MARTIN HEIDEGGER'S PHILOSOPHY OF RELIGION**
   John R. Williams
   1977 / x + 190 pp.
3. **MYSTICS AND SCHOLARS**
   The Calgary Conference on Mysticism 1976
   Edited by Harold Coward and Terence Penelhum
   1977 / viii + 121 pp. / OUT OF PRINT
4. **GOD'S INTENTION FOR MAN**
   Essays in Christian Anthropology
   William O. Fennell
   1977 / xii + 56 pp.
5. **"LANGUAGE" IN INDIAN PHILOSOPHY AND RELIGION**
   Edited and Introduced by Harold G. Coward
   1978 / x + 98 pp.
6. **BEYOND MYSTICISM**
   James R. Horne
   1978 / vi + 158 pp.
7. **THE RELIGIOUS DIMENSION OF SOCRATES' THOUGHT**
   James Beckman
   1979 / xii + 276 pp. / OUT OF PRINT
8. **NATIVE RELIGIOUS TRADITIONS**
   Edited by Earle H. Waugh and K. Dad Prithipaul
   1979 / xii + 244 pp. / OUT OF PRINT
9. **DEVELOPMENTS IN BUDDHIST THOUGHT**
   Canadian Contributions to Buddhist Studies
   Edited by Roy C. Amore
   1979 / iv + 196 pp.
10. **THE BODHISATTVA DOCTRINE IN BUDDHISM**
    Edited and Introduced by Leslie S. Kawamura
    1981 / xxii + 274 pp.
11. **POLITICAL THEOLOGY IN THE CANADIAN CONTEXT**
    Edited by Benjamin G. Smillie
    1982 / xii + 260 pp.
12. **TRUTH AND COMPASSION**
    Essays on Judaism and Religion in Memory of Rabbi Dr. Solomon Frank
    Edited by Howard Joseph, Jack N. Lightstone, and Michael D. Oppenheim
    1983 / vi + 217 pp.
13. **CRAVING AND SALVATION**
    A Study in Buddhist Soteriology
    Bruce Matthews
    1983 / xiv + 138 pp.
14. **THE MORAL MYSTIC**
    James R. Horne
    1983 / x + 134 pp.
15. **IGNATIAN SPIRITUALITY IN A SECULAR AGE**
    Edited by George P. Schner
    1984 / viii + 128 pp.
16. **STUDIES IN THE BOOK OF JOB**
    Edited by Walter E. Aufrecht
    1985 / xii + 76 pp.
17. **CHRIST AND MODERNITY**
    Christian Self-Understanding in a Technological Age
    David J. Hawkin
    1985 / x + 188 pp.

EDITIONS SR

1. **LA LANGUE DE YA'UDI**
   Description et classement de l'ancien parler de Zencircli dans le
   cadre des langues sémitiques du nord-ouest
   Paul-Eugène Dion, O.P.
   1974 / viii + 511 p.
2. **THE CONCEPTION OF PUNISHMENT IN EARLY INDIAN LITERATURE**
   Terence P. Day
   1982 / iv + 328 pp.

3. **TRADITIONS IN CONTACT AND CHANGE**
Selected Proceedings of the XIVth Congress of the International Association for the History of Religions
Edited by Peter Slater and Donald Wiebe with Maurice Boutin and Harold Coward
1983 / x + 758 pp.
4. **LE MESSIANISME DE LOUIS RIEL**
Gilles Martel
1984 / xviii + 484 p.
5. **MYTHOLOGIES AND PHILOSOPHIES OF SALVATION IN THE THEISTIC TRADITIONS OF INDIA**
Klaus K. Klostermaier
1984 / xvi + 552 pp.
6. **AVERROES' DOCTRINE OF IMMORTALITY**
A Matter of Controversy
Ovey N. Mohammed
1984 / vi + 202 pp.
7. **L'ETUDE DES RELIGIONS DANS LES ECOLES**
L'expérience américaine, anglaise et canadienne
Fernand Ouellet
1985 / xvi + 672 p.

STUDIES IN CHRISTIANITY AND JUDAISM / ETUDES SUR LE CHRISTIANISME ET LE JUDAISME

1. **A STUDY IN ANTI-GNOSTIC POLEMICS**
Irenaeus, Hippolytus, and Epiphanius
Gérard Vallée
1981 / xii + 114 pp.
2. **ANTI-JUDAISM IN EARLY CHRISTIANITY**
Vol. 1, **Paul and the Gospels**
Edited by Peter Richardson with David Granskou
1986 / x + 232 pp.

THE STUDY OF RELIGION IN CANADA / SCIENCES RELIGIEUSES AU CANADA

1. **RELIGIOUS STUDIES IN ALBERTA**
A State-of-the-Art Review
Ronald W. Neufeldt
1983 / xiv + 145 pp.

COMPARATIVE ETHICS SERIES/ COLLECTION D'ETHIQUE COMPAREE

1. **MUSLIM ETHICS AND MODERNITY**
A Comparative Study of the Ethical Thought of Sayyid Ahmad Khan and Mawlana Mawdudi
Sheila McDonough
1984 / x + 130 pp.

Also published / Avons aussi publié

RELIGION AND CULTURE IN CANADA / RELIGION ET CULTURE AU CANADA
Edited by / Sous la direction de Peter Slater
1977 / viii + 568 pp. / OUT OF PRINT

Available from / en vente chez:
Wilfrid Laurier University Press
Wilfrid Laurier University
Waterloo, Ontario, Canada N2L 3C5

**Published for the
Canadian Corporation for Studies in Religion/
Corporation Canadienne des Sciences Religieuses
by Wilfrid Laurier University Press**